BLOOD
ON THE CROSSBAR

BLOOD
ON THE CROSSBAR
THE DICTATORSHIP'S WORLD CUP

RHYS RICHARDS

First published by Pitch Publishing, 2022

Pitch Publishing
9 Donnington Park,
85 Birdham Road,
Chichester,
West Sussex,
PO20 7AJ
www.pitchpublishing.co.uk
info@pitchpublishing.co.uk

ISBN 978 1 80150 174 3

Typesetting and origination by Pitch Publishing
Printed and bound in Great Britain by TJ Books, Padstow

Contents

For Rhian, Hedd and Aneirin.

This book is dedicated to

Las Madres de la Plaza de Mayo

and all the disappeared.

Acknowledgements

FIRSTLY, THANK you to my family, without whose support and guidance none of this would be possible. To my wife, Rhian, thank you for your understanding and patience and thank you for keeping me grounded in the 21st century, when 1978 was taking up such a space in my brain. Thank you to my children, Hedd and Aneirin, and my dog Medi for always keeping me busy and reminding me why I do this.

I owe a huge debt of gratitude to all the people who helped with the research for this book. Thank you for unlocking the doors that led to so many incredible discoveries. Muchas gracias a mi amigo Fernando Spannaus, whose first-hand knowledge and incredible stories shaped so much of this book; thanks also for helping to put into context things that can only be understood by someone fluent in Porteño.

I'm incredibly grateful for the help of Dr Pete Watson, who was always at the end of a telephone to give me advice, armed with an encyclopaedic knowledge of Latin American football, culture and history.

Diolch Morgan Isaac, who was the first person I reached out to when I decided to write about this World Cup. Another diolch to Morgan's father, Russell Isaac, for providing behind-the-scenes stories from Scotland's training camp in Alta Gracia, Córdoba.

Bedankt Freek de Jonge and the late Bram Vermeulen, who fought so tirelessly with Amnesty International to cast a spotlight on the atrocities of the dictatorship, and from whom this book gets its title.

I would also like to thank Marina Franco for her incredible work writing about Argentine exiles who fought back against the dictatorship from overseas, and for putting me in contact with former members of Boycott du Mondial Committee of football in Argentine (Committee to Boycott the World Cup in Argentina or COBA).

Thank you to Bob Cox, who led the campaign in the Argentinian media to discover the fate of the disappeared, it was an honour to put your stories into print.

Thank you to everyone who was willing to be interviewed; your incredible insights and memories have added colour to the infamous stories of 1978. In no order: Clive Thomas, Raanan Rein, Hossein Nayebagha, Tim Vickery, Stuart Horsfield, Barry Davies, Gary Thacker, Ronnie McDevitt, John MacLaverty, Nima Tavallaey Roodsari, Liliana Andreone and many more who were willing to help.

Finally, thank you to everyone at Pitch Publishing for putting your faith in me to tell this story.

Introduction

25 JUNE 1978, Estadio Monumental, Buenos Aires. General Jorge Videla hands Daniel Passarella the Jules Rimet Trophy. Argentina are champions of the world. A defining night in the lives of both men as they realise conflicting dreams.

For Videla, a victory for the regime. The legitimisation of a much-maligned military junta, with the eyes of the world upon them. For Passarella, a victory for the people. For those in the stands, who could have easily found themselves instead in military detention centres, the proximity of the most notorious of which was particularly poignant. Within earshot of the sounds of jubilation emanating from the home of Club Atlético River Plate, was Escuela Superior de Mecánica de la Armada (ESMA). The building was officially the school of mechanics of the navy but in practice it served as a rudimentary centre of detention, torture and murder, where opponents of the dictatorship were exterminated during Argentina's 'national reorganisation process'.

The tournament takes place amid a 'dirty war', where kidnap, torture and murder are practised on an industrial scale. The euphoric cheers of Estadio Monumental in 1978 are a jarring contrast to the sounds two years prior. The sound of military vehicles churning up the roads of Buenos Aires precede years of chilling silence as General Jorge Videla's military junta seize power from Isabel Perón, third wife and widow of Juan Perón. Videla's right-wing authoritarian government would be responsible for the deaths and disappearance of between 15,000 and 30,000 Argentine nationals, political activists, left-wing sympathisers and subversives. Prisoners are tortured in detention centres, children are abducted from their parents and given to families of the military, and political enemies are taken on 'death flights' – drugged and thrown from aeroplanes into the Río de la Plata.

In the middle of the Cold War, the tournament takes place during a critical juncture in Latin America's history, with dictatorships in place across the continent. For Argentina's regime, this World Cup served as a public relations exercise, where they had the opportunity to showcase the best of their nation, embracing the outside world and leaving behind decades of isolationism.

The shadow of the dictatorship loomed heavily over César Luis Menotti's supremely talented Argentina team and has long undermined a squad who have fought for generations to be remembered for their abilities rather than their association with the military. Menotti was a staunch socialist and the unlikeliest figurehead for the national team, but a born winner with a philosophy for attacking, open football that symbolised Argentina opening its doors to the world.

Despite only 16 teams competing in the 1978 World Cup, the legacy of the tournament is scorched into the footballing memory of these nations. From the finalists, who left the greatest player in the world at home, to the undefeated Brazilians, who claim to have been the victims of a match-fixing conspiracy that eliminated them. But this isn't exclusively the story of politicians or footballers. This is the story of the people: Argentine exiles, Parisian students, two Dutch comedians and the mothers of Plaza de Mayo, who every Thursday march in front of Casa Rosada, the residence of Argentina's president, desperate to discover the fate of their missing children.

The Hosts

The death of General Actis

The decision to award the 1978 World Cup to Argentina was announced in 1966. In the 12 years between the decision and the staging of the event, eight different people would lead the country. There would be two *coups d'état* and a military junta would be established, only to be toppled by the prodigal return from exile of Juan Domingo Perón. Finally, in 1976 a military junta would be established to oust Perón's widow, the unelected former vice-president Isabel Perón.

With the country teetering dangerously close to civil war throughout the early to mid-1970s, there would have been every reason to assume that staging a World Cup would be a step too far, or an unwanted distraction for the Argentinian government. However, the junta pushed on with staging the tournament. Buoyed by their recent claim of power, the dictatorship saw the social and political opportunities to establish their regime in the global gaze. General Jorge Rafael Videla was the de facto leader of Argentina's sixth military junta, and although to modern, Western sensibilities the idea of a military coup is horrifying, in South America at the time it was seen by many as an established mode of toppling lame or corrupt governments. Indeed, at the time the majority of citizens would have believed the military to be better equipped to deliver the World Cup than 'Isabelita's administration'. A hangover from the days of the wars of independence on the continent, militaries – no longer fighting conquistadors – now looked inwards and saw themselves as 'guarantors of social order'.[1]

As de facto leader of Argentina, Videla delegated the organisation of the World Cup to a newly created committee, the Ente Autarquico Mundial (EAM). General Omar Actis was tasked with heading up EAM and organising the hosting of the tournament. The general had retired from active military duty in 1972 and was assisted by naval captain and eventual vice-admiral, Carlos Lacoste, right-hand man and close friend of Admiral Emilio Massera. Argentine journalist Ezequiel Fernandez described Actis as an austere man, who wanted an austere World Cup.[2] The retired general felt that Argentina had no need to comply with the demands of FIFA president João Havelange, who promised to deliver the first World Cup in colour. The organisation also expected the host nation to update its stadiums, ensuring the facilities were state of the art.

Actis's appointment was far from a universally popular choice within the junta. His moderate approach to matters

1   Dr Peter Watson (teaching fellow of Latin American studies at the University of Leeds). 2020. *These Football Times* podcast, *Political Football: The Story of the 1978 World Cup: Violence, Protests, Controversy and a Stunning Home Glory.*

2   *A Dirty Game.* Documentary dir. Jaap Verdenius and Kay Mastenbroek, 2002.

and criticism of the tournament's expenditure was detested by Massera, who believed it needed to be delivered at any cost. Massera considered delivering the World Cup to be vital to the image of Argentina, a notion on which he and General Jorge Videla clashed. Despite Videla being an ever-present figure at Argentina matches throughout the World Cup, the man who had never set foot inside a stadium prior to the tournament initially considered the World Cup to be an unnecessary extravagance. Admiral Massera, an intimidating figure, either by hook or by crook convinced Videla that the World Cup was wholly necessary, and the tournament took place as he had intended.

General Actis was assassinated on 19 August 1976; shot by five gunmen en route to his first press conference since the establishment of the military junta. Actis was reportedly expected to criticise the vast expenditure on the tournament at a time of soaring inflation. The general's murder was officially cited as an assassination carried out by a left-wing terrorist organisation, which were commonplace prior to the coup but had significantly reduced at the time of his murder. The *New York Times* remarked: 'There was a noticeable lull in terrorist killings of this type.'[3]

Over time, opinion has shifted on the responsibility for the assassination. Most sources now accept that Actis was murdered by forces within the junta, horrified that he would expose their recklessness with the economy and derail the World Cup plans. According to Dr Pablo Albarces of the University of Buenos Aires, 'Everybody

---

3   Juan de Onis. 'Guerillas kill 2 in Argentina', *New York Times*, 20 August 1976.

in Argentina, including the generals, knew he had been killed by the navy.'[4]

After General Actis's death the responsibility of organising the tournament would fall to Lacoste. Still fiercely loyal to his superior, Lacoste's ascension meant that Massera now had a direct hand on the tournament. Lacoste's navy connections would serve his career well as he would eventually become caretaker president of Argentina in an 11-day handover period between Roberto Viola and Leopoldo Galtieri. Indeed, Lacoste would be a beneficiary of nepotism for the rest of his days. One of his more profitable friendships was with none other than FIFA president João Havelange, who made him vice-president of FIFA in 1982. When democracy was restored in Argentina, Lacoste was charged with embezzlement of funds from the World Cup's organisation committee and investigated for the murder of General Actis. Despite these accusations, Havelange campaigned tirelessly for Lacoste to retain his role within FIFA.[5] This demonstrated how intertwined the dictatorship in Argentina was with world football's governing body at the time and explains some of the influence Argentina had over things that would benefit the team, such as the kick-off time in their infamous second-round match versus Peru and the appointment of the referee for the final.

Lacoste's approach to the World Cup was more carefree than Actis's measured, conservative method and mirrored

4   Alan Tomlinson and John Sugden. 2016. *Football, Corruption and Lies: Revisiting 'Badfellas', the Book FIFA Tried to Ban.* Routledge.
5   David Yallop. 1999. *How They Stole Our Game.* Poetic Publishing.

Massera's 'deliver the tournament at any cost' mantra. Lacoste's ascension to the head of the EAM meant that the men who ran the tournament were the same men who ran the detention centres, including Admiral Emilio Massera. A cabal of Argentina's most powerful men was involved in the day-to-day running of the detention centres, with the flagship torture centre, ESMA, designed and maintained by the Navy.[6]

Why host the World Cup?

Dr Peter Watson – teaching fellow of Latin American studies at the University of Leeds – speaks of the opportunity of 'nation branding'.[7] This is the idea that a major sporting event can bring tangible economic and social prosperity to a host country, where a nation can show off its infrastructure, organisation and capabilities to host people from all over the world. The 1978 World Cup provided Argentina with all the necessary ingredients for a much-needed nation-branding exercise. If successful, the military would be able to rebrand the nation, promoting law, order and patriotism, while pushing threats of communism and anarchism to the fringes of society.

The World Cup was long overdue in Argentina. From a sporting point of view, Argentina holds a superiority complex over its neighbours, and members of the Argentine Football Association (AFA) would have been embarrassed

---

6   Malcom Coad. 1980. 'The "disappeared" in Argentina 1976–1980'. *Index on Censorship*, 9(3): 41–43. doi:10.1080/03064228008533069

7   Interview with Dr Peter Watson 2021 – teaching fellow of Latin American studies at the University of Leeds.

that Uruguay, Brazil and Chile had beaten them to the punch in hosting the World Cup. Argentina has historically had close ties with Europe, due to its colonial history with Spain and the mass immigration of Spanish, Italian and, to a lesser extent, British people. The UK's legacy in Argentina is defined by the round ball, the game of the refined and a gift from middle-class Europeans to Argentina. The opportunity to stage the world's greatest tournament would symbolise Argentina's arrival at the top table of global powers. It was an aching ambition of many of the generals, despite their ambivalence towards the game itself.

In sporting terms, Argentina's relationship with Europe is a paternal one. '*Somos tu padres* – We are your fathers' is a phrase heard often in Argentinian football, where one team (the father) displays its dominance over their rival (the son). Toppling the European giants was a rite of passage for Argentina: a victory over Europeans, particularly Spain and the UK due to the historical context, was viewed as evidence of a maturing football nation. To all involved in the organisation of the tournament, hosting the World Cup was the equivalent of inviting your parents round for dinner in your first grown-up flat.

The World Cup was also an opportunity for the junta to flex its muscles, to show how secure the country was, that they had overcome the left-wing subversives and were now an established, secure state. During this Cold War era, many nations across Latin America were struggling with armed conflict between 'left-wing agitators' and totalitarian regimes, and a successful tournament would signal a victory for law and order in the eyes of the military.

The junta would have been helped by their opponents, Los Montoneros, promise of a relative ceasefire during the World Cup. The Montoneros – an armed left-wing guerrilla militia – vowed not to execute any operations within 600 metres of any of the World Cup venues and to ensure that no spectators, journalists, tourists, teams or delegations were harmed.[8]

Indeed, scores of the left-wing, Perónist guerrilla group supported the hosting of the tournament on Argentinian soil. Their fight with the military junta was a battle for hearts as well as minds and to oppose the staging of the World Cup would have been ideological suicide. For the people of Argentina, the national team, La Albiceleste, were a source of great national pride, a rare beacon of unity in an increasingly fractured society. Professor Raanan Rein notes:

'By 1978 the guerrilla movements lost much of the popular support they enjoyed in 1975–1976. Pretending to represent the popular will, movements such as the Montoneros of the People's Revolutionary Army could not allow themselves to turn their back on the most popular sport in the country. Most Argentines wanted their country to host the World Cup games and hoped for their nation to win the cup. As they were losing the military battle, Montoneros and the People's Revolutionary Army were desperate to maintain some popular support. Therefore,

---

8   Nicolas Sagaian. 'Montoneros operations during the 78 World Cup, the offensive that wasn't'. Papelitos.com

formally or informally, the guerrilla movements had to reach a truce with the military dictatorship.'[9]

Having suffered as many as 3,000 casualties between 1976 and 1977,[10] the fragmented and almost decimated factions launched a propaganda war with the government – moving away from the bombs and using stickers instead. Popular slogans used in their literature were 'Argentina Campeon – Videla to the wall' and 'This match shall be won by the people'. These slogans clearly demonstrated that the Montoneros were supporters of the national team, seeking to challenge the regime's attempt to use the team to represent them.[11]

Hosting the World Cup was also an opportunity for the junta to put a face to their regime. They were up against a one-man cult of personality in the ghost of Juan Perón, a personality that still exists in Argentina today in the ideology of Perónism. The opening ceremony would have been the first time many had heard Videla speak. To compare with the classic Dutch 4-3-3, the junta were very much a three-pronged attack: army, navy and air force – the three branches of the armed forces, rather than a one-man show. Although a household name, General Jorge Videla was not a charismatic character; he was the antithesis to populist right-wing leaders such as Hitler and Mussolini.

Former editor of the *Buenos Aires Herald*, Argentina's premiere English language newspaper, Robert Cox recalls

---

9   Interview with Raanan Rein, 2020.

10   Nicolas Sagaian. 'Montoneros operations during the 78 World Cup, the offensive that wasn't'. Papelitos.com

11   Nicolas Sagaian. 'The Silent Resistance'. Papelitos.com

Videla as 'an uninteresting man. Completely lacking in any charm. Not a menacing guy, a little weasel with a thin moustache.'[12] In fact, it was Videla's lack of charisma that made him the ideal candidate to lead the junta. The army was split between supposed moderates and extremists, and Videla was viewed as a safe pair of hands, necessary to placate the divisive elements of the armed forces. It was widely assumed at the time that whoever led the army would one day become the de facto leader of the country, such was the regularity of military coups in this era of Latin American history. So, to no one's surprise, the commander-in-chief of the army assumed the post of President of the Republic after the 1976 coup.

Prior to the disappearance of thousands of citizens deemed as 'subversives' by the military, there was great hope that Videla's regime could finally bring peace to the troubled streets of Argentina. Cox himself admits that he 'wanted to believe in Videla because he stood between the people and the extreme right wing. The ones who believed in the conquests. They had ideas of conquests throughout Latin America, they looked at themselves as Christians who were fighting for the Catholic faith and Western civilization. They were fighting what they thought would be the Thirdrd World War. Which nobody else had recognised.' Lieutenant Colonel Hugo Ildebrando Pascarelli of the Argentinian army stated: 'The struggle we are engaged in does not recognise any natural or moral limits; it is beyond any discussion of what is good or evil.'

---

12   Interview with Robert Cox, former editor of the *Buenos Aires Herald*.

This example of hyperbolic rhetoric demonstrates the lengths the military were willing to go to to establish their order. The junta frequently referred to themselves as 'the moral saviours of the west'.[13]

The military, the media and the Mothers of Plaza de Mayo

Crucial to the success of the military was controlling the messaging of the World Cup. Massera, more than Videla, saw the opportunity to communicate directly with people in their homes – to take inspiration from old enemy Eva Perón and flood the radio waves during a time of exceptional nationalism, to be the voice of Argentina. At least in this respect the Montoneros could find a level playing field. During Argentina's second match of the tournament, against France, the Montoneros managed to jam the signal and interrupt the transmission. Although the images weren't disrupted, the organisation was able to transmit its own commentary, a 13-minute, uninterrupted message where they spoke of 5,000 dead and 20,000 disappeared citizens at the hands of the dictatorship.[14]

In contrast to the guerrilla radio transmissions of the Montoneros, the established media in Argentina was broadly behind the military and the staging of the World Cup, thanks in no small part to intimidation from the dictatorship towards the media. At first the press was wined

---

13 Quote by Ezequiel Fernandez, Argentine journalist. *Dirty Game.* Documentary dir. Jaap Verdenius and Kay Mastenbroek, 2002.
14 Nicolas Sagaian. 'Interferences by Montoneros during the 78 World Cup – Radio Liberacion'. Papelitos.com

and dined by the dictatorship, who even gave journalists a tour of ESMA, the notorious detention centre, although they were careful to avoid showing them the places of torture. Cox recalls, 'They [the dictatorship] were trying to improve their relationship with the press. Initially they tried to suppress, but then they realised they couldn't shut things down, so they tried to control [the press].'

The government scheduled a briefing between the military and media prior to the tournament. Cox said: 'Before the World Cup, they called us all in [the media]; the minister for the interior Albano Harguindeguy, a big fat guy who looked like Goering, said, "You behave yourselves, you don't report anything [negative]. The world is watching Argentina and everything is fine here."' Of course, none of the journalists asked any questions. The message was clear, they were to toe the party line and showcase the best of the tournament, no lenses were to be pointed internally at the dictatorship. Investigative journalism was not a discipline encouraged by the Argentinian military, as Cox discovered when he first arrived. 'In my first press conference, I was astonished that nobody took any notes. Because at the end, you got a press release from the government. And you published it, just as it was.'

Nonetheless, Cox had pertinent questions that he wanted to ask the government, particularly about the names of journalists who were beginning to number among the disappeared. 'At that time I was pursuing why so many journalists were being kidnapped. I followed him [Harguindeguy] into his office because I had a list of journalists that were missing. Where are they? What's happening? Harguindeguy denied any knowledge of the disappearances of the journalists.'

During this era the television and radio were taken over by the government but newspapers still enjoyed relative independence. The printed media were able to question or criticise the government but the large publications broadly chose not to, understandably for self-preservation upon fear of death. Without media coverage of the industrial-scale disappearances, many of the stories passed by word of mouth. Cox recalls, 'There wasn't any good knowledge, apart from what people saw in the street, and chose not to see. You saw these thugs gunning through the streets in their unmarked cars. The Ford Falcon took on a sinister meaning. They were used by the death squads, and they took people off to be murdered. People managed not to see that, people were able to enjoy the World Cup. Some people didn't know, and some people chose not to know.'

The *Buenos Aires Herald* was an outlier in the press and under the stewardship of Cox began to ask questions of the junta. In 1959, when Cox arrived, the editors weren't particularly interested in reporting on Argentina. Instead they focused on international news. Their concern was the readership, which was mainly foreign businessmen and the remnants of the British community. However, things would change after the coup as they began to print the names of disappeared journalists each week. Cox laments that reporters from Argentina's biggest newspaper, *Clarin*, were reticent to hold the dictatorship to account and wouldn't question them on anything of value. Cox recalls speaking to Videla and asking, 'Señor Presidente, what about the kidnappings?', when a *Clarin* reporter interjected and said, 'We appreciate you have to do things a certain way. Like Julius Caesar,' appealing to Videla's ego and an administration always seeking to be seen as noble.

To many in the media, the oppression and control of the dictatorship was seen as a means to an end. Cox suggests that they believed they would improve their human rights record once they had expelled the dissidents. They allowed militia groups to act on behalf of the dictatorship and didn't challenge their behaviour. The groups would raid houses based on the most elementary of evidence and arrive at the wrong places. They would steal possessions and make tremendous mistakes. The pratfalls of these militia groups were never reported in the newspapers.

Cox's reporting of the disappearances would soon put him under the spotlight of the military, whose officials arrived at his house, armed with machine guns and took him away. He was taken to a recognised prison in police headquarters, used to torture people. 'The first thing I saw, painted on a huge wall in front of me, was a huge swastika with the words "Nazi Nationilismo".' Cox was charged with 'publication of information about subversive activities' and questioned before being released and moved to the nearby Hotel Sheraton. His detainment was reported in international newspapers, proving that the news about the nature of the autocratic government was beginning to spread overseas.

Much is made of the relationship between Nazi Germany and Argentina in the mid-20th century. The relationship between the German and Argentinian military was somewhat symbiotic as the Germans trained the Argentinian military and the latter would pay tribute to the former in its military uniform and trademark goose-step when marching. Even former high-ranking Nazis such as Adolf Eichmann were able to disappear to Argentina following the Second World War. In a 1980 report on the detention centres, it was discovered that 'overt Nazism is practised widely in the camps. Jewish prisoners are singled out for especially harsh treatment and Nazi regalia, including flags, are openly displayed,' echoing Cox's experience.[15]

For many of the domestic media, the arrival of the foreign press was seen as an opportunity to get the real story of Argentina out. The group most desperate for foreign intervention were Las Madres de Plaza de Mayo, the group of mothers who marched together around the plaza campaigning for answers on the whereabouts of their missing children. They were desperate to discover the fate of their children and met a wall of silence domestically. The dictatorship identified this threat and produced a smear campaign, portraying these women as the 'mad women of Plaza de Mayo'. Haydée Gastelu, an original member of the group, interviewed by Uki Goñi, addressed this, saying, 'Of course we were mad. Mad with grief, with impotence. They took a woman's most precious gift, her child.' Gastelu's son numbered among the disappeared, a student abducted and murdered during the dictatorship's sweep of intellectuals.

---

15   Malcom Coad. 1980. 'The "disappeared" in Argentina 1976–1980'. *Index on Censorship*, 9(3): 41–43. doi:10.1080/03064228008533069

Las Madres de la Plaza de Mayo's greatest hope and the dictatorship's greatest threat were one and the same, the foreign press. Crucially, in opening its doors to the world, the dictatorship had invited unwanted attention to its darkest secret. Robert Cox identifies the staging of the World Cup as the catalyst for the investigation into the disappeared: 'That's the time [1978 World Cup] the foreign press began taking an interest, which enraged the military. That started to help the situation. People in Argentina began taking an interest in what was happening.'

Groups had popped up in France, the Netherlands and elsewhere in Europe to protest about the human rights abuses in Argentina and to challenge the staging of the World Cup. Amnesty International began a campaign to brief journalists travelling to Argentina to cover the tournament about the atrocities taking place there. One of these interactions between Mothers of Plaza de Mayo member Marta Moreira de Alconada Aramburú and Dutch journalists illustrates the desperation of the mothers and how the arrival of the foreign press was an enormous source of hope for them. She cried, 'We just want to know where our children are. Alive or dead, we want to know where they are. We don't know who to turn to anymore: consulates, embassies, ministries, churches – they've all shut their doors on us. That's why we're begging you to help us, you are our last hope. Please, help us. Help us, please. You are our last hope.'[16]

---

16 Ailin Bullentini. 'The international press and the mothers of Plaza de Mayo, the other side of the World Cup', Papelitos.com

The dictatorship's treatment of Las Madres would become increasingly heavy-handed since the group's inception in April 1977. Later that year, founding member Azucena Villaflor was abducted from her home in Avellaneda following the publication of a newspaper advertisement naming the disappeared children of the mothers. Villaflor was transported to the ESMA detention centre and never seen alive again. Almost 30 years later, in 2003, the body of Villaflor was exhumed and discovered to have suffered injuries consistent with impact against a solid surface following a fall – suggesting that she was a victim of the 'death flights'. The murder of Villaflor was attributed to notorious torturer and naval officer Alfredo Astiz, nicknamed the 'blonde angel of death'. Astiz was sentenced to life in prison in 2011 for his role in the kidnap and murder of Las Madres founders Villaflor, Esther Ballestrino and Maria Ponce. Astiz was also convicted, *in absentia* in France, for the murder of French nuns Alice Domon and Léonie Duquet in 1977, after their disappearance in Argentina.[17]

The military were hamstrung to do anything to harm foreign press in the way they could harm Villaflor and could do little to dissuade journalists arriving in Argentina from speaking with critics of the government. What they were able to do, however, under the guise of security, was control who the travelling footballers and their nation's delegates spoke to. In partnership with FIFA, players and officials were explicitly banned from engaging with Las Madres

---

17 'Argentina "Angel of Death" Alfredo Astiz convicted', BBC website, 2011.

de la Plaza de Mayo. This did not stop Las Madres from sending letters to the players and to journalists, requesting their help in amplifying their voices.

Many urban myths exist around the relationship between the players and Las Madres. One is that Swedish goalkeeper Ronnie Hellström had attended a march with Las Madres. Hellström was attributed with the quote: 'It was an obligation I had with my conscience,' describing his meeting with the group. However, years later he would pour cold water on this fable in an interview with Argentine journalist Ezequiel Fernandez, saying, 'It wasn't me. No. I remember seeing them, but I didn't go to the Plaza. A couple of players went, but I don't remember who.'[18]

The player in question was Dutch defender Wim Rijsbergen. Injured during the Netherlands' final group match against Scotland, Rijsbergen remained with the Dutch squad for the second round but would play no further part in the tournament. With more free time on his hands than his compatriots, he enjoyed a little more freedom to explore the city. 'We were not allowed to leave the hotel. Only one player from our team saw the Madres. He left the hotel and told us.'[19] These are the words of Arie Haan and Ernie Brandts, members of the Dutch 1978 World Cup squad, and the player in question was, of course, Rijsbergen. Thanks to the efforts

18 Julio Boccalatte, Perfil del unico jugador Holandes que pudo haver la visita Rijsbergen, en bicicleta a ver a la Madres, Pagina 12, 2022.
19 Julio Boccalatte, Perfil del unico jugador Holandes que pudo haver la visita Rijsbergen, en bicicleta a ver a la Madres, Pagina 12, 2022.

of Amnesty International and Dutch comedy duo, Bram Vermeulen and Freek de Jonge, the Dutch squad were probably the one most aware of the atrocities taking place in Argentina. Their presence in the tournament had been highly controversial in the face of a boycott campaign that gathered great momentum. Rijsbergen's understanding of the situation was deepened by his meeting with Las Madres and he would remain in contact with them for many years, forging a long-term friendship with one member, Nora de Cortiñas.

The mothers were unaware of the true horrors and wanted to know where their children were being held. The belief at the time was that they were imprisoned somewhere in the country, with many believing they were held in tropical locations near the border with Paraguay. The reality, of course, was much more gruesome. Within the walls of ESMA, 3,000 detainees were murdered. In the early days this was in the most primitive of fashion: shot and burned on the barbecue. The perverse act echoed the Argentinian tradition of a Sunday 'asado'. Much like the Nazis' final solution to exterminate the Jews, the dictatorship faced a logistical problem of disposing of the bodies from their city centre location. Soon they would take to the skies and throw their victims out of aeroplanes into the Río de la Plata. They had to keep flying further out, as the bodies kept washing ashore in Mar del Plata.

Las Madres begged for information as they faced complete radio silence from the authorities. No information, no reassurances and no acknowledgement. Cox states, 'The World Cup was so noisy, the celebrations so loud, they drowned out the sound of the disappeared.' None of the major newspapers printed the stories of the disappeared, other than the *Buenos Aires Herald*'s list of names. Cox laments, 'All they had to do was print a letter from one of the mothers, but they chose not to. There was a reason. Argentina had lived under military rule so many times. The first coup was in the 30s. During military dictatorships, you learned as a journalist, you wrote what the government told you.' Perhaps the *Herald*'s publication in the English language, or Cox's status as a British citizen, meant they weren't scarred by Argentina's autocratic military history, which allowed them to be bolder in their stance, questioning the military.

Despite the wall of silence domestically, the foreign press began taking an interest in the human rights abuses, which Cox describes as 'enraging the military'. In addition to ESMA, other detention camps were established around the country. Detention centre Club Atlético was renowned for detaining socialist 'dissenters', sometimes housing as many as 1,500 prisoners, far surpassing its 200-person capacity. 'El Banco' boasted a surveillance office, focusing on foreign visitors during the World Cup, principally journalists. The military were demonstrably fearful of what journalists would discover during the tournament and with whom they would speak. Prisoners in these camps who had connections with foreign journalists were tortured and interrogated to discover what messages they had shared with the outside world.[20]

---

20 Malcom Coad. 1980. 'The "disappeared" in Argentina 1976–1980'. *Index on Censorship*, 9(3): 41–43. doi:10.1080/03064228008533069

The legacy of Argentina 1978

While it's true that sport doesn't exist in a vacuum, the days and weeks of the 1978 World Cup were a reprieve for many Argentines from the world that surrounded them. Whenever La Albiceleste took the field, the country, albeit temporarily, was in ceasefire. Guerrillas and generals, left wing and right wing, torturers and tortured, faced the same direction, towards a field or a television set, and idolised the same national heroes.

The streets of Buenos Aires were no stranger to bloodshed in the 1970s but the city basked in the glow of World Cup fever for those few weeks in 1978. Argentine journalist and broadcaster Fernando Spannaus recounts, 'It was the best time to be in Buenos Aires, ever. It was freedom. At a glance.'[21] Many of the restrictions on personal freedom were lifted during this time and, after Passarella's men had triumphed in the final, it's said that as much as 60 per cent of Buenos Aires took to the streets to celebrate with their compatriots. The sounds of motorists blasting their horns in unison with the chants of 'AR-GEN-TINA' formed the soundtrack of the junta's united nation. But under the surface, deep divisions remained.

Claudio Tamburrini, a former goalkeeper for Almagro, imprisoned for being a political activist, speaks of the perverse ceasefire during the World Cup when he states, 'Sport makes torturers and tortured embrace after the goals are scored. During the World Cup, Argentinians replaced critical political judgement with

---

21 Interview with Fernando Spannaus, 2021.

sporting euphoria.' However, the unity provided by these moments of sporting ecstasy was short-lived. 'They went back to torturing us afterwards,' former prisoner Adolfo Pérez Ezquivel laments.[22] It's impossible to unweave the intertwined experiences of prisoners and torturers during the 1978 World Cup. Perhaps it speaks of the success of the government's strategy that for 90 minutes, while Argentina took the field, the whole country was united. Videla used the platform of the opening ceremony to speak of 'the peace we all wish for. As people with dignity and freedom,'[23] and for a limited time the promise of peace had come to pass.

Robert Cox believes that the World Cup victory and subsequent explosion of national pride emboldened the more extreme elements of the military: 'I think they thought, we've done it. Now we've succeeded, nobody's going to care about what we do. After this, their torture and murder went ahead with impunity. But at least during the celebrations of the World Cup, I was hopeful, thinking, perhaps Argentina will get out of this horror.'

Cox's stay in Buenos Aires was coming to an end. Following an attempted kidnapping of his wife Maud, his son David received a letter containing a death threat. In his final meeting with the president, Videla asked Cox to stay in Argentina. He vowed to give Cox protection from the militia groups and stated, 'I wish I could go home. But, if I left, a general would come with his sword and swamp the country with blood.'

---

22 *Pele, Argentina and the Dictators.* Goalhanger films. 2020.
23 General Jorge Videla's speech during the opening ceremony.

Videla would later, on his deathbed, confide in a trusted journalist that the military had decided to kill 'between 5,000 and 6,000 people' but, of course, this is a very conservative estimate, with thousands more known to have been murdered by the state.[24] In such times, when an arbitrary figure can be plucked out of thin air as a justifiable number of citizens to exterminate, it's impossible to consider the dictatorship as a pragmatic mediator between extremists.

Alfredo Gonzalez and Horacio Gullermo de la Paz authored a 1980 report, 'Testimony on Secret Detention Camps in Argentina', in which they stated that the military junta 'never intended to limit its attentions to the guerrillas'. The men spent the World Cup in El Banco detention centre, escaping when in transit in 1979 and finding asylum in São Paulo, Brazil. According to their estimates, fewer than one in five of the detainees were members of armed opposition groups such as the Montoneros or had any such connections. Instead, having seized control during the coup in 1976 and ridden the wave of extreme nationalism during the World Cup triumph of 1978, the dictatorship sought to crush any and every dissenting voice in Argentina.[25]

---

24 Interview with Robert Cox, 2021.
25 Malcom Coad. 1980. 'The "disappeared" in Argentina 1976–1980'. *Index on Censorship*, 9(3): 41–43. doi:10.1080/03064228008533069

El Flaco

CONFORMITY. OBEDIENCE. Faith. Attributes valued by right-wing dictatorships. It is one of football's great paradoxes that the man to lead Argentina to the 1978 World Cup would be the antithesis to this totalitarian template.

César Luis Menotti, or El Flaco (the thin guy) as he was affectionately known, was born in Rosario in 1938. After a decade-long professional career representing Boca Juniors and Rosario Central, as well as stints in Brazil and North America, El Flaco would make his way to the managerial dugout. With a trademark cigarette in hand, he would steer a legendary Huracán team to 1973 Torneo Metropolitano victory before taking the helm of the national team. A young manager with an exciting philosophy, taking over the national side after domestic success is hardly a story unique to Argentina. His appointment after Argentina's humbling exit at the 1974 World Cup was entirely logical from a football standpoint. His status as national coach during the junta's regime, however, was an extremely uncomfortable truce.

Menotti was a member of the Communist Party in his youth and is a lifelong socialist. A deep thinker, who wears his principles on his sleeve, Menotti was an awkward figurehead for the national team. The military was desperate to tie itself closely to the Albiceleste but in Menotti they had a coach who was openly at the opposite end of the political spectrum. For all its storied ruthlessness, the dictatorship displayed pragmatism in equal parts. After the chaos of the previous World Cup, success at home in '78 was vital. In short, winning with a rebel at the helm was better than losing with a stooge.

The 1974 World Cup was a humbling experience for La Albiceleste; a combative yet unimaginative team were thrashed 4-0 by the Netherlands. Johan Cruyff's Oranje had put on an exhibition. Displaying their brand of total football, they left an exhausted, humiliated Argentina in the dust at Gelsenkirchen. While heads were spinning in Germany, back in the AFA headquarters heads were being scratched.

In the south of Buenos Aires, in a barrio named Parque Patricios, an unfashionable team named Huracán were becoming the darlings of Argentinian football. Usurping the established oligopoly of Buenos Aires's 'big five', Huracán played an attractive, attacking brand of football that fired them to a domestic title in 1973, and a Copa Libertadores final in 1974, losing to compatriots Independiente.

There was a home-grown solution to La Albiceleste's woes. Huracán's coach, César Luis Menotti, was tasked with reforming the national team. The overhaul was a difficult ask. Argentina's tough, isolationist, physical game would be replaced with a philosophy Menotti created from his own mould, a globalist, attractive and ambitious style. Menotti drew inspiration from Europe, particularly the 4-3-3 formation popular in the Netherlands, which Argentina would use throughout the 1978 World Cup. From Huracán's factory line of talent came World Cup winners Osvaldo Ardiles and crowd favourite René Houseman. Although the left-wing philosophy of El Flaco was incompatible with the rigid conservatism of the junta, his style of football paid tribute to an old, classical style of South American football. This seduced the administration in the way that conservatives are attracted to nostalgia.

Menotti loathed Argentina's low-risk approach to football, famously saying, 'In football there are risks, because the only way you can avoid taking risks in any game is by not playing.' Although ideologically opposed, Menotti's philosophy on risk mirrors that of the junta in staging the World Cup. With hindsight, we see Passarella holding the trophy aloft into a swollen Buenos Aires sky, sending the nation into ecstasy. But the very notion of staging the World Cup wasn't without significant risk. Economically, staging the tournament was at best perilous and at worst completely callous. It's estimated that as much as 11 per cent of the country's budget was spent on the World Cup. During this time inflation had soared to as much as 300 per cent.

The economic risk proved unsuccessful, despite anecdotal beliefs that hosting major tournaments provides economic growth for host nations. A 2018 study by the Federal University of Paraíba has discovered that hosting World Cups has had a negative effect on income per capita for seven of the nine host nations up to the 2018 World Cup, including Argentina 1978.[26] But Menotti was not burdened by economic factors. His less tangible task was the same as the dictatorships: to unite the people of Argentina.

In both a sporting and a social sense Argentina was at a crossroads. As a new man would steer La Albiceleste towards the World Cup, a new regime would introduce Argentina to the rest of the world. Due to the synchronicity of these events in the mid-1970s it's natural to link the two things but, perhaps unsurprisingly, Menotti always sought to distance himself from the government. He has long refuted any attempts to link the Argentina squad with the government, calling it a 'calumny' or slander to say that the government was responsible for the successes on the pitch.[27] The perceived symbiotic relationship between national team and dictatorship is an unfortunate albatross that hangs around the neck of the 1978 squad but it is important to consider these things in context and to remove the blinkers of modern Western standards.

Menotti has been criticised by revisionists for allowing himself to be the figurehead of a team so closely aligned with a right-wing dictatorship. Menotti himself would have lived under numerous military governments and, crucially in Argentina, it was an established model for the military to remove civilian governments that were alleged to have

26 Jorge H.N. Viana, Antonio Vinicius Barbosa, Breno Sampaio. 2018. 'Does the World Cup get the economic ball rolling? Evidence from a synthetic control approach'. *EconomiA*, 19(3).
27 Mariano Verrina. 'Menotti: I kept my word, I did what I had to do'. www.papelitos.com.ar

become corrupt. Many in Argentina celebrated the removal of Isabelita's civilian government. Citizens were angry at the perceived nepotism of installing Juan Perón's widow as president when elections were merely a year away.

Isabel Perón was considered by many to be ineffective at dealing with the guerrilla attacks that were plaguing the capital city, as bombs were detonated by groups that spanned the left-right political spectrum. Former editor of the *Buenos Aires Herald*, Robert Cox, recounts: 'Like Heinz beans, there were 36 different varieties of guerrilla groups at the time, ranging from extreme right to extreme left.'[28] Many hoped the junta could clean up the streets of Argentina. Of course, with the benefit of hindsight, we're able to understand that 'cleaning up' encapsulated the murder of thousands of citizens categorised as subversives.

Menotti himself was no stranger to the conflict: 'They shot my house twice. It was almost a Perónist basic unit. My father militated in Perónism and was a defender of Perón; my mother, on the other hand, hated Perón and defended Evita.'[29] El Flaco, although politically conscientious, wouldn't have been privy to the end game of the government. Despite General Jorge Videla's eagerness to utilise the national team as a symbol for the government, football men weren't in the inner circle of trust. In fact, it was only on Videla's deathbed that he confided in someone he believed to be a trusted journalist that the junta had

---

28 Interview with Robert Cox, 2021.
29 Mariano Verrina. 'Menotti: I kept my word, I did what I had to do'. www.papelitos.com.ar

planned all along to murder Argentinian citizens.[30] Menotti has stated that he was unaware of the full scale of the atrocities, despite the murmurings at the time: 'I knew there were detainees and political prisoners. What I didn't imagine was, for example, that people were thrown from the aeroplanes or so many other atrocities that were known later.'[31]

Menotti typifies the conflict many Argentines would have felt as the national team lifted the Jules Rimet Trophy. Although ideologically opposed to the junta, El Flaco was completely devoted to the national team. His philosophies about how football should be played and the responsibility of the national team to the people of Argentina were as rich as his political principles: 'There's a right-wing football and a left-wing football. Right-wing football wants to suggest that life is a struggle. It demands sacrifices. We have to become of steel and win by any method.' El Flaco, of course demanded a 'left-wing' style of football, whereby the ethics of fair play and a responsibility to entertain were non-negotiable. This would never cede, even for victory.

A most emotional triumph on home soil arrived on 25 June 1978 at Estadio Monumental. Menotti describes his memory of the event: 'Happiness. I kept my word. Winning the World Cup here. I feel like I did what I had to do.'[32] El Flaco's happiness seems to be charged with relief. It's unclear to whom Menotti is referring when he speaks of

30 Interview with Robert Cox, 2021.
31 Mariano Verrina. 'Menotti: I kept my word, I did what I had to do'. www.papelitos.com.ar
32 *Ibid.*

keeping his word. Could it be to the government, who so brazenly equated success on the field as affirmation for themselves? Or to the people of Argentina, who so desperately needed positive, public role models? Menotti nailed his colours to the mast in an interview years later when he stated, 'Our football belongs to the working class and has the size, nobility and generosity to allow everyone to enjoy it as a spectacle.'

The little-known story of the botched kidnap attempt of Menotti's wife hints at the pressure faced by the coach at the time. Robert Cox claims that, instead of Menotti's wife, a very similar-looking woman, a family friend, was bundled into one of the dreaded Ford Falcons used by the notorious death squads. One can only speculate the fate Menotti would have faced had the team suffered the same humiliation as four years before in West Germany.

What is clear is that, despite the pressure, El Flaco was graced with a talented, resilient and ambitious squad. He referred to them as 'an invincible team' that boasted the attacking prowess of 'El Matador' Mario Kempes, fellow World Cup Final goalscorer Daniel Bertoni and striker Leopoldo Luque. The attack married well with the miserly defence led by Daniel Passarella that made it through the second round unbreeched and the industrious midfield containing rising star Osvaldo Ardiles.

Despite the pressure, El Flaco's extraordinary confidence in the team was well warranted. His faith in his players came from the abundance of time he was afforded with them. An alien concept in modern football, where the riches of clubs dictate the time players, commonly seen as a club's asset, spend with their national team. In 1978 Menotti spent six months with his squad, establishing a style of play, honing partnerships and experimenting with different players. Squad member Ricky Villa recalls: 'From the January to the June the whole squad was together, at a camp just outside Buenos Aires. The word for that in Spanish is *concentracion*.'[33] Menotti allowed the players their freedom during the camp, as they were allowed to visit families at weekends, but as the tournament loomed on the horizon, restrictions were tightened, meaning they had to remain on camp at all times during the final month. The strict conditions imposed by the coach somewhat belie the laissez-faire, long-haired, coffee-shop philosopher image of Menotti. Perhaps feeling the pressure from the AFA and, effectively, the military, that pressure was inevitably pushed down to the players.

Despite finding it difficult to spend time away from family, the newly married Villa admits that the strict conditions were successful, saying, 'It worked. Menotti changed the whole mentality of Argentinian football. He brought in discipline. He challenged us to be more professional.' Menotti had high expectations of his players, personally and professionally. The long time in camp allowed him to assess the personalities of his players as well as their abilities with a football. This inevitably led to some players being disappointed that they would miss out on the tournament, despite taking part in the training camp.

---

33 Brian Viner. 2006. 'Ricky Villa – I recognise I am a little part of English football history'. Independent.com

Such was the embarrassment of riches available to Menotti at the time that he opted to leave out a 17-year-old Diego Maradona from the final squad. Menotti believed that the young genius wasn't equipped to deal with the pressure of the World Cup on home soil. El Flaco was curt with the devastated teenager, sparing him the flattery of inflating his ego: 'I simply had 22 to register of 25 players I had. Three of them had to be excluded. I had told them I was going to proceed like this. What did they gain if I told them that they were amazing players but had to be cut out?'[34]

Perhaps Menotti's blunt honesty was an attempt to introduce the young man to the cut-throat nature of the game. His rationale for his decision is perhaps best outlined in a scouting report he prepared for FC Barcelona in 1978 on the 17-year-old Argentinos Juniors prospect, which has since been published. In it, he describes Maradona: 'Young. He was born on 30/10/1960. He has prodigious technical qualities, easy dribbling. He has a straight-line vision facing the goal, but he knows how to get rid of the ball for the best placed team-mate. Extraordinary reflexes. He protects the ball very well to play it immediately with great efficiency. His short passes and shots are pure wonder. Prodigious changes of pace.'

Villa corroborates Menotti. Recalling the selection dilemma, he stated, 'Menotti's only worry was he was too young. In training, Diego was superb. I remember talking to Ossie and Kempes about it. We all thought he had to be in the team. But unfortunately for me he played in my

34 'Behold, The Champions!' www.papelitos.com.ar

position. When he did come into the side after the World Cup, I never played for the national team again.'[35]

Maradona would get his chance to play for Menotti a year later when he represented Argentina at the 1979 Junior World Cup in Japan. Menotti coached the junior team at this tournament and, yet again, Argentina lifted the trophy. Maradona was able to shake off the disappointment of being omitted from the senior squad by scoring six goals and winning player of the tournament. On his path to becoming a global cultural icon, Diego's stock had raised considerably domestically. As with the 1978 senior squad, the dictatorship saw the value in promoting young, talented and admired sportsmen as the international face of the country. Diego, his team-mates and the trophy were paraded around the country as symbols for the future of Argentina.

By this point the dictatorship was facing international pressure, as opening the doors to the world by hosting the World Cup had let the cat out of the bag on some of the atrocities committed. In 1979 a delegation from the International Court of Human Rights would visit Argentina to investigate. At this point American PR agency Burson Cohn and Wolfe were hired by the military, at great cost, to design the slogan '*Los Argentinos somos derechos y humanos* (We Argentinians are human and right)'. The tactics of the dictatorship were yet again laid bare. The use of 'We Argentinians' is interesting and a clear attempt by the government to intertwine itself with the people of

---

35 Brian Viner. 2006. 'Ricky Villa – I recognise I am a little part of English football history'. Independent.com

Argentina in a display of unity. Yet again a world-beating football team led by César Luis Menotti would be hijacked by the dictatorship as a symbol of its benevolence.

Despite his pride at the World Cup wins, it's clear that Menotti laments the use of the victories by the dictatorship. Rarely is the sporting prowess of the 1978 squad mentioned without the footnote of the match-fixing allegations that haunted the Peru game, or the image of General Jorge Videla in the stands during matches. Despite his joy in bringing the trophy to Argentina, El Flaco often speaks of his shame of how the memory has been tainted by association: 'It really is a shame not to recognise everything that those players did, that they played for free all their lives, that they never claimed a prize.'[36]

36 Mariano Verrina. 'Menotti: I kept my word, I did what I had to do'. www.papelitos.com.ar

Group 1: Argentina, France, Italy and Poland

Italy vs France: 2 June 1978 – Estadio José María Minella, Mar del Plata

Group 1 would begin with an afternoon clash between European juggernauts Italy and France in Mar del Plata. The same evening, hosts Argentina would begin their challenge for the Jules Rimet Trophy, taking on Hungary in Buenos Aires. The tournament had kicked off the previous night with holders West Germany taking on Group 2 rivals Poland but the opening fixtures in Group 1 meant home interest had reached boiling point.

Dino Zoff led out the Italians against a French team making their first World Cup appearance in 12 years. The French side contained a 22-year-old playmaker who would go on to shine on the global stage, Saint-Étienne's Michel Platini. Indeed, the French contained a healthy blend of experience and youthful promise, skippered by legendary defender Marius Trésor of Marseille. Coach Michel Hidalgo targeted a place in the second round for the returning Frenchmen but recognised that starting the tournament strongly was essential, stating, 'I believe

Argentina have already claimed one of the second-round places, so the fight is between ourselves, Italy and Hungary for the other place. It is important that we beat Italy.'[37]

France would take heed of Hidalgo's desire for a strong start and made an immediate impact as forward Didier Six's searing pace took him past two Italian defenders, running the length of the left-hand side of the Italian half. Six fired a left-footed cross on to the head of Bernard Lacombe, who headed past a shell-shocked Dino Zoff. The Italians had been caught cold.

A young Italian team showed their maturity as they found a foothold in the match and pressed for an equaliser. This arrived in shambolic fashion as a wayward shot was redirected on to the post by Roberto Bettega, his header thumping the stanchion of crossbar and post before rebounding back into the box. The ball pinballed between Italian forwards and French defenders before Paolo Rossi unwittingly diverted the ball into the net. It was a scruffy goal befitting the cabbage-patch surface of the Mar del Plata pitch. As French defenders stared at each other in bewilderment, the Italians players embraced in celebration.

Rossi's goal was not one to savour from an aesthetic point of view but the Tuscan's first goal for the Azzurri was significant in not only restoring parity for his team but also launching his career as one of the national team's most beloved goalscorers. Prior to this tournament, Torino's Francesco Graziani had been expected to lead the line. Six years Rossi's senior, Graziani had three

---

37 David Miller. 1978. *World Cup – The Argentina Story*. Frederick Warne Publishers.

years' more experience in the blue shirt and was a trusted member of the squad that had qualified for the tournament. However, underwhelming displays in the World Cup warm-up matches meant that Italian coach Enzo Bearzot opted for the more versatile Rossi, who during the tournament frequently switched the point of reference for Italy's attack, drifting out to the wings and swapping positions with the Juventus duo of Bettega and Franco Causio. Rossi, the slim marksman, had suddenly grown into the Azzurri shirt that had previously dwarfed him. In fact, 1978 proved to be a breakthrough year for Rossi as he finished top scorer in Serie A with newly promoted Vicenza, his 24 goals firing the Biancorossi to an incredible second-place finish.

At half-time Bearzot replaced midfielder Giancarlo Antognoni with Renato Zaccarelli. The substitute would quickly repay his coach by firing Italy into the lead ten minutes into the second half. A well-placed drive found the corner of the net, with the French goalkeeper perhaps unsighted, rooted to the spot. In typical fashion, the Azzurri kept the French at arm's length to see out the rest of the match. France mustered a few more chances, most notably a Lacombe header that floated just above Zoff's bar, but Italy's organisation and composure allowed them to thwart any further French attacks. Marco Tardelli, who would become a household name four years later for his World Cup-winning goal and passionate celebrations, showed great discipline and concentration in shepherding the enigmatic Platini to the fringes of the action.

This would be a World Cup too soon for a talented French team, which would reach the bronze play-off in Spain four years later. However, France's preparation for the World Cup hadn't run smoothly. On 23 May 1978 coach Michel Hidalgo was driving with his wife in Bordeaux, his destination the train station, where he was meant to travel to Paris to meet with the team prior to their departure for Buenos Aires. During the journey, Hidalgo's car was forced to the side of the road by another vehicle, from which emerged four armed men, who instructed Hidalgo to exit his car. One of the men frog-marched him into the nearby woods, while the rest waited by the car. Hidalgo, understandably fearing for his life, got into a struggle with the armed assailant and managed to wrestle the weapon from the man. As the would-be kidnapper fled the scene, Hidalgo returned to find his wife and car unharmed, then he drove to the nearest police station to hand over the weapon. The police later discovered that the weapon was not loaded.

Unperturbed by the attempted kidnapping, Hidalgo joined the national team in Paris. That evening the French press agency AFP received a phone call from someone who identified themselves as the kidnapper, citing raising awareness of the humanitarian atrocities in Argentina as their motive. Hidalgo was known to be left-leaning in his politics but insisted in an interview with *Le Monde* newspaper that 'boycotting the World Cup is not the best way to understand and help these people'.[38] As pressure to

---

38 Nahuel Lag. 'The attempt to kidnap Michel Hidalgo'. papelitos.com/ar

boycott the World Cup was building in Europe, the players and staff would have felt relieved to board the plane for Buenos Aires.

Argentina vs Hungary: 2 June 1978 – Estadio Monumental, Buenos Aires

Argentina had selected a squad of 20 domestically based and two internationally based players for the tournament. Both Mario Kempes, nicknamed 'El Matador', and Daniel Bertoni plied their trade in La Liga, at Valencia CF and Sevilla, respectively. Córdoba-born Kempes had returned to the international fold in 1978 after spending a year in international exile. Although the majority of South American teams selected domestic players, Menotti decided that Kempes possessed too much quality to leave in Spain. Kempes arrived at the tournament following an insatiable season, plundering 28 goals and the Pichichi trophy for the second season in a row. His 1978 haul in Spain was the highest since countryman Alfredo Di Stéfano managed three more in 1957. Bertoni had yet to represent Sevilla but, following the World Cup, he would spend two successful seasons in Andalucía, scoring 30 goals in 71 matches.

In the absence of teenage wonderkid Diego Maradona, Menotti selected Daniel Valencia and Norberto Alonso as the attacking midfielders. The former represented Talleres, who had narrowly missed out on 1977's Torneo Nacional, finishing runners-up. Although not considered a generational talent, like the prodigious Maradona, Valencia was a respected, creative footballer whose maturity made him a safer bet than the boy who would become 'El Pibe de Oro' (The Golden Boy). Alonso had returned to River Plate after a sabbatical in France with Marseille. The Buenos Aires club formed the spine of the national team, with Ubaldo Fillol in goal, Passarella at centre-back and Leopoldo Luque leading the line.

Menotti valued continuity and familiarity. He selected players who had formed strong relationships at club level, which meant that five of the squad represented River Plate. *Superclasico* rivals Boca Juniors, by contrast, didn't have a single representative in the squad, despite being Intercontinental champions in 1978 and back-to-back winners of the Copa Libertadores. Left-back Alberto Tarantini had recently departed Boca Juniors after a bitter contract dispute and entered the World Cup as a free agent. As a valuable commodity in football's biggest shop window, Tarantini's performances earned him a move to England with Birmingham City.

Boca Juniors' best chance at a representative for the squad would be at right-back, where Vicente Pernía had represented La Albiceleste throughout the previous year. Menotti faced a straight choice between him and Jorge Olguín of San Lorenzo. The two players contrasted in terms of personality and playing style, and the debate on who to select was divisive among fans of the national team and an obsession of the media. 'Olguín o Pernía, Pernía o Olguín?' Menotti would be asked to the point of exhaustion in the lead-up to the tournament. Pernía was an archetypal, muscle-bound right-back who delighted in the physical aspect of the game and was very difficult to pass. Olguín had begun his career as a forward, had 'improvised' on the wing during his time at San Lorenzo, but was mainly deployed as a centre-back at his club.[39] Comfortable on the ball, Olguín provided Argentina with more of an attacking threat down the flanks, complementing Tarantini on the opposite side of the pitch.

As with Maradona, Menotti offered little explanation in public on his selection of Olguín over Pernía and would become frustrated with the media scrutiny of selection of individuals, proclaiming, 'Y dale con Pernía?' to journalists. He was highlighting the frustrations of being asked the same questions about his team. 'Y dale con Pernía?' would become a catchphrase, repeated more than 30 years later by River Plate coach Marcelo Gallardo in 2012, when he had become exacerbated at explaining his selections to the media.

Without an explanation from Menotti, Argentinians were left to their own devices to surmise why Olguín was given the nod over Pernía. Argentinian TV personality Mario Sapag lampooned the dilemma in a famous comedy sketch, implying that the selection was down to their personalities. Pernía was portrayed as sad – 'Pernía esta triste' – and Olguín was said to be joyful, even down to the sound of his name. This would become another catchphrase, one that Olguín said had followed him for years and led to teasing of his children at school, who carried the same 'joyful' surname.[40]

---

39 Jorge Olguín interview with *El Grafico*, 2014.
40 *Ibid.*

In footballing terms, the selection was more likely to be down to style of play. Menotti was noted as an admirer of the Dutch style of total football and had selected players who were comfortable playing in different positions. Olguín offered more versatility than Pernía due to his experience at centre-back and brief spell of moonlighting as a winger at San Lorenzo. Pernía had also disappointed his coach in the colours of Argentina, collecting a red card against Scotland during their 1977 tour of South America.

The 22-man squad selected, there was now the small matter of beginning the World Cup campaign, with the dictatorship in attendance. General Jorge Videla was not a common sight at the side of a football pitch but during the tournament he would attend every Argentina match, in civilian clothes. 'Videla had never set foot on a football pitch in his life. Until the World Cup of '78, when he went to seven football matches in a month,' according to journalist Ezequiel Fernandez Moores.[41]

Argentina kicked off their campaign that evening in Estadio Monumental, home of Club Atlético River Plate. The hosts got off to the worst possible start as Hungary's Károly Csapó fired the underdogs ahead, redirecting a rebound past Ubaldo Fillol in goal. Hungary's advantage would be short-lived as the hosts found a way back into the match within five minutes. In trademark fashion, winger José Valencia carried the ball purposefully through the Hungarian midfield and, as he accelerated, the opponents' defence had no option

---

41 *Pele, Argentina and the Dictators.* Goalhanger films. 2020.

but to upend him in the crudest fashion. Mario Kempes stood over the free kick with the opportunity to punish Hungary's cynical play. His powerful drive was blocked by Hungarian goalkeeper Sándor Gujdár, only for River Plate's Leopoldo Luque to react quickest, firing the ball past the keeper. Argentina's barrel-chested, moustachioed hitman had got La Albiceleste off the mark and sent a sold-out Estadio Monumental into ecstasy. In equal parts relief and jubilation, the Argentina players embraced under the approving gaze of the dictatorship.

Argentina enjoyed the lion's share of goalscoring chances for the remainder of the match but had to wait for their winner. After a goalmouth scramble, River Plate's Norberto Alonso and Sevilla-bound Daniel Bertoni combined to score the winner. Both on as substitutes, and due to the bizarre decision to number the shirts alphabetically, the forwards numbered 1 and 4, respectively, celebrated near the corner flag. Argentina managed the remaining seven minutes perfectly as Hungary's discipline fell apart. The Hungarians received two red cards in the final minutes for reckless challenges, and the 11 men triumphed over the remaining nine.

The two red cards did little to dispel the prevailing idea that Argentina would receive favourable treatment from the officials during the tournament. Hungary manager Lajos Baróti had previously stated to legendary football journalist Brian Glanville that 'everything, even the air, is in favour of Argentina'. His worries would become a self-fulfilling prophecy in Buenos Aires, as his exasperated players remonstrated with Portuguese referee

Antonio Garrido, their frustrations igniting a fractious final ten minutes.

Having weathered an early scare, Argentina had negotiated their first hurdle unscathed. Their team was functional, if not yet completely fluid, and their centre-forward Luque was off the mark. As with all centre-forwards, goals were the most sacred commodity for the man from Santa Fe, who would finish his international career with a ratio of a goal every other match. Luque would also go on to enjoy a prolific tournament in front of goal but, from a personal point of view, the tournament was coloured by both triumph and tragedy. Luque's alertness in front of goal to score the opener belied the fact that he had been playing the match with the weight of a terrible tragedy on his mind.

'Uppermost in my mind was that earlier that day the brother of a close friend of mine had disappeared. His body was later found by villagers on the banks of the River Plate with concrete attached to his legs.'[42] Luque didn't reveal whether the victim was an enemy of the military but the method of murder suggests involvement from the death squads. For Leopoldo Luque, the path to glory was not a straight line and he would be faced with further tragedy the next time he put on the shirt of the national team.

Italy vs Hungary: 6 June 1978 – Estadio José María Minella, Mar del Plata

Italy faced a much-changed Hungary four days later in Mar del Plata. Suspensions following red cards to two of

---

42 Will Hersey. 2018. *Remembering Argentina 1978: The Dirtiest World Cup of All Time*. Esquire.com

Hungary's forwards against Argentina meant that the two Lászlós (Fazekas and Pusztai) joined Sándor Pintér in a three-pronged attack. The pitch had taken its toll on a few other members of the 11 that had faced the hosts, with Hungary fielding a new goalkeeper in Ferenc Mészarós, deputising for Sándor Gujdár. Mészarós would have a busy afternoon as Italy sought to reach the second round with their second win of the tournament.

The Azzurri's passage to the latter stages was assured thanks to a ruthless display from Roberto Bettega, who was at the heart of all of Italy's attacks, seemingly playing on a different surface to the beleaguered Hungarians as he led them around the butchered turf on strings. However, Hungary had created the match's first moment of quality as Fazekas gracefully swayed past two Italian defenders but, faced with Dino Zoff inside the 18-yard box, seemed to tense up and lifted his shot over the bar. The missed opportunity sparked the Italians into life as Rossi once again found his name on the scoresheet, following in Tardelli's long drive and scrambling the rebound past the goalkeeper. Rossi's second goal of the group stage further enhanced his reputation as the penalty box's most ruthless finisher.

Italy doubled their lead within a minute as Zombori's loose pass into heavy Italian traffic was picked off in a dangerous position in Hungary's half. Causio picked up the ball and lofted a first-time pass into the Hungary box, which caused chaos among the defenders. On hand to benefit from the mix-up was Bettega, who powered through dithering defenders, controlled the ball on his thigh and fired a low shot beyond the goalkeeper and into the net.

In the second half, Italy put the game beyond doubt. A quick interchange of passes, a lay-off to Benetti and a low, powerful laces-first finish ended the match as a contest. Benetti's rocket from the edge of the box gave the goalkeeper no chance as it rifled into the bottom corner, giving the Italians an unassailable three-goal lead. Hungary were awarded a dubious penalty with ten minutes remaining, which substitute András Tóth scored to add some respect to the scoreline, but they were well beaten and eliminated from the tournament.

Argentina vs France: 6 June 1978 – Estadio Monumental, Buenos Aires

Later in the evening, hosts Argentina were given the opportunity to join Italy in the second round, provided they could overcome France. What followed was an all-time classic and one of the matches of the tournament.

After dispatching an ill-disciplined Hungary, Argentina faced a sterner task against France. Expectation and excitement were high as the match began, with those not in attendance in Buenos Aires crowded around their black-and-white television sets. Although everyone in the country was watching the same thing, not everyone was receiving the same sounds through their TV. A two-kilometre radius in the city centre of La Plata listened to a message from Los Montoneros, who had hijacked the audio for the match. As the match kicked off, instead of the sounds of the commentator in Estadio Monumental, listeners heard the voice of Mario Firmenich, the commander-in-chief of Los Montoneros, the left-wing, Perónist organisation at war with the dictatorship.

Firmenich spoke about the state terrorism of the military and the 'painful reality' of thousands of disappeared Argentinians, held captive or murdered by the dictatorship. He condemned Videla and the junta, labelling them as savages that had created 'the most painful balance that exists in our memories in only two years. Over 5,000 dead, around 20,000 disappeared.' In a call to arms, Firmenich stated, 'It's the duty of every Argentine to show the world the real Argentina.'[43]

The desire of Los Montoneros to show what they deemed to be the real Argentina, echoes statements made by General Videla at the time. In Videla's speech at the opening ceremony, the general spoke of a nation given an opportunity to coexist in unity and diversity, thanks to the hosting of the World Cup. The Montoneros, of course, poured cold water on this notion and sought to peel back Videla's statesmanlike façade, highlighting the savagery of the junta in dealing with dissenters. To them, revealing this was to show the real Argentina.

The Montoneros operation took place on the fifth floor of Hotel La Plata, using a transmitter fed through the battery of a Ford Falcon, ironically the vehicle favoured by the military death squads as their mode of abduction. The operation was considered to be one of the most successful in the history of the group, considering they had been

---

43   Nicolas Sagaian. 'Radio Liberacion – Interferences by Montoneros during the 78 World Cup'. Papelitos.ar

forced underground over the course of the previous year, losing numerous members. It was the first time the leader of Los Montoneros had been able to speak directly to the public in years, and the message would be amplified by the interest in the story from local and international press. The tactic would be used again by the group later in the tournament. The operation was relatively low-risk as by the time the army had reached the hotel the people responsible had long gone, leaving behind a message scrawled on the walls: 'Only the people can save the people'.

Following a resounding victory for Los Montoneros over the army in this particular battle of cat and mouse, matters turned back to the field, 60 kilometres north in Buenos Aires. The young French team were in no way overawed by the occasion and settled into the opening rhythm of the match better than their hosts. Early on, midfielder Henri Michel received the ball 30 yards from goal on the right-hand side. Three Argentina defenders stood off Michel as he floated a cross into the box into the path of striker Bernard Lacombe, who stooped to meet the ball with a diving header. Lacombe was unable to apply enough power to trouble Fillol, who saved the ball comfortably at his feet; however, the move should have set off alarm bells for Argentina's defence. Lacombe was alone in the box and had the ball not reached him at an awkward height, he would have been able to strike it with more power or even take a touch, such was the space he was afforded. No Argentinian defender had tracked the run of Michel Platini either, had Lacombe nodded the ball into his path.

Argentina were then given another warning, as Didier Six faced down Olguín on the left flank. Six's perpetual motion allowed him to pass Olguín easily and he fired a quick cross low into the box. Forward Dominique Rocheteau's reactions were far sharper than those of the flat-footed defence, but he sent his shot the wrong side of Fillol's post. The French attack was purring as Argentina's defence was left reeling.

Argentina needed a foothold in the match, which came as Osvaldo Ardiles carried the ball in the French half. A one-two between the two sons of Córdoba, Kempes and Ardiles, sent the latter into the box. Kempes's return ball was slightly overhit and pushed Ardiles away from goal. The midfielder's deceptive strength on the ball, despite his slight frame, allowed him to evade heavy French challenges. An attempted sandwich tackle saw two French defenders on the floor as Ardiles retained possession. He took the ball to the byline, inviting the tackle from French skipper Trésor.

The imposing Trésor knew that any contact could result in a penalty and he instead hoped that Ardiles would run out of room, as he attempted to shepherd the diminutive midfielder and the ball out of play for a goal kick. Ardiles, however, was able to drag a cross back towards the crowded penalty spot. Kempes had followed his pass but, ultimately, a mix-up saw him block an attempted shot and the ball spilled out to Luque, whose shot was cleared off the line. As both teams had now registered chances, the nervous energy and tempo of the match increased significantly.

Argentina's best chance fell to Kempes, who thumped a volley against the bottom of France's upright from four yards. He had followed in a deliciously floated ball, which landed on his favoured foot, only to snatch at the shot, blasting it at the near post. Argentina's highest-rated player was clearly feeling the enormity of the pressure on his shoulders and, at this point in the tournament, seemed to be snatching at chances, as if fearful that more time on the ball meant more time for mistakes.

Despite his two misses, Kempes's influence on the match was growing and he was beginning to show why he was heralded as the home nation's great hope. Picking the ball up in his own half, 'El Matador' charged at the French midfield, drawing Trésor out of the defensive line in the middle of the park and daring a challenge from the Frenchman. Trésor obliged and, as he lunged for the ball, found that Kempes was no longer there. He had drawn the flying challenge and glided past the defender with ease. Kempes pushed the ball out to Valencia on the left wing. He feinted to cross and then squared the ball back to Kempes. As French defenders sought to make amends, rushing out to Kempes, he struck a powerful shot that again blasted against the post, shaking the frame of the goal.

Viewers would have been forgiven for thinking they were watching a video replay of the same incident just before half-time, as Kempes received the ball in the centre of the pitch. Dominique Bathenay, on his return to the French team, believed he could see enough of the ball to hook a leg and dispossess Kempes. Kempes had anticipated the challenge and dragged the ball back with his heel, changing direction and leaving Bathenay on the turf in no-man's land. With acres of space now ahead of him, Kempes drove forward as he had earlier, drawing a languid challenge from Michel and easily gliding past him. In passing Michel, the ball pitched up slightly, allowing Kempes to loft it over the defence. Luque controlled the ball on his chest, shrugged off the challenge from Trésor and fired a left-footed shot goalward. The shot was blocked by the falling figure of Trésor, whose arm swatted the ball out for a goal kick, completely accidentally. René Houseman raised a hand to claim a penalty, conducting the partisan crowd who were now screaming a cacophony of obscenities at the officials. Luque shrugged his shoulders nonchalantly, asking the ref to consider the possibility of a penalty.

The referee, Jean Dubach of Switzerland, had seen enough to consult his linesman and, after a brief discussion, Dubach pointed to the spot. The Swiss had been about 40 yards behind play and was unsighted, much to the disbelief of the French players. This was not a typical handball penalty in 1978, when most accidental handballs were shrugged off as part of the game. Barry Davies, BBC commentator, described it as 'the most ridiculous penalty I've ever seen'.[44] Daniel Passarella made no mistake from the spot, firing an unstoppable shot into the bottom-left corner. The captain ran away in celebration, leaping into the air and embracing his team-mates. Argentina had weathered the early French storm and reached half-time in the ascendancy.

---

44   Interview with Barry Davies 2021.

The interval did nothing to reduce the heat from the match. Ten minutes into the second half, Valencia's booming 25-yard half-volley dipped under the bar of French goalkeeper Bertrand-Demanes. The stopper had to spring to tip the ball over, his strong hand enough to prevent a spectacular goal. In diving backwards, the keeper landed awkwardly on the post and had to be substituted for Dominique Baratelli.

Injured and fuelled by a perceived sense of injustice, France continued the second half in breathless fashion. On the hour mark they found themselves back in the match. Patrick Battiston, attacking from right wing-back, pushed Argentina's defenders further back until they reached the edge of their penalty area. He clipped a ball over the head of Tarantini, which fell in between the Argentina centre-backs. The ball bounced tantalisingly, igniting a foot race between Rocheteau and Fillol, who charged from his line. Rocheteau reached the ball first and lofted the ball over the head of the onrushing River Plate keeper and on to the crossbar. The ball bounced back into play, evading the defenders who had chased it in. Rocheteau controlled the ball into the path of Michel Platini, who crashed a powerful shot into the empty net.

France were good value for the equaliser and the momentum seemed to be shifting in their favour. Michel Platini was growing into the match and the crowd at Estadio Monumental were witnessing the growth of a future superstar as he glided past two challenges in the middle of the park, before threading a pass to Didier Six. The striker took a touch that left him clear of Passarella's desperate challenge. He carried the ball closer and struck it early, before Fillol had set himself to save the shot. The ball evaded Fillol but crucially trickled past the post.

Argentina were reeling and it was now their turn to look skywards and curse the cruel hand of fate when they faced an injury setback. Sensing France's growing dominance and feeling the need for fresh legs, Menotti replaced Valencia with Alonso. However, Alonso didn't last ten minutes before he was forced off with an injury, replaced by Ortiz.

The momentum had passed between both teams numerous times in the second half alone but would take one more decisive jerk in the direction of Argentina with 20 minutes remaining. Ardiles's through ball found Luque with his back to goal, just outside the 'D' of the box. Luque's first touch was heavier than he had intended, causing the ball to pop up into the air but 70 minutes of breathless football had taken its toll on French bodies and minds, and with fatigue setting into both, the defence hadn't closed Luque down. The man from Santa Fe had enough time to wait for the ball to bounce, allowing it to reach optimum height before taking his shot. As soon as Luque's boot made contact it was clear France were in trouble. The ball was struck with equal measures of spite and precision as it flew into the bottom corner of the French goal. It resembled a cruise missile, such was the speed and accuracy of the drive, leaving the French goalkeeper haplessly clutching at the Buenos Aires air. Upon the ball hitting the net, the stadium erupted with emotion. The deafening roar was one of a crowd appreciative of the quality of the strike but also aware of how significant the next goal in the match would be. The unbridled joy among spectators and players alike erupted into the Buenos Aires sky, as Argentina claimed the lead.

Luque sprinted towards his team-mates, arms aloft in a gesture reminiscent of Juan Perón's famous pose on which the World Cup logo was based. Luque was mobbed by his team-mates, the relief palpable in their embrace. Argentina had a lead to defend and France were now left to rue their missed chances in the lead-up to the goal. Two minutes later, with just 15 minutes remaining to play, Didier Six once again called goalkeeper Fillol into action. A sublimely struck left-footed volley required every sinew of strength from the goalkeeper, who was able to divert the ball wide at full stretch, sending France's hopes of reaching the second round with it.

In the dying embers of the match France were left feeling a huge sense of injustice as their penalty appeals following Galván's foul on Six were waved away by the referee, who was far closer to this event, which seemed to be a far more clear-cut decision than Trésor's ambiguous handball. However, fortune favoured the home team as the French pleas were ignored. Barry Davies deemed the penalty to be a stronger shout than Argentina's and the prevailing wisdom among neutrals was that Argentina had got away with it.

Nevertheless, a fine French team exited the tournament with two losses in their opening matches. Argentina would progress, although not unscathed as they finished the match with ten men, minus an injured Leopoldo Luque, who had damaged his elbow. He missed the celebrations at his home stadium against France and didn't return to the team camp at José C. Paz as he was taken to hospital for treatment. He would wake to find the faces of family members around his hospital bed. However, they hadn't visited to enquire about the elbow but to deliver devastating news. 'I thought they had come because of my injury, but it wasn't. My dad came up to me and gave me the news that my brother [Oscar, nicknamed 'Cacho'] had been killed in a car accident.'[45]

Luque's brother Cacho had been travelling to Buenos Aires in a small truck they'd borrowed from a neighbour. Poor driving conditions and heavy fog meant the vehicle crashed into stationary truck in San Isidro, 30 kilometres north of the capital city, killing Cacho.

Leopoldo Luque was one of the most vocal members of the 1978 squad who criticised the dictatorship. Luque has consistently sought to distance the success of the squad from the military, and he said, 'Not one of the military leaders at the time shook my hand to offer their condolences. No one cared. So, I said "this is how it is". That's why it really annoys me when people connect us. We had no relationship whatsoever.' Neither the military nor the AFA contributed towards the funeral, or procedure to transfer Cacho's body back to his family home. Instead, the Argentinian squad collected the money from their common fund to pay for the transfer.[46]

---

45   *Pele, Argentina and the Dictators.* Goalhanger films. 2020.
46   Eddie Corp. 2021. 'The drama and glory of Leopoldo Luque'. digismak.com

Grieving and injured, Luque missed out on the final group match against Italy, which would determine the winner of the group. The striker returned to his family home to console his parents. Granted compassionate leave by Menotti, he was told, 'Do what you need to do, but don't forget we need you here.' Menotti's words would prove prophetic as Argentina, minus their powerful forward, faced their final group match against a formidable Italian team.

France vs Hungary: 10 June 1978 – Estadio José María Minella, Mar del Plata

Before establishing who would take top spot in the group, the two teams yet to record a point faced off in Mar del Plata. Wounded by two losses, in matches they could have won in different circumstances, France took to the field with a score to settle. The 22,000 in attendance would have been forgiven for not recognising the French team. Although coach Hidalgo had shuffled the pack, making seven changes from the loss to Argentina, it was what the team was wearing that was particularly unfamiliar. France had only packed their away kit and were surprised to discover that Hungary had also arrived in their away kit. What made this problematic was the fact that both kits were white. As the designated home team, the fault for the mix-up fell on France and they were faced with a dilemma. Their home kit had been left 400 kilometres north in Buenos Aires.

France's solution was to borrow a set of home kit from local team, Club Atlético Kimberley. For the first time in their history, France would take to the field in red socks, blue shorts and, thanks to the generosity of 'Los Verdiblancos', green-and-white shirts. However, disguised as a fifth division Argentinian team, France's performance was one from the top tier. Centre-back Christian Lopez fired them into the lead after 20 minutes. Receiving a square pass, 30 yards from goal and under no pressure from Hungarian defenders, he arrowed an unstoppable shot into the top corner. Marc Berdoll consolidated the lead 15 minutes later, as he dragged three Hungarian defenders across the quagmire in front of the penalty box, keeping his footing and composure on an awful surface, before firing a low shot back across the goalkeeper into the opposite corner.

Sándor Zombori scored Hungary's goal of the tournament with five minutes remaining of the half. The midfielder exchanged a one-two on the edge of the French box, controlling the ball expertly with his left foot, before opening his body and placing a curved finish into the top left-hand corner of the goal. But any hopes Hungary may have had of registering a point were swiftly extinguished within 60 seconds as Rocheteau scored France's third goal and ended the match as a contest. The man from Saint-Étienne negotiated a crowded penalty area, arriving on to a low cross first and diverting a smart shot under goalkeeper Sándor Gujdár.

The second half petered out without incident as both teams exited the tournament having shown glimpses of quality but second best to the teams that would compete that evening in Buenos Aires.

Argentina vs Italy: 10 June 1978 – Estadio Monumental, Buenos Aires

Argentina were without the injured duo of Leopoldo Luque and Norberto Alonso for the Group 1 finale against Italy, requiring César Menotti to tinker with their starting XI. Following his 20-minute cameo from the bench against France, Oscar Ortiz started the match on the wing, replacing Huracán winger René Houseman. The task of leading the line in the absence of Luque fell to Sevilla's Daniel Bertoni, making his first start of the tournament. Italy were unchanged from their win against Hungary.

The crowd at El Monumental was as consistently fervent as the two previous matches, creating a pulsating, partisan atmosphere designed to intimidate officials and opposition alike. However, on this evening Argentina found their opponents unbowed and the man in the centre circle unperturbed by the atmosphere around him.

In the opening minute Italy set out their stall, showing their hosts that they were happy to engage in a physical battle. During a break in play, Juventus's midfield enforcer Romeo Benetti stepped over a prone Américo Gallego on the floor and, in passing, raked his studs along the leg of the midfielder. The act was unseen by Israeli referee Abraham Klein, but the message had been delivered to the Argentinian midfield – Italy were not to be intimidated.

Argentina started the match well. Passarella lofted a through ball high into the Buenos Aires sky; Kempes brought the ball down on his chest on the edge of the penalty area and laid it off to Ardiles, whose left-footed shot didn't carry enough venom to trouble Zoff, who was able to collect the ball. Italy's main threat during the first half came from set plays, as Rossi flicked on a corner into the middle of the box towards Bettega. Rossi's flick was slightly too high for his co-striker, who was unable to meet the ball cleanly, instead shooting the ball into the turf. The scuffed shot crucially took enough pace off the ball for Fillol to react quickly enough between the posts to push the ball over the bar from point-blank range.

During the first half, Argentina struggled to assert any dominance in midfield and Italy were able to nullify attacks by deploying forward Franco Causio in a deeper role. The striker dropped back when the hosts were in possession, allowing Italy to outnumber their opponents in midfield. Too often Gallego and Ardiles found themselves without options in the middle of the park and unable to play through the Italians.

Kempes's free kick summoned a fantastic save from Zoff in the first half's only true moment of quality. From 30 yards, Kempes struck his kick with venom as it soared over the wall, only to dip violently towards the top left-hand corner of Zoff's goal. The ball seemed destined to nestle neatly into the angle between post and bar, only for Zoff to claw it away with his fingertips, at full stretch. The Italian captain had saved a certain goal and El Matador had yet to register a goal at the tournament. Then Zoff doubled down on his heroics from the ensuing corner, as he dived low to save Passarella's towering header. The Argentina captain was unusually short for a centre-back, standing no higher than 5ft 8in but leapt high above the stationary Italian defenders. His header was straight from the coaching manual, heading the ball low into the ground, making it difficult for Zoff. However, the goalkeeper was equal to the attempt, displaying quick reflexes to get down low and gather the ball.

The first half ended 0-0, much to the chagrin of the home fans, who had seen referee Abraham Klein wave away two penalty appeals. The 22 players trudged off after a 45-minute stalemate without protestation but the crowd was apoplectic. Klein later stated, 'The crowd were very upset. I had no problem with the players; they respect me. The crowd, you know, they pay and when they pay they can tell you whatever they think about you and your mother.'[47]

Klein, aware of the reception he would receive from the crowd, hatched a plan to protect himself from the vitriol of the stands. Italy returned to the field to a torrent of abuse; next out of the changing rooms came the home heroes, Argentina. Klein opted to coincide his return to the pitch with Argentina's, following Menotti's men on to the pitch. The home crowd had no opportunity to hurl abuse at Klein as they were swept along on a wave of enthusiasm, cheering their 11 countrymen back on to the field of play.

As the second half progressed and the game matured, both teams exchanged long-range shots until Italy orchestrated a training-ground move of sheer artistry that would leave Argentinian defenders clutching at thin air. From a throw-in, Antognoni passed the ball through a crowd to Bettega, who, in one movement, played the ball

---

47 Rob Smyth. 2012. 'The forgotten story of Abraham Klein, the "master of the whistle"'. *The Guardian*.

with the outside of his boot to Rossi, and spun his defender. Rossi fed the ball back to Bettega, who had now stolen a yard on his defender. With one touch, Bettega fired the ball past the advancing Fillol. In three touches, Italy had carved through Argentina's defence and scored the opening goal.

Italy had 20 minutes left to protect their lead and, as in their opening match against France, they were able to see out the match in a composed way. Their biggest scare came when Américo Gallego weaved his way through the box, falling at the feet of centre-back Antonio Cabrini, who nervously glanced at referee Klein as the Italian team held their breath. To a chorus of whistles from the crowd, Klein emphatically waved away penalty appeals and play moved on. Argentina's undefeated beginning to the tournament was evaporating before their eyes. Without any further threats on the Italian goal, the final whistle blew and Italy had topped the group.

Referee Abraham Klein managed a volatile match with aplomb, never succumbing to the influence of the partisan crowd and officiating with unwavering impartiality. He conceded that refereeing a match of such magnitude, in a cauldron atmosphere and under the gaze of the dictatorship, wasn't an easy task. Many referees may not have been strong enough to be impartial. In Simon Kuper's book, *Ajax, The Dutch, The War*, he stated: 'I think all referees are fair, but not all of them are brave.'[48] However, Klein's bravery would ultimately rule him out of refereeing the final. Although nobody acknowledged this publicly, it's

---

48 Simon Kuper. 2011. *Ajax, The Dutch, The War: Football in Europe During the Second World War*. Orion.

indisputable that the military in Argentina were unhappy with Klein's performance in the match against Italy and didn't want La Albiceleste to be officiated by him again. The Argentina players themselves bore no ill will towards the referee; to a man they shook hands with the official at the end of the match and accepted the result with dignity and professionalism. Commentators from around the world praised Klein, as British journalist Brian Glanville wrote: 'There was nothing more impressive in this World Cup, than the way he stood between his linesmen at half-time, scorning the banshee whistling of the incensed crowd.'[49]

Despite the global admiration of Klein's fairness and impartiality, the dictatorship scapegoated the Israeli for his decisions not to award the home team a penalty. World Cup organiser Carlos Lacoste's close friendship with FIFA president João Havelange meant that the military was able to enjoy massive influence over the appointment of officials and, as a result, Klein missed out on officiating the final.

Group 1 was complete; France and Hungary had been eliminated. Group winners Italy would remain in Buenos Aires to join the rest of Group A in the second round. Argentina, however, would be in Group B, which would take place in Mendoza and Rosario. Although not the desired path of the military and the AFA, it would be in Rosario that La Albiceleste would find their mojo and El Matador would find home comforts in front of goal, in the stadium where he had represented Rosario Central with distinction. Argentina would also be strengthened by the

---

49 Rob Smyth. 2012. 'The forgotten story of Abraham Klein, the "master of the whistle"'. *The Guardian*.

return of Leopoldo Luque for the second stage. He had buried his brother on the day of their defeat to Italy and, after the funeral, his father told him he needed to return to the national team. His father said, 'You have to go back. You fought all your life for this, you deserve it. And besides, they lose without you.'[50]

50 Eddie Corp. 2021. 'The drama and glory of Leopoldo Luque'. digismak.com

Group 2: Mexico, Poland, Tunisia and West Germany

THE 1978 World Cup didn't open with the hosts in Group 1 but with the reigning champions in Group 2. Alongside West Germany were Poland, who had emerged from the previous World Cup with a creditable third place, CONCACAF champions Mexico and the unfancied Tunisia, who had finished in fourth place in 1978's Africa Cup of Nations earlier in the year.

The West Germans entered the World Cup as holders and recent European Championship finalists, losing in a famous penalty shoot-out to Czechoslovakia, remembered for Antonín Panenka's innovative, chipped penalty. However, the champions had lost the spine of their World Cup-winning team following the international retirements of Franz Beckenbauer, Wolfgang Overath and Gerd Müller. Another omission was 1974 World Cup Final goalscorer Paul Breitner. The Bayern Munich product had returned to Germany, spending a season with Eintracht Braunschweig after his three years in La Liga with Real Madrid. He was a polarising, yet fascinating member of the 1974 squad, whose public persona was full of contradictions. A much-publicised spat with West Germany's coach Helmut Schön meant he wasn't considered for selection to the squad.

Following the bust-up, Breitner provoked the ire of his compatriots, stating, 'I don't feel German at all, and I certainly don't feel Bavarian.' The man from Kolbermoor had gone from national hero and World Cup Final goalscorer to unpatriotic pariah of the national team. Some German fans had even campaigned for Breitner to return his 1974 winners' medal. Breitner had an overtly political personality and idolised left-wing icons such as compatriot Karl Marx and Argentine revolutionary Che Guevara. His outspoken nature and larger-than-life personality was at odds with the stoic, humble Schön and led him to being dubbed 'the newest hero of German counter-culture' by the *New York Times*.[51] In his youth, the Bavarian had participated in the 1968 protest movement, which in West Germany was typified by students protesting to remove government officials with links to Nazism.

Prior to his departure to Spain, Breitner had bemoaned the culture of Bayern Munich as a football club. Criticising the 'nouveau riche, money-based aristocracy' of Bayern, he sought a dream move to La Liga giants Real Madrid.[52] Breitner's penchant for sports cars and good living were often cited by critics as contradictory to his socialist ideals. Dubbed a champagne socialist by detractors, he conceded that the only thing that saddened him about his departure was leaving his expensive cars behind in Bavaria. Breitner also campaigned to receive a portion of the half-

---

51   Robin Hackett. 2011. 'Paul Breitner: Playing on the left'. ESPN.com
52   *Ibid.*

a-million-pound transfer fee that Madrid had parted with, declaring the transfer process as 'unlawful and contrary to human rights'.

Much like his politics and personality, Breitner's style of football was tough to pin into a corner. An attacker by trade, he was converted to a left-back during his apprenticeship at Bayern Munich, before switching to midfield in Madrid. He would enjoy a profitable midfield partnership with Karl-Heinze Rummenigge upon his return to Bayern, then he would eventually return to the West German national team for the 1982 World Cup. It's interesting that his sabbatical from representing West Germany in World Cups took place when the tournament was hosted by an administration so at odds with his left-wing politics and has led to suggestions that his absence was due to objections with the nature of Argentina's dictatorship.

However, his omission was personal, rather than political. Breitner endured an uneasy relationship with the German football federation (DFB) and wasn't suited to what he believed to be the monotony of international football. He described his experience as 'airport, hotel, airport' and bemoaned the lack of financial incentives in representing his country as he had previously agitated for a showdown with the DFB about win bonuses.

Breitner's career was as complex as his personality, characterised by a prodigious return to both Bayern and the national team. His opposition to General Videla's military junta meant that his exile from the national team during the 1978 World Cup was timely. His suggestions that he 'did not feel German' at the time period points to an awkward time for German identity. In 1975 West Germany had swayed politically to the right. Chancellor Helmut Schmidt was far more conservative than his predecessors and a period of austerity followed. If the late 60s and early 70s were marked by the establishment of Germany's first welfare state, then the mid-70s were characterised by a period of economic crisis management, following a global recession.

On international matters, West Germany had deemed it necessary to cooperate with Argentina's military junta as it feared that, without the military, Argentina could fall back into 'leftist authoritarian adventures', which West Germany believed to be extremely dangerous.[53] At this time, the West Germans would have been extremely anxious about the global rise of left-wing activism, with Latin America particularly susceptible. Echoing the 1968 student protests that Paul Breitner had so passionately identified with, West Germany was reeling from the 'German autumn' of 1977.

Throughout the 1970s West Germany suffered attacks from the Red Army Faction. This was a left-wing guerrilla organisation rooted in the 1968 protests that targeted the industrialists and elites of West Germany, with particular focus on those with Nazi pasts. On 5 September 1977 a chauffeured car carrying Hanns Martin Schleyer was travelling through Cologne. Following the murder of banker Jürgen Ponto and Attorney General

---
53 Nils Havemann. 2014. 'The Federal Republic of Germany and the 1978 Football World Cup in Argentina: Genesis and deconstruction of a propagandistic myth'. *The International Journal of the History of Sport*, 31(12): 1509–1518. DOI: 10.1080/09523367.2014.90727

Siegfried Buback, Schleyer was an obvious target for the Red Army Faction. Schleyer was one of West Germany's most powerful industrialists, a high-profile member of the conservative Christian Democratic Union Party and, crucially, a former member of the SS. His driver was forced into evasive action and slammed on his brakes as a woman pushing a pram stepped out into the street. Schleyer's police escort crashed into the back of his car, as the woman pulled two machine guns out of the pram. Further accomplices arrived at the ambush, opening fire on both cars, killing four of the convoy. The Red Army Faction members pulled the still-alive Schleyer out of the car, kidnapping him.

A month later, on 13 October, Lufthansa Flight 181 travelling between Frankfurt and Palma de Mallorca was hijacked by four armed militants: two Palestinian and two Lebanese. Among the demands of the hijackers was the release of Red Army Faction prisoners from Stammheim prison, a maximum-security facility in Stuttgart. The West German government remained steadfast in refusing to negotiate with the hijackers. Five days later, after the plane had landed in Mogadishu (its sixth redirect), in cooperation with Somali authorities, German unit GSG 9 stormed the plane. They killed the four hijackers and liberated the 86 passengers.

Following the botched negotiation, Red Army Faction members in Stammheim communicated a suicide pact, using smuggled transistor radios. Andreas Baader, Gudrun Ensslin and Jan-Carl Raspe synchronised their suicides on 18 October 1977. The event was dubbed 'death night' by the media. The response from the Red Army Faction was swift and brutal, as the body of kidnapped Hanns Schleyer was discovered in the boot of an Audi 100 on the same day. The death of founding members, and success of Operation Feuerzauber in liberating the hostages of Lufthansa Flight 181, was a deathblow to the first wave of the Red Army Faction. Nonetheless, the violence of the German autumn had scarred the West German republic.

Due to the involvement of the Popular Front for the Liberation of Palestine in the hijacking of Lufthansa Flight 181, West Germans feared the global reaches of like-minded left-wing guerrilla groups. As a result, they had a vested interest in the success of Argentina's military junta. Left-wing terrorism was regarded as a 'spider's web, whose filaments transcended German borders', as West German authorities in communication with Argentinian generals discovered that German Red Army Faction members had been in communication with left-wing guerrilla groups in Argentina.[54]

Due to the nature of General Jorge Videla's dictatorship, there were numerous West Germans on the left of the political spectrum who opposed the staging of the World Cup in Argentina. The West German members of Amnesty International formed a campaign that focused on the motto 'Yes to football, no to torture', referencing the human rights violations that were taking place in detention centres dotted around the country.

54 Nils Havemann. 2014. 'The Federal Republic of Germany and the 1978 Football World Cup in Argentina: Genesis and deconstruction of a propagandistic myth'. *The International Journal of the History of Sport*, 31(12): 1509–1518. DOI: 10.1080/09523367.2014.90727

The West German support of Amnesty International's boycott campaign was at odds with the West German state, which sought cooperation with the dictatorship. During the dictatorship's rule between 1976 and 1983 West Germany sold 4.5 billion Deutschmarks worth of arms to Argentina. As a result, campaigns such as 'Yes to football, no to torture' were 'incompatible with the silent democracy approach towards Buenos Aires'.[55]

As was typical across the nations competing in the tournament, there were factions of citizens that vehemently opposed the staging of the World Cup in Argentina on humanitarian grounds. However, the campaigns to boycott, or to raise awareness of the human rights violations were grassroots campaigns. The governments and governing bodies chose diplomacy and sent their teams regardless.

For West Germany, as defending champions, to boycott the tournament was unthinkable. A boycott was not the goal, instead the World Cup could be used as a platform to amplify the human rights violations in Argentina to the average German. Helmut Frenz, the German executive secretary of Amnesty International, insisted that the organisation wasn't creating propaganda for or against the World Cup, declaring: 'We are opposed that the roar of football fans be used to drown out the screams of those being tortured in Argentina.'[56] Frenz had first-hand experience of Latin America's military dictatorships, as

55 Felix A. Jiménez Botta. 2017. 'Yes to football, no to torture! The politics of the 1978 football World Cup in West Germany'. *Sport in Society*, 20(10): 1440–1456.

56 *Ibid.*

the German-Chilean pastor had been expelled from Chile for his role in the investigation of the mass disappearances during Pinochet's regime.

Amnesty International's tactic of using the World Cup to shine a light on Argentina's regime can be traced back to the friendly between West Germany and Argentina in Boca Juniors' home ground, La Bombonera. The reigning world champions defeated their hosts 3-1, but a comfortable victory led to uncomfortable questions for the DFB. On Christian talk show *Wort zum Sonntag* (*Word on Sunday*) theologian Helmut Franz suggested that the friendly was an opportunity for West Germany to put the Argentinian dictatorship under the microscope and ask questions about the disappeared people and allegations of human rights abuses. He asked, 'It was a friendly! Who are our friends over there? The oppressors or the oppressed?' Franz continued, '[The DFB should have] confronted the military dictators with the human rights violations in their country and demanded the freedom of political prisoners.' DFB president Hermann Neuberger was enraged by the programme's interference and implored it to focus on its religious output and steer clear of politics. Neuberger declared that 'human rights violations occurred all over the world and focusing "disproportionately" on Argentina smacked of left-wing political bias'.[57] He clearly echoed the sentiments of the West German government, which deeply feared the risk of left-wing activism.

---

57   Felix A. Jiménez Botta. 2017. 'Yes to football, no to torture! The politics of the 1978 football World Cup in West Germany'. *Sport in Society*, 20(10): 1440–1456.

Opponents of the dictatorship in Argentina were seen as likely bedfellows with Red Army Faction sympathisers, and thus any public condemnation of the regime in Argentina was feared to be an endorsement of left-wing agitators. Perhaps due to West Germany's dangerous place on the precipice in the 1970s war on terrorism and recent history of bloodthirsty dictatorship, Neuberger mirrored the government's 'silent diplomacy' rhetoric. He stated in an interview with magazine *Sports Illustrierte*: 'I am very careful with the term dictatorship.' He instead showed willingness to accept that the junta was on a journey to 'healthy democracy' after its guerrilla war.

Amnesty International faced silence from the DFB and quickly changed tack, instead engaging directly with West Germany's football players. They sent letters to each member of the squad, detailing the atrocities that were taking place in Argentina. They highlighted the numbers of disappeared, kidnapped and imprisoned people at the hands of the junta, including 17 Germans in their number. The letter emphasised the proximity of the detention centres to the stadiums – hidden in plain sight – and drew comparisons between the 1978 World Cup and Hitler's 1936 Olympics in Munich. The letter included a petition, demanding the end to human rights violations in Argentina and requesting that the West German government accept 500 Argentine enemies of the state as refugees.[58]

Amnesty International's attempts to engage the players directly proved far more fruitful than the stonewall they

---

58 *Ibid.*

received from the DFB. The West German media were fascinated by the responses of the players, which were documented in the popular current affairs magazine, *Bild*. The opinions of the squad covered the whole political spectrum. Captain Bertie Vogts echoed the standpoint of the DFB and conservative press, believing that the criticism displayed left-wing bias. Conservatives alleged that the criticism of Argentina's right-wing administration was disproportionate to the scrutiny of socialist administrations around the globe. Conservatives criticised the motives of Amnesty International, believing that they were attempting to capitalise on the Cold War and that their goal was to 'damage [West German] relations with the military government in Argentina' rather than 'humanitarianism'.[59] Goalkeeper Sepp Maier was a supporter of Amnesty International's campaign. It was rumoured that, during the tournament, he had marched with Las Madres de Plaza de Mayo, but this was later disproven.

The petition's most vocal and famous supporter was none other than the Bavarian in exile, Paul Breitner. In his interview with *Bild*, Breitner described coach Schön, the DFB and president Neuberger as politically ignorant. Breitner accepted that the champions had to travel to Argentina but the team had a moral responsibility not to be seen to endorse the regime and should refuse the handshake of the generals. Breitner vehemently opposed

---

59 Philipp Rock. 2010. *Macht, Märkte und Moral: Zur Rolle der Menschenrechte in der Außenpolitik der Bundesrepublik Deutschland in den Sechziger und Siebziger Jahren* [Power, Markets, and Morality: The Role of Human Rights in the Foreign Policy of the Federal Republic of Germany in the Sixties and Seventies]. Frankfurt: Peter Lang.

the West German team being paraded as part of the junta's perverse sideshow, when thousands of people were being tortured during the tournament – echoing Amnesty's message of 'Fussball ja, volter nein'. He stated, 'Our team will go to Argentina to play football, not make politics. But it can prevent being used as a marionette for the political games of Argentinian generals.'[60]

West Germany entered the World Cup as reigning champions but far from favourites. High-profile retirements, Breitner left at home and political divisions among the team meant that things were less than harmonious in the camp. All things considered, neighbours Poland would have been confident that they could triumph over rivals West Germany in topping the group.

The 1970s and 80s were considered a golden era of Polish football. The 'Bialo-czerwoni' (red and whites) began the decade by winning a gold medal at the 1972 Olympics in Munich. En route to defeating Hungary in the final, Poland defeated East Germany in Nuremberg. They would then dazzle the German public once more, two years later at the 1974 World Cup, as marksman Grzegorz Lato's golden boot-winning performance inspired them to a third-place finish. The talented Poles harboured genuine aspirations of success in Argentina.

Poland's ambitions were matched by a Mexico team whose qualification came due to their victory in the 1977 CONCACAF Cup, winning easily with a 100 per cent

---

60   Jan Eckel. 2012. 'Humanitarisierung der internationalen Beziehungen?' [Humanitarisation of foreign relations?]. *Geschichte und Gesellschaft*, 38(4): 603–635.

record and scoring 20 goals, conceding only five. Group 2 was completed by North Africans Tunisia, considered to be the minnows of the group. Expectations for the Eagles of Carthage were humbler than their Group 2 counterparts, as no African or Arab team had ever won a match at the World Cup to this point.

West Germany vs Poland: 1 June 1978 – Estadio Monumental, Buenos Aires

The opening match of the tournament took place in front of almost 68,000 fans, but prior to a ball being kicked was the small matter of the opening ceremony. Newspaper *La Nacion* had printed a detailed schedule of the events in that morning's edition. The doors would open at 10am, five hours before kick-off, with the opening ceremony scheduled to begin at 1pm. The military school's band provided the entertainment as groups of students contorted around the pitch to their beat, spelling out words with their bodies. They formed the words 'Argentina 78' followed by 'Mundial FIFA' for the entertainment of those in the stands and watching at home on television. Like their compatriots who would take the field to play Hungary the following day, the Argentine students wore the blue and white of their country.

The expectations on their performance were also incredibly high and the piece was choreographed down to the most minute detail by the national director of physical education, Héctor Barovero, along with Professor Beatriz Marty de Zamporolo. The ceremony and general organisation of the opening fixture were praised by the largely partisan domestic press. They commented on the bilingual stewardesses who were able to coordinate the press and travelling supporters, helping them reach the stadium. Much was made of the conduct of the supporters, aided by helpful stewards who 'entered without pushing, running nor flooding and left as if they were leaving Colon Theatre'.[61]

It had been much documented how the tournament was vital to the public relations of the new Argentinian junta and, as such, the opening ceremony was the first glimpse behind the curtain. The ceremony was Argentina's first opportunity to introduce the world to its new regime and an opportunity for Argentina to reveal the human face to the *coup d'état* that swept to power two years before. For many in attendance it would have been the first time they had seen General Jorge Videla speak publicly. In civilian clothing – a grey, double-breasted pinstripe suit – Videla was introduced as 'General Lieutenant, Mr Jorge Rafael Videla, president of the nation'. This unremarkable man, with his toothbrush moustache, as *Buenos Aires Herald* editor Robert Cox describes, welcomed the world to Argentina: 'Ladies … gentlemen. Today is a joyous day for our country, the Argentine nation.' He continued to reference the visiting nations' 'good faith in a climate of affection and reciprocal respect'. The good faith shown towards the hosts, of course, was not granted unconditionally or unanimously, with so many in attendance torn over whether the host nation was fit to put on the tournament.

---

61   Ailin Bullentini. 'The inaugural ceremony of the 78 World Cup'. Papelitos.com/ar

Videla mentioned the word 'peace' a further five times in his speech, briefly deviating to mention friendship. Evidently, the dictatorship wanted to publicly broadcast the power of the tournament in unifying the nation and promoting a peaceful image of Argentina. It's unclear whether Videla was preaching to the converted or sending a message to the subversives. Nonetheless, his speech was received warmly by many, with Barry Davies of the BBC stating, 'Videla made quite a good speech at the opening about joining the world. The Argentine man in the street welcomed the world because of their love of football, they had a good team and thought they would do well. Both military and man in the street wanted it to go well, but for different reasons.'[62]

With Videla's words about peace and unity ringing in their ears, the teams played out 90 minutes without a goal or even a booking. Much of the match was played at testimonial pace, with neither West Germany nor Poland showing much aggression in front of goal. The ceasefire in Estadio Monumental left the teams to share the spoils, with a point each. Poland were more than equal to their opponents and created a great second-half chance that they agonisingly missed. Captain Kazimierz Deyna took a free kick from 25 yards out. His shot-come-cross whipped across the surface of the six-yard box, as forward Andrzej Szarmach strained every sinew of his body to divert the ball into the net, but it rolled just out of the reach of his studs for a West German goal kick. The reigning champions

---

62 Interview with Barry Davies 2021.

created very little in front of goal and were disjointed throughout. Manager Schön wrote the 90 minutes off as a poor match and the performance was roundly criticised back in West Germany. Günter Netzer, who represented West Germany at the 1974 World Cup and was now manager of Hamburger SV, was particularly scathing in his appraisal, stating that West Germany produced a 'shocking performance. Germany are without a leader, without ideas, even without skill.'[63]

Tunisia vs Mexico: 2 June 1978 – Estadio Gigante de Arroyito, Rosario

The following day Tunisia faced Mexico in Rosario. As West Germany were without their afro-wearing king of counter-culture, the burden of 70s cool fell upon the shoulders of Mexico. Adorned in their uber-chic kits, designed by Levi's, the Mexican squad were undoubtedly the most stylish in the tournament. Midfielder Leonardo Cuéllar embodied the look of the time with his oversized afro and beard, looking every inch the 70s icon.

The ostentatious stylings of the Mexican team were appreciated by a humble attendance of only 17,346 in Rosario, but they witnessed a historic match that would embarrass CONCACAF champions Mexico and put North African football on the map. Mexico began strongly and took the lead just before half-time, Antonio de la Torre's speculative cross stiking a Tunisian hand, leading

---

63 David Miller. 1978. *World Cup: The Argentina Story*. Frederick Warne Publishers.

to Scottish referee John Gordon pointing to the spot. Vázquez Ayala took the subsequent spot kick, placing the ball in the bottom-right corner, as goalkeeper Mokhtar Naili was unable to get a glove to the ball, despite diving the correct way.

Tunisia found themselves level ten minutes later as defender Ali Kaabi fired a low drive through a crowded penalty area, past an unsighted José Pilar Reyes. Tunisia then edged in front with ten minutes of play remaining. A sweeping, one-touch move found Néjib Ghommidh inside the 18-yard box. A couple of touches and two strides later Ghommidh took the ball past the Mexican defence and, having drawn Reyes to the edge of the box, he used the outside of his right boot to guide the ball past the onrushing goalkeeper. It was a goal born out of high-octane, high-risk football and finished with aplomb.

Ghommidh then turned provider for the third Tunisian goal, which confirmed their victory. Picking the ball up 25 yards from goal, he spotted a run from full-back Mokhtar Dhouieb on the right flank. With the Mexican defence flat-footed, Ghommidh threaded the ball outside, to the edge of the 18-yard box. Without breaking stride Dhouieb received the ball at full speed and took a touch, before lofting the ball over the goalkeeper and into the roof of the net. Two moments of supreme quality played at breakneck speed had punished the Mexicans, and Tunisia were good value for their 3-1 win. The Eagles of Carthage celebrated on the pitch of Estadio Gigante de Arroyito, etching their name in history as pioneers of African football.

West Germany vs Mexico: 6 June 1978 – Estadio Chateau Carreras, Córdoba

Holders West Germany heaped further misery on Mexico four days later in Córdoba. Helmut Schön's men dusted off their goalscoring boots, punishing the hapless Mexico. Cologne's Dieter Müller's fabulous goal opened the scoring for West Germany. Receiving the ball with his back to goal, he deftly controlled it with his left foot before swerving to his right, leaving his defender rooted to the spot. A further touch with his right foot to take the ball from under his feet took him to the outside of the box. From 20 yards, he sent a low drive into the bottom right-hand corner, scoring one of the goals of the tournament.

Dieter's namesake Hansi doubled the lead. Receiving Heinze Flohe's perfectly weighted through ball in the right-wing position at the edge of the box, he took a touch with his left foot to take the ball past the defender and unleashed a fierce shot across the keeper that doubled West Germany's lead. Karl-Heinze Rummenigge ended the contest before the half-time break, scoring a superb individual goal. Picking the ball up in his own half, Rummenigge strode the length of the Mexican half, easily sidestepping the only tackle attempted 25 yards from goal. Mexico's threadbare defence retreated, without challenging the ball carrier. Rummenigge poked the ball past the goalkeeper to confirm the victory.

The Germans would further impose their superiority, adding a fourth before half-time. Rainer Bonhof stood over a free kick around 30 yards out, ten yards from the touchline. Noticing the lack of concentration in the defensive wall, he shifted the ball to his left. Heinze Flohe found himself unmarked and, due to the glacial speed of Mexico's covering defence, he was allowed to take a shot. Flohe obliged and his left-footed piledriver flew into the top corner, allowing goalkeeper Reyes no chance to save it.

Rummenigge and Flohe added to Mexico's misery in the second half, both scoring goals of real quality again. West Germany were completely ruthless in Córdoba, hammering Mexico 6-0 and conducting their own miniature goal of the tournament competition. At this point, the champions would have been very confident about their progress in the tournament. But Argentina's second city would yet prove to be an unhappy hunting ground for the West Germans.

Poland vs Tunisia: 6 June 1978 – Estadio Gigante de Arroyito, Rosario

Poland finished the second round of fixtures in second place in the group after a 1-0 win against Tunisia. Ali Kaabi, the man who scored Tunisia's first-ever goal in a World Cup, became the villain this time. Following a Polish one-two pass, a lofted ball hung in the Rosario sky, just outside the six-yard box. Kaabi missed the ball completely when attempting his clearance. Grzegorz Lato gambled on Kaabi's airstrike and pounced between defender and goalkeeper, firing a half-volley low past the goalkeeper and finishing the move he started at the edge of the 18-yard box.

Tunisia followed up their fine showing against Mexico by producing an accomplished display in the second half, which left a strong Poland team clinging on for the win, desperately counting down the minutes to the final whistle. The Eagles of Carthage's best opportunity fell to skipper Témimi Lahzami, who saw his effort crash against the crossbar and bounce to safety, taking Tunisia's hopes for a well-deserved point along with it.

West Germany vs Tunisia: 10 June 1978 – Estadio Chateau Carreras, Córdoba

Following the six-goal demolition of Mexico, perhaps West Germany feared that they had used up their quota of goals for the group stages. Those fears were realised when they faced a resolute Tunisian team in Córdoba. The Eagles of Carthage, fresh from a stellar display against Poland and with a feeling of injustice coursing through their veins that they hadn't achieved a well-deserved draw, were a match for the reigning champions.

The West German's best chances in the first half all came from set pieces, the most notable of which produced a fine save from goalkeeper Mokhtar Naili. A clearance from a corner kick fell to Rainer Bonhof at the edge of the box and the Borussia Mönchengladbach legend half-volleyed a missile goalward with extreme prejudice. Naili met fire with fire and required every inch of his strength to palm the shot over the bar and into the Córdobese sky. West Germany continued to play in front of Tunisia but were unable to penetrate their defence in any meaningful manner.

Hammadi Agrebi produced the best chance of the first half, leaving hearts in mouths in the West German defence. Agrebi found Akid at the edge of the box, and his lofted return pass reached Agrebi at a narrow angle just outside the six-yard box. Agrebi fired a powerful half-volley that rose over goalkeeper Sepp Maier and dipped the other side of his head. Maier had to watch the ball pass over him, hoping that it wouldn't curve goalward. Fortunately for the Bayern Munich keeper, the ball curved the other way, narrowly passing the outside post.

Naili in the Tunisian goal enjoyed a comfortable second half, stopping every shot as the Tunisian defence forced West Germany to shoot from distance. The only time the Tunisian defence found themselves stretched came from a break that allowed Klaus Fischer a one on one with Naili. The Tunisian won the duel, narrowing the angle and making himself a human wall that the Schalke 04 striker found impassable, firing low into Naili's arms. Accepting that it wasn't their day, West Germany settled for the 0-0, handing over the initiative to Poland, who had to beat Mexico to top the group.

Poland vs Mexico: 10 June 1978 – Estadio Gigante de Arroyito, Rosario

The door was open for Poland to progress as group leaders, the only obstruction being already eliminated Mexico. They were still stinging with embarrassment following their two losses and began the game with purpose, demonstrating that they wouldn't simply step aside for Poland. From a free kick near the corner flag, Cuéllar found Hugo Sánchez. The powerful forward, who would later go on to play for both Atlético and Real Madrid, rose highest with an acrobatic bicycle kick but his athletic strike sailed over the bar. Sánchez turned provider for Cristóbal Ortega later that half, as his low drive found the Club América forward at the edge of the six-yard box. Ortega fired a shot across the box that ricocheted around and out for a corner.

Just before half-time Poland seized the opportunity to go ahead. Ortega was dispossessed on halfway, near the touchline. The ball found Poland captain Kazimierz Deyna, whose first-time left-footed pass threaded through the Mexican defence to forward Lato. Lato skipped a challenge and squared the ball into the box for strike partner Zbigniew Boniek. Salivating at the ball served up to him, Boniek managed to compose himself, sort out his feet and calmly side-foot a volley past the goalkeeper. Boniek celebrated by collecting the ball and booting it into the air, before pumping his fist to fire up his compatriots. The goal had alleviated any nerves in the Poland team, their relief clear to see. Poland ended the half on top, so leading the group table.

However, the Polish players' relief was short-lived, as Mexico's only goal from open play during the tournament arrived soon after half-time, levelling the scores. The inspired Ortega received a lofted pass, anticipated the challenge of midfielder Wojciech Rudy and calmly dinked the ball on the volley past him. As Rudy had committed to the tackle, he was unable to catch the overlapping full-back, Ignacio Flores. He charged forward towards the penalty box, weaved around the defence and hit a low cross towards the penalty spot. Arriving at the opportune moment was Victor Rangel, whose miskick trickled over the line, much to the disappointment of goalkeeper Jan Tomaszewski, who had seemingly lost his bearings, preoccupied by Flores's run.

Mexico's time in the sun was short-lived as they conceded within a few minutes, surrendering the lead to Poland. Deyna capitalised on a game of penalty box pinball and fired a left-footed screamer into the top corner from 20 yards, leaving Mexico's goalkeeper clutching at thin air. The goal must have been particularly sickening for Mexico after failing to capitalise on their own goalmouth scramble minutes earlier, when Cuéllar's shot was blocked on the goal line.

The rest of the match was played out in quality fashion, with both teams enjoying good chances. Inspired by Deyna's emphatic top-corner finish, Boniek surpassed that strike with a fine goal of his own. Receiving a pass and with 30 yards of Rosario turf in front of him, Boniek took a touch to settle himself before hitting a swerving thunderbolt that left the goalkeeper helpless. The ball appeared to be heading towards the centre of the goal before veering into the top corner at the last fraction of a second.

Poland finished the group with two wins and a draw and topped the standings, meaning they would be in the same second-round group as Group 1 runners-up Argentina. West Germany would fall into the same second-round group as Group 1 winners Italy.

Group 3: Austria, Brazil, Spain and Sweden

MUCH TO the chagrin of the dictatorship, the logo of the 1978 World Cup (designed two years prior to the coup) would pay tribute to the late Juan Domingo Perón. The light arms on a white background were designed as a homage to Perón's signature arms-lofted gesture. While the colour scheme was uniquely Argentinian, the symbolism was implicitly Perónist. In his thesis, 'The nation arrested: Propaganda and human rights at Argentina '78', Liam Macheda describes the logo as an 'evocative symbol that could not be mistaken for belonging to any other tournament except an Argentinean one'.[64]

From the World Cup logo's homage to Juan Perón's lofted-arm celebration, to Mario Kempes's flagrant, goal-saving handball, the 1978 World Cup is famous for its participants' use of their hands. This chapter will recall the forgotten incident that took place during the hugely controversial Group 3 match between Brazil and Sweden, when a footballer raised his fist in defiance of the dictatorship.

---

64   Liam Macheda. 2019. 'The nation arrested: Propaganda and human rights at Argentina '78'. University of Oregon.

Group 3 delivered little in terms of goals but delivered much in controversy. The quality of football, or lack thereof, was in part due to the quality of surface in one of the group venues. The newly laid pitch at Estadio José María Minella in Mar del Plata cut up as soon as studs met grass, leaving the surface resembling the fields of rural Patagonia, where the gauchos famously roamed.

The group began with an upset. Austria, having qualified for their first World Cup in 20 years, triumphed over a Spanish team that had only tasted defeat once since failing to qualify for the previous World Cup.

Austria vs Spain: 3 June 1978 – Estadio José Amalfitani, Buenos Aires

Austria faced off against Spain at the home of Vélez Sarsfield, Estadio José Amalfitani. The stadium had been renovated in time for the World Cup, adding an upper tier and increasing the capacity to accommodate almost 50,000 spectators. Fortunately for the organisers, who had been disappointed by attendances at some of the group matches, the opening fixture of the group drew a respectable 40,000 fans, eager to see the European teams compete.

Spain were expected to triumph over Austria but found themselves trailing early on. Walter Schachner opened the scoring after ten minutes with one of the goals of the tournament. Receiving the ball on halfway, near the touchline, Schachner set his sights on the Spanish 18-yard box, threatening to cut inside. Instead, the Austrian forward continued his run out wide, gliding past defenders rooted to the spot. He found himself at the edge of the six-yard box and unleashed an arrowed strike into the roof of the net, the ball whistling past the ear of the oncoming Miguel Ángel.

Spain's No. 7, Dani equalised with a smart finish at the midway point of the first half. A misguided clearing header sent the ball directly into the air. Showing great poise at the edge of a crowded 18-yard box, Dani tracked the flight of the ball before drilling a volley low into the bottom corner. 'La Roja' were level but the Austrians were not to be denied their victory, as Hans Krankl's instinctive finish claimed a famous 2-1 win. Krankl reacted first to a loose ball into the box, placing his shot into the bottom corner. Krankl, mobbed by jubilant team-mates, had secured the Austrians' maiden win of the tournament.

Brazil vs Sweden: 3 June 1978 – Estadio José María Minella, Mar del Plata

Whenever Brazil enter a World Cup, they do so under an extraordinary weight of expectation from their home supporters. Regardless of their modest fourth-place finish in 1974, they were expected to be among the contenders in Argentina '78. Brazil's 1978 vintage is an interesting one, a team in transition between Mário Zagallo's all-conquering 1970 team and Telê Santana's insouciant, aesthetically beautiful 1982 one. It's important to also consider the fact that Brazil were a wounded beast after their humbling exit at the previous tournament, where they got lost on the carousel of Johan Cruyff's total football and were crushed under the wheels of the Oranje machine.

Rather than lick their wounds, Brazil were inspired by their conquerors and determined to emulate them the next time they were on the world stage. Their admiration of the Dutch team of '74 bears no resemblance to how they viewed them just two years previously. The then world champions Brazil hosted the Brazil Independence Cup in 1972 to commemorate the 150th anniversary of the country's declaration of independence. The tournament acted as a de facto World Cup, to whet the appetite between 1970 and 1974, and was the brainchild of former president of Brazilian football, and future FIFA president, João Havelange.

The tournament, which welcomed teams from Europe and South America, also included all-star teams from Africa and CONCACAF. The purpose was three-fold: firstly Havelange needed something on which to anchor his challenge for the next FIFA presidential election, to showcase the growing economy of 1970s Brazil, and for the national team to cement their status as the world's premier football team. However, the tournament wasn't very well attended by Europe's best-known teams, as the Europeans cared little for their future president's campaign of vanity and didn't want to suffer a bloody nose in South America, two years out from a World Cup. Brazilian football expert Tim Vickery recalls finding a Brazilian football annual of the era that poured cold water on the profile of some of the European absentees. Despite acknowledging that the loss of West Germany and Italy harmed the legitimacy of the tournament, Brazilian journalists didn't consider the Dutch to be much of a loss to the 'minicopa', declaring that 'between ourselves, no one is going to miss Holland' in the publication.[65]

The 'minicopa' went to script, with Brazil beating Portugal, the nation from whom they had declared their independence, in the final and João Havelange being declared FIFA president in 1974. The sting in the tail, however, was that the Netherlands would arrive on the international scene just two years later, boasting the world's greatest player and handing Brazil a chastening beating en route to a World Cup Final.

Brazil coach Cláudio Coutinho had been on the coaching staff since 1970 and had witnessed European teams gradually overtaking their South American counterparts, with superior technique and tactical nous. Coutinho, much like all Brazilian technocratic coaches of the era, was obsessed with Dutch football, from the Feyenoord of the early 1970s to Cruyff's Ajax and the national team. In an interview with English journalist Tim Vickery, Zico revealed that 'we were trying to copy Holland, but we couldn't do it. We didn't have the cultural base to do it.'[66] Brazil's most creative player, and the heir to the throne of Pelé spoke of his frustration of being born in a different age, with a keener focus on tactics and formation stifling some of his creativity in a way that his predecessor never experienced. 'I would prefer to go free, but that is not practical. Europe has forced us to play more

---

65 Tim Vickery. *The Brazilian Shirt Name* podcast – Episode: 3 July 1974 – Netherlands v Brazil – Total Football.

66 Interview with Tim Vickery 2021.

systematically, because they don't allow us space to play, like in 1970.'[67]

Coutinho's position as coach was an unenviable one. He was tasked with introducing a new style of football to a young, inexperienced team, shouldering great pressure from the Brazilian media. He underlined his challenges when he claimed, 'We have already got the most difficult thing to find – talent. I cannot provide that. But I can provide determination, discipline, teamwork.'[68] Discipline was a particular challenge for Coutinho as much of the team was 25 or under, with captain Rivellino at 32 tasked with being the mature sage on the pitch. The principle of teamwork was also a challenge for Coutinho, who found his position as coach constantly undermined, with suggestions he would lose his job before the second round had taken place due to underwhelming performances in the first group stage. The coach was treated with ridicule by English sources, seen as an easy fall guy as he was a military man, and there was a prevailing sense of 'let's hang all the crimes of the dictatorship on him'.[69]

Much like most of Latin America, Brazil was under a military dictatorship during this time. This lasted for over 20 years and shared many similarities with Argentina's junta: CIA-supported (as part of Operation Condor), heavily focused on law and order (reflecting the motto of the nation 'order and progress') and notable for its brutal suppression of opponents. The Brazilian dictatorship also

---

67   Graham McColl. 2010. *How to Win a World Cup*. Bantam Press.
68   *Ibid.*
69   Interview with Tim Vickery 2021.

had a successful football team that could be exploited as part of the nation's branding. The 1970 World Cup-winning team arrived during a time referred to as 'The Brazilian Miracle', a period of economic boom, which saw average annual gross domestic product rise by 10 per cent between 1969 and 1973 under the rule of President Medici.[70] The right team at the right time.

Despite the precarious nature of his position, Coutinho was tremendously respected in his native Brazil and, following the World Cup, he would excel domestically as the architect of the great Flamengo team of the time, laying the foundations for Flamego's 1981 Intercontinental Cup triumph over Liverpool.

If the cauldron of Buenos Aires's El Monumental brought pressure on Argentina, then Brazil found their own pressure cooker 400 kilometres south in Mar del Plata. It was here that they would make their bow in the tournament, facing Sweden. In the cafés and bars the length and breadth of Brazil, you will find people of an age to remember the 1978 World Cup happy to list the nefarious tactics used by the host country to make Brazil's participation in the World Cup as difficult as possible, the first of which was the location of Brazil's matches. Many Brazilians believe their team was sent to Mar del Plata, with its agricultural pitch, to prevent them playing decent football and to sap the energy from their legs. In truth, during the first round they did look lethargic and toothless. But then none of the teams competing in Group 3 emerged

---

70   Bruce Handler. 1975. 'Plying High in Rio'. *New York Times* archive.

with enhanced reputations, producing only eight goals in total, while the rest of the groups averaged 17 goals.

Brazil's opening match versus Sweden was steeped in controversy and is commonly remembered for a contentious refereeing decision. The match began in expected fashion with a talented Brazil team dominating the early proceedings. Two through balls sliced open the Swedish defence, only for chances to be spurned by Toninho and Reinaldo. Sweden then took the lead against the run of play, striker Thomas Sjöberg stabbing the ball into the net after a smart exchange of passes in the final third. The goal lifted Sweden and they troubled Brazil once more, Larsson hitting the crossbar with a header from a free kick. Larsson found himself the loneliest man in Estadio José María Minella, unmarked in the box, with only a shuddering crossbar for company, as a bewildered Brazil defence cast accusatory looks at one another.

Brazil equalised just before half-time. Cerezo's looped cross found the feet of striker Reinaldo. After a brief scramble, he fired home. In the half a second it required for him to find the net and vault the onrushing goalkeeper, the Atlético Mineiro hitman had to decide whether to celebrate the goal with his signature clenched fist salute. The celebration was the source of much debate at the time as a clenched fist paid homage to the Black Panther party and was an anti-racist and socialist symbol. Reinaldo's openness about his politics was a source of great division back home in Brazil, with many speculating that his left-wing tendency was the reason he found himself out of the team on occasion. Although Reinaldo's politics wouldn't have been popular with the dictatorship, his 28 goals in 18 matches during that season's Campeonato Brasileiro made him undroppable.

Much like the Argentinian dictatorship was forced to tolerate a left-wing manager in Menotti, Brazil had to accommodate the like-minded Reinaldo as their target man. Prior to the team's departure, Medici's successor, President Ernesto Beckman Geisel, met with the squad and coaching staff. The president, in a way that only dictators can, reminded Reinaldo of his responsibilities as a representative of Brazil, informing him that it was in his best interests to conform with their expectations. 'The general said that I shouldn't talk about politics because they took care of that,' Reinaldo said. Geisel insisted that Reinaldo celebrate with open arms as it was 'more beautiful' than the clenched fist. Of course, the dictator wasn't concerned with the aesthetics of Reinaldo's celebrations, rather the prospect of his star striker embarrassing the dictatorship on the world stage with a gesture that was linked to Marxism. The Brazilian government expected obedience from their sportsmen and Geisel wanted Reinaldo to echo Pelé's sentiments when asked about Brazil under Emilio Medici's rule in 1972. Pelé declared, 'There is no dictatorship in Brazil. We are free people. Our leaders know what is best for us and govern in a spirit of toleration and patriotism.'[71]

Geisel's plea was ignored a half-second after the ball hit the net. Reinaldo, through instinct or defiance, raised his clenched fist. His socialist principles were broadcast

---

71 Marius Lien. 'A troubled history'. *The Blizzard*, 13.

to the global audience. He would later raise both arms in celebration, unwittingly channelling Perón, as asked by Geisel, although this wouldn't have placated the dictator. Reinaldo would play in the next game against Spain but then wouldn't feature again until the third-place play-off, by which time Brazil were out of the running for the Jules Rimet Trophy. The striker found himself out of favour in the national team, his appearances sporadic, before finally being dropped from the '82 World Cup squad.

When the Brazil squad returned to their hotel, Reinaldo received a letter addressed from Venezuela. Inside was a report on Operation Condor, the CIA campaign designed to assassinate political enemies in Latin America. The letter alleged that former Brazilian president Juscelino Kubitschek, assumed to have died in a car accident, had been assassinated. 'The document was in Spanish. I didn't understand everything. I had a bomb in my hands. I was terrified, so I kept the envelope in the bottom of my suitcase and didn't show anyone.'

Reinaldo's act of defiance had cast him as an anti-authoritarian poster boy. This may have limited his appearances in Brazil's No. 9 shirt but made him a person of interest for left-wing guerrilla groups. He held on to the letter until his return to Brazil, when he passed the letter on to his friend and musician Gonzaguinha, who was involved in left-wing activism. Despite his ideology, Reinaldo was clearly spooked by the letter and didn't mention its contents publicly for decades. In 2014 an inquiry by the National Truth Commission into Brazil's human rights violations concluded that Kubitschek wasn't the victim of an assassination. The contents of the letter received by a terrified Reinaldo were deemed in retrospect to be nothing more than hearsay.

It's difficult to attribute Reinaldo's omission from the national team to any one thing. His politics, during a time when left-wing sentiments were brutally suppressed by an authoritarian government, presented awkward dilemmas for national coaches. However, Telê Santana subsequently made Socrates captain for the 1982 World Cup, a man who famously campaigned for democracy in Brazil and wore his socialist principles on his sleeve. It's suggested that Socrates's middle-class upbringing allowed him more leniency than working-class Reinaldo from the coaching staff. This leniency also applied to Socrates's penchant for a heavy-drinking, heavy-partying lifestyle. Injuries no doubt played a part in Reinaldo's limited appearances, as he suffered from knee problems throughout his career. The heavy pitch in Mar del Plata would only have exacerbated any lingering injuries. Tim Vickery laments that 'we'll probably never know the true reasons. If there is one reason.'[72]

Back in Mar del Plata, the match seemed destined to finish as a 1-1 draw until the final seconds, when Brazil were awarded a corner. Crucially, substitute Nelinho dawdled, incorrectly placing the ball outside the corner arc. Replacing the ball had eaten up what was left of the time and, as the corner took flight, referee Clive Thomas spun to face the halfway line and blew his whistle, indicating time

---

72 Interview with Tim Vickery 2021.

was up. Unbeknown to Thomas, Zico had risen to meet the cross that had fizzed across the six-yard box and headed the ball into the net, believing he had won the match. Thomas could have avoided controversy by whistling before the corner or waiting and allowing the phase of play to be completed, but the Welshman, christened 'The Book' for his literal application of the laws, wouldn't sacrifice his principles for the easy decision. It became one of the most controversial decisions in World Cup history, as it denied Brazil what would have been a crucial win in their opening fixture. A handful of Brazilian players briefly remonstrated with Thomas, trying to establish whether he had blown for full time before or after the goal. According to BBC commentator Barry Davies: 'A lot of people left the stadium not realising what the real result was.'[73]

Thomas recalls that refereeing Brazil's opening fixture wasn't a task that his fellow professionals were envious of: 'Nobody wanted to ref Brazil.'[74] The intimidating Havelange was president of FIFA and a Brazilian national. The thought of upsetting Havelange was a cross the referees didn't want to bear. Despite the famous images of the Brazilian players remonstrating with Thomas, he insists that once the decision was made and explained to them, they accepted it without further protestations. The same was not true about Havelange, and Thomas would not referee another match in Argentina. After full time, the referees' assessor knocked on the door, shook hands with the other three officials and ignored Thomas.

73 Interview with Barry Davies 2021.
74 Interview with Clive Thomas 2021.

Thomas recounts that the next day, in the hotel during the debrief, the other referees were all able to pick holes in his performance, to the disappointment of Thomas, as he believed the other refs were unwilling to put their heads above the parapet themselves.

After the spark of the first round of fixtures, the rest of the group rarely threatened to combust. Austria followed up their win over Spain with 1-0 win over Sweden. They were good value for their second success of the tournament, with Krankl earning and converting the penalty for the only goal of the match. Meanwhile, Spain and Brazil played out an uneventful 0-0 in Mar del Plata, with both teams opting to shoot from distance rather than play intricate football on a poor surface. Brazil's Rivellino drew the most eye-catching save with a powerful drive. The 0-0 draw suited Brazil far more than Spain.

An unremarkable 90 minutes in Mar del Plata proved to be a catalyst for an explosive 48 hours in Brazil's camp. Reports were emerging of a fractious atmosphere, following midfielder Dirceu's public criticism of veteran midfielder Rivellino and the coach Coutinho. Rivellino and Zico were also reportedly unhappy with their coach. These reports intensified the scrutiny on the squad, amplifying the pressure to perform. After their opening two matches Brazil were wilting under the pressure, barely scraping along. This reportedly prompted the president of Brazil's football federation, Admiral Helenio Nunes, to challenge Coutinho's autonomy in selecting the team, so for the rest of the tournament, the side was to be selected by committee. Coutinho had also reportedly offered his resignation in the aftermath of Nunes's attempted coup, an offer that was refused by his president.

Coutinho's account of the situation conflicts with this rumour. Writing for theantiquefootball.com, Shahan Petrossian reveals, 'Months later in an interview, he denied the alleged "sacking" during the finals, as well as any problems with Rivellino and Zico. No one will ever know what really happened during the closed meeting that night following the match vs. Spain.'[75] Admiral Nunes later seemingly admitted that team selection became a democratic process, declaring that 'the players and the wise directors imposed their points of view on Coutinho, and made him change that sad panorama to save the honour of Brazilian football'.[76]

For Brazil a 1-0 victory over Austria in their final group match saw both nations progress at the expense of Spain and the winless Sweden. Coutinho, if he was believed to be the man with the final say over selection, dropped Zico and Rivellino from the starting XI. Brazil and Austria both finished the group on four points, separated only by goals scored, 3-2 in Austria's favour. As unlikely group winners, they would enter the second round in Group A, playing their matches in Buenos Aires and Córdoba. The South Americans, in second place, were left to rue their draw against Sweden and dream about how different things may had been had Zico's 'winning goal' arrived a fraction of a second earlier.

---

75 Shahan Petrossian. 'Brazil's tour of Europe 1978', theantiquefootball. com

76 Graham McColl. 2010. *How to Win a World Cup*. Bantam Press.

Nevertheless, despite a squad reportedly at loggerheads and a coach humiliated by his federation, Brazil had qualified for the second round, where they would find themselves alongside bitter rivals Argentina in Group B, playing in Rosario and Mendoza. Despite their starring role in the most controversial moment of the group, Brazil would yet play a bit part in the most debated match in World Cup history 18 days later. The Brazilian fans, upset by the referee's decision in their opening match, would later be incandescent, adding the host nation's creative scheduling and allegations of match-fixing to their list of grievances.

Blood on the Crossbar

IN JANUARY 1978, two men named Bram Vermeulen and Freek de Jonge met in Schiller Café, Amsterdam. The Dutchmen were part of an alternative cabaret act known as Neerlands Hoop that specialised in social and political commentary. Freek de Jonge had a contact at Amnesty International, which was compiling evidence of human rights abuses in Argentina under their military junta. The two men vowed that afternoon that the focus of their art would be to do everything possible to showcase the atrocities taking place in Argentina. Together with Amnesty International and with the support of the Young Socialist organisation in the Netherlands, De Jonge and Vermeulen made their declaration: 'We're going to organise resistance and take it to the extreme, the Netherlands shall not go to the World Cup.'[77]

The boycott campaign began in earnest that afternoon in Amsterdam and would grow throughout the Netherlands as Neerlands Hoop toured the country spreading their message. Their cabaret shows focused on

---

77   *A Dirty Game.* Documentary dir. Jaap Verdenius and Kay Mastenbroek, 2002.

the crimes of the dictatorship in Argentina and the use of the World Cup as a sports-washing project, whereby the military was using the tournament as a means to improve its image and sweep human rights violations under the carpet.

The title of their show was *Blood on the Crossbar*, highlighting the culpability of football in the atrocities taking place in Argentina. During their stage show, the band performed with the backdrop of a mocked-up World Cup logo, placing a skull between the blue waves. The message was clear: the tournament couldn't be separated from the bloodshed, and to take part in the tournament was to endorse the dictatorship and its crimes.

Vermeulen stated, 'We made our objective clear – the Dutch should not go to the World Cup. Because you can't organise a World Cup in a dictatorship.' The duo were, however, pragmatic enough to realise that to challenge the Dutch football association (KNVB) to boycott the World Cup was a monumental task. Not only was football the most popular sport in the Netherlands, but as finalists four years prior they stood a good chance of winning the tournament and becoming world champions. Vermeulen quantified his statement, adding: 'Of course, you have to have a multi-layered plan. The real objective was maximum attention for the situation in Argentina.' In this respect, although the World Cup was identified by Argentina's General Emilio Massera as a vital opportunity to improve the image of Argentina, the opposite was equally viable. The staging of a World Cup provided opponents of the dictatorship with a platform to expose the horrors that were taking place under the rule of the military. The World Cup presented an opportunity, a catalyst for change.

The campaign couldn't have come at a more critical juncture, as the same month that the duo met in Schiller Café, 27 Argentine corpses washed ashore in neighbouring Uruguay. The victims were undoubtedly taken on the military's infamous death flights and thrown into the Río de la Plata that separated the two countries. The arrival of the bodies in Uruguay symbolised the fact that the knowledge of the military's atrocities was beginning to reach people beyond the shores of Argentina.

As *Blood on the Crossbar* toured around the country, performed in front of raucous, like-minded audiences, De Jonge and Vermeulen's message was gathering momentum. However, the boycott had yet to cross political or class divides, as the movement was embraced mainly by middle-class liberals and artists. Felix Rottenberg, the chairman of the Young Socialists, was an early ally of the duo. He ruefully conceded, 'There was no mass movement of people from the left. This is football, you don't fight football.'

De Jonge and Vermeulen, despite their better judgement, had picked a fight with football. Regardless of their attempts at dialogue, they were stonewalled by the KNVB. The duo extended an olive branch to the association but were met with hostility. Karel Jansen, a representative of the Dutch players' union, illustrated the association's view of the duo, recalling, 'They [KNVB] saw them as a provocation.' A group creating problems on the eve of a World Cup.

Vermeulen was affronted by the KNVB's stance, branding it immature and ignorant. Bemoaning the unwillingness to address the greater issue of human rights violations, he mimicked the KNVB: 'How dare you touch football?' adding, 'They were scared we would snatch their favourite toy.' The duo were discovering the blinkered vision that sport can cause, as the potential for the Dutch to become world champions had caused an ethical blind spot for the KNVB.

This ethical dilemma has been a historical problem for sporting boycotts, as South African-British politician Peter Hain discovered during his 1969 'stop the tour' campaign earlier that decade. The campaign sought to stop the 1969/70 South African cricket and rugby union tours of Great Britain, due to the ongoing apartheid in South Africa. The campaign faced unprecedented criticism, with campaigners assaulted on the field as they attempted to disrupt matches. The campaign also faced criticism from fellow anti-apartheid campaigners who felt that disrupting sport was a step too far. Hain commented, 'What I'd call "soft L liberals" said, you can't touch sport.'[78] Hain felt the wrath of his detractors when he was forcibly ejected from Swansea's St Helens ground during a rugby match between local team Swansea RFC and South Africa, following a demonstration on the pitch. The anger of those in the stands towards the disruption of their game shows the importance of sport to the working classes – in Wales rugby union is very much a working-class game and Swansea is a working-

---

78 Interview with Peter Hain 2020.

class city. To those working classes, sport can be crucial, as its meritocracy provides a freedom of self-expression.

The class battle is something Freek de Jonge and Bram Vermeulen had to experience as they struggled to move their campaign from its perception as a middle-class vanity project. Legendary Dutch midfielder and member of the '78 squad, Johan Neeskens, embodied a working-class Dutch culture. Although a very wealthy man playing in Barcelona, his hard work and industry on the field saw him painted as the antithesis to Cruyff's refined image. Although a grand over-simplification to decree Neeskens as a misfit, arriving in the great cosmopolitan Ajax team from unfashionable RC Heemstede, he embodied a hard-working everyman image that his namesake Cruyff did not. Neeskens echoed the trope heard so frequently by Vermeulen and De Jonge, stating, 'You don't mix politics and sport. Otherwise, you can't play any match. There's shit everywhere in the world. If you boycott Argentina you have to boycott Soviet Russia and Bulgaria.'

There was a distinct divide between international and domestic attitudes towards a potential boycott of the tournament. In contrast to Vermeulen and De Jonge, Argentinian guerrilla group Los Montoneros opposed a World Cup boycott, knowing that they would be fighting against the current of patriotism in Argentina. In Argentina, even enemies of the dictatorship broadly supported the staging of the tournament. The campaigns to boycott it were uniquely foreign, usually spearheaded by Argentine exiles. The noise created by the *Blood on the Crossbar* tour was key to spreading this information.

At loggerheads, the boycott campaign and the KNVB both looked to the Dutch government for support. Prime minister Dries van Agt, the leader of the centre-right Christian Democratic Appeal, was reportedly sympathetic to Neerlands Hoop's cause; however, the government insisted that it was a matter for the KNVB.

Wallis de Vries, the deputy secretary for culture and sports, confirmed this, saying, 'How does a government deal with an independent organisation [KNVB]?' The Dutch government's policy of non-intervention in sporting matters was a source of great frustration for both sides. Neerlands Hoop were still insistent with their objective to make it 'impossible' for the Netherlands to send a team to the World Cup, whereas the KNVB desperately sought an endorsement from the Dutch government to quell the rising calls for a boycott. Instead, the government declared that the KNVB was 'fully and solely responsible for Dutch football', much to the frustration of both parties. Meanwhile, the Dutch socialist party formally passed a motion to support the boycott, but the party represented few people in the Netherlands, having failed to win a seat in the house of representatives 1977 election. The party, with its roots in Maoism and Marxism, had yet to establish a crossover appeal necessary to grow De Jonge and Vermeulen's campaign from its core audience.

The frustrations the duo were beginning to feel as their campaign came up against a brick wall were outlined in the lyrics of the song 'Ik tel mijn idealen'. De Jonge sang: 'Tomorrow another day has passed in Chile, Russia, Uganda, Argentina. I count my ideals and

I lose them day by day.' In the face of their frustrations, the KNVB made some headway, succeeding in getting the foreign ministry and Dutch embassy to advise them in Argentina. This followed a fruitful meeting with the ministry where the KNVB insisted a boycott would be off the table. To the naked eye, the KNVB had succeeded in getting an endorsement of sorts from the Dutch government. Much to the frustration of De Jonge and Vermeulen, they would never get their confrontation with the Dutch team or KNVB. As they staged a protest at Amsterdam's Schiphol airport, the Dutch squad was ushered in through a back door and flown to Argentina under the cover of darkness.

The Netherlands played their group matches in Mendoza and Córdoba, the opening two taking place in Mendoza, the city at the foothills of the Andes. The rural location of the training camp meant the players were kept far away from the powder keg of Buenos Aires, which hosted demonstrations from Las Madres de Plaza de Mayo. Unknown to the players, the camp was surrounded by the military. The location was equipped with military posts and anti-aircraft guns. The Dutch squad's existence in Mendoza was in a bubble, impregnable from the outside world.

On arrival in Argentina, convinced by the KNVB, the foreign office issued the Dutch squad with a strict code of conduct. Paramount to this code were three key rules:

1. The players were to make no mention of politics in interviews and to speak exclusively about football.

2. The players were not to be seen with any government or military officials.
3. The players were not allowed to visit any areas of potential political activity.

Freek de Jonge and Bram Vermeulen's assertion that sending a team to Argentina was an endorsement of the dictatorship was dismissed out of hand by the KNVB. However, the KNVB was worried that the players could be exploited for political gain and as such tried all it could to isolate them from the goings-on in Argentina. This frustrated the players immensely, as they were isolated in such a remote location, deep in the foothills of the Andes.

However, Dutch fears were realised following an explosive publication in the newspaper *El Gráfico*. Upon their arrival in Argentina, the press were given an information pack on each player in the squad, which contained facts such as each player's height, weight, dominant foot, etc. However, most significant of all, printed at the bottom was each player's signature. On the eve of the World Cup Final, *El Gráfico* printed an open letter from Dutch captain Rudi Krol, which contained his thoughts on the tournament. He praised the organisation of the tournament, the fantastic hospitality they had received from their hosts and the military itself. Of course, Krol had written no such letter, he had given no interview and the signature at the foot of the letter was a forgery.

The KNVB's fears had been realised: the players had been used by the military. Even with a retraction, readers of *El Gráfico* would still believe that the Dutch squad had endorsed the government – a strike for the military's public relations machine. Prior to the tournament, the KNVB had never shared these concerns with the players themselves. Defender Jan Poortvliet was asked whether the KNVB ever shared with the squad that they could be used for PR. He replied, 'No. Nothing. We didn't pay any attention to human rights.'

Ultimately, both the KNVB and Neerlands Hoop suffered losses. The boycott campaign was unsuccessful and, upon arrival in Argentina, the Dutch players were used as stooges by the military. However, both can point to the romance in glorious failure. For the Dutch squad, the romance was in the long walk off the ticker tape-strewn El Monumental pitch that led them on the path to become football romantics' favourite nearly men. For Vermeulen and De Jonge, their romance is their part as a cog in the machine that would eventually bring down the dictatorship.

Group 4: Iran, the Netherlands, Scotland and Peru

DURING A time when murder and disappearances were commonplace in the host country, it feels hyperbolic and vulgar to use the 'group of death' trope when speaking about the trivial matter of football. However, in a different time and place, Group 4 would be labelled as just that. It contained four teams who harboured genuine aspirations to reach the second round. Of these, two had set their sights on lifting the Jules Rimet Trophy. Group 4 contained 1974 finalists, the Netherlands, Ally MacLeod's much-fancied Scotland, Asian Cup champions Iran, and Copa América holders Peru. Taking place in Mendoza and Córdoba, the group had its own microclimate, which produced iconic goals, an unlikely winner and even a failed drugs test.

The 1978 World Cup came during the twilight years of Peru's golden generation. La Blanquirroja (the red and whites) had established themselves as a force in Latin American football during the 1970s, thanks to a quarter-final appearance in Mexico 1970 and their sophomore Copa América title five years later. Following an eight-year absence, the tournament returned in 1975 and a surprise victory for Peru upset the established hierarchy of Latin American football. Since the inception of the tournament, the giants of the continent – Argentina, Brazil and Uruguay – had passed the cup among themselves, the oligopoly interrupted only three times in 50 years. However, the '70s marked a new dawn for the Peruvian national team.

Success at the World Cup offered both sporting and social opportunities for Peru. Dr Pete Watson says that football is often used as a 'nation-building project', whereby the success of a team is used to inspire and unite a nation's people. The 1978 Peruvian squad certainly contained many ingredients of a nation-building project, the most important of which is, of course, a successful team. Second, the 1970s squad was the first to contain players representative of a diverse Peru. In 1978 it included non-European-looking Peruvians, the two most notable being Teófilo Cubillas and Hugo 'El Cholo' Sotil. The nickname El Cholo referenced Sotil's indigenous origin.

A successful stint at the World Cup was an opportunity to address what Watson describes as Peru's historic problem of assimilating indigenous people into what was perceived to be the Peruvian nation. 'In the 150 years since Peru's independence the question of how to include indigenous people in the identity of the nation has been problematic for the republic.'[79] Understandably, alongside the obvious sporting ambitions of the players, the government of Peru would have taken a keen interest in the marketability of a successful team.

---

79 Interview with Dr Peter Watson 2021 – teaching fellow of Latin American studies at the University of Leeds.

Football was no exception to this historic problem of black and indigenous representation. As far back as 1930 the great Alianza Lima team, representative of the black, working-class community of La Victoria, wasn't embraced by the nation, as the elites were uncomfortable with black players representing Peru. The Peruvian football federation in fact refused to recognise Alianza's fourth title win in 1934, such was the lack of acknowledgements from the nation's elites. The 1970s saw the first attempts to address this ethnic imbalance, as now the national team featured notable players of a darker complexion. An ethnically diverse team, representative of all corners of Peru would inspire viewers back home and thrill those in the stands.

In contrast to Peru's enthusiasm, the Netherlands approached the tournament minus their talisman, the world's greatest footballer: Johan Cruyff. They also faced the added pressure of unprecedented protests against the team's mere presence in Argentina. Cruyff's absence has often been incorrectly attributed to his objection to Argentina's military regime, as his politics were famously at odds with the right-wing sentiments of the Argentinian junta. At the time, Cruyff stated that he didn't have the required focus to represent his country at the World Cup. He revealed that the commitment to playing at the World Cup required an extended period away from his family, a sacrifice he was unwilling to make. Years later, in his autobiography *My Turn*, Cruyff would shed further light on this, revealing that his family suffered a terrible ordeal when their Catalunya apartment was broken into, as the burglars robbed them at knifepoint. Cruyff's guilt that he could not protect his family meant that he was uneasy leaving them to fly to the other side of the world. Cruyff declared, 'After the kidnapping attempt, I never had a moment's doubt about not going to Argentina. Anyone who would leave his family behind in those circumstances would be out of his mind.'[80]

Perhaps understandably the expectations back in the Netherlands were somewhat muted, considering they were missing their best player. Oranje supporters were split on Cruyff's decision, one group launching the 'Pull Cruyff across the line' campaign, inundating the player with requests to change his mind. Cruyff claimed, 'I was sent postbags full of requests from Dutch fans … but the safety of my family had to come first.'[81]

Once it was clear that he would not compromise, other fans derided Cruyff for turning his back on the team. Some suggested that he had assimilated to life in Barcelona and was now more Catalan than Dutch.[82] This mindset had also briefly permeated the team itself two years prior at the 1976 European Championships. Cruyff and Barcelona team-mate Johan Neeskens were granted permission to meet up with the Dutch training camp a few days later than the rest of the squad.

Upon their arrival, a sardonic Willy van der Kuijlen remarked, 'Here come the kings of Spain.' This comment touched a nerve with Cruyff, who issued the coaching staff

---

80 Johan Cruyff. 2016. *My Turn*. Pan Macmillan.

81 *Ibid.*

82 Interview with Andy Bollen, author of *Fierce Genius – Cruyff's Year at Feyenoord*.

with an ultimatum: either Van der Kuijlen was to leave the squad or he would.[83]

Unsurprisingly, the greatest player in the world remained and Van der Kuijlen left the squad, along with goalkeeper and PSV Eindhoven team-mate Jan van Beveren. The spat is often attributed to a supposed feeling among PSV representatives in the national squad that they weren't held to the same standards as Ajax or Feyenoord players. The two Johans' connections with Ajax were probably more important in this example than the fact that they played in Spain. Van der Kuijlen clearly felt that the former Ajax players were afforded luxuries that he, as a PSV player, wouldn't have been. The whole debacle is another chapter in the anthology of Dutch teams going to tournaments with talented squads, seemingly intent on falling out with one another.

Cruyff expressed regret that he didn't attend the 1978 World Cup. Covering the final for BBC, he spoke of his frustration of watching the match, unable to prevent what he was seeing as Argentina triumphed over his Oranje team-mates in El Monumental. He said, 'I had a hard time in the studio. Would we have won if I could have been there? I think, quite honestly, that we might have done.'[84]

With or without the great Cruyff, the Dutch path to the final would be no simple procession. Their opponents hadn't arrived to merely play the part of villains in a total

83 Gary Thacker. 2021. *Beautiful Bridesmaids Dressed in Oranje: The Unfulfilled Glory of Dutch Football*. Pitch Publishing.

84 Johan Cruyff. 2016. *My Turn*. Pan Macmillan.

football pantomime; they faced a difficult group – filled with ambitious competitors.

Iran came into the tournament as the three-times champions of Asia. The team were considered the pet project of Shah Mohammad Reza Pahlavi and a huge nationalist symbol for Iran. The tournament would be the final bow for this team, who returned home to a very different country. Just a year later the Islamic revolution would take place and the shah would be replaced by Ayatollah Khomeini. It would be 20 years before Iran qualified for another World Cup and the collapse of the shah's team would lead to a period in the football wilderness for the nation.

Much like the hosts, the fingerprints of their government were all over the Iranian national team. It was heavily rumoured that those with progressive, left-leaning tendencies were less than popular with the team. One of the most curious characters in the Iranian squad was Hassan Nayebagha. The midfielder was an outspoken critic of the shah, as he felt the regime was anti-intellectual; however, he was a favourite of coach Heshmat Mohajerani and thus selected for the World Cup following Iran's strong showing at the 1976 Olympics in Montreal. Nayebagha had originally stated that he would boycott the tournament, due to his opposition to Argentina's right-wing dictatorship. Despite this, Mohajerani's influence was sufficient to persuade his player to join up with the squad. As the writing was on the wall for the shah, Nayebagha was hopeful for the post-imperial Iran he would return to after the World Cup. He believed the country would move forward towards democracy and economic growth and this would only be strengthened by a strong World Cup showing.

Ultimately, the midfielder would be disappointed by the revolution. He deemed Khomeini's rule to be a religious dictatorship and he would soon join the People's Mojahedin Organization of Iran (MEK), a group violently opposed to Khomeini's regime. The left-wing militant body is designated as a terrorist organisation in Iraq and Iran, plus the European Union (until being delisted in 2009). Nayebagha would mentor young defender Habib Khabiri, who would in 1983 be arrested for membership of the MEK, then tortured and executed by Khomeini's regime. Nayebagha cites the execution of his protege as the reason he will never reconcile with Iran's administration.

After his spectacular goal against Kuwait in 1978, the 23-year-old Khabiri wasn't selected for the World Cup. Much like their Dutch counterparts, Iran had entered the World Cup missing a talismanic player. His omittance and subsequent execution makes him somewhat of a cult hero for many Iranians. Iranian football commentator Manook Khodabakhshian refers to Khabiri as a James Dean figure, a 'rebel without a cause',[85] a stark difference to the terrorist portrayed by the state.

Iran would be joined by another nation with much to gain from a strong World Cup showing. Scotland rose to become the football power of the British Isles in the late

---

85   Ian Thomsen. 1998. 'Political football Americans will experience the deep-seated nationalism of World Cup play when the U.S. meets Iran in an emotional test for both sides'. *Sports Illustrated*.

'70s, winning the British Home Championship in 1977, a triumph that included a famous win against England at Wembley, prompting a pitch invasion from the raucous Tartan Army that the goalposts simply couldn't survive. Scotland further cemented their claim to dominance of the British Isles by qualifying for the tournament at the expense of Wales. In a controversial move, Wales's home fixture versus Scotland was played in England, at Liverpool's Anfield stadium. The Football Association of Wales (FAW), hamstrung by the fact that Cardiff's Ninian Park was unavailable due to crowd trouble in the 1976 European Championship, chose Anfield over Wrexham's Racecourse. Although the Racecourse is the oldest international football ground in the world and boasted a bear-pit partisan atmosphere, it was dwarfed by Anfield in terms of capacity. The FAW saw an opportunity to line their pockets and, thus, thousands of Scottish supporters made the journey to Liverpool, outnumbering their Welsh counterparts. The travelling Tartan Army's trip south ended in delirium as they secured a controversial 2-0 win, with Scotland opening the scoring from the penalty spot as the referee mistook Joe Jordan's blatant handball for the red sleeve of a Welshman. Nevertheless, Scotland went on to secure their place at the World Cup, emerging from a qualifying group that also contained Czechoslovakia.

Despite the nefarious circumstances that won the match in Anfield, and Scotland's modest third place in the 1978 British Home Championship, there was little doubt that Scotland were the power in British football. There was a justifiable air of extreme confidence around the Scottish football squad, which mirrored the new-found confidence and belief of the Scottish nation in the late '70s. The 1970s was a time of a great sea change in British politics and this decade saw the rise of the Scottish National Party (SNP). The SNP's brand of left-wing civic nationalism was a growing force in Scotland and the decade saw them claim their first seats in Westminster. Like their group rivals Iran and the hosts Argentina, there was much political capital in a successful Scottish national team. The SNP had even tried to recruit national team manager Ally MacLeod. Although a staunch patriot, apolitical Ally politely rebuffed their approaches.

In MacLeod, Scotland had found the poster boy for their confidence. The Glaswegian blended self-assurance with charm and swagger and was prone to making bold claims about the strength of his teams. He believed he was born to succeed and stated that Scotland were not only going to Argentina to compete but that they would return with the World Cup in hand. The Scotland team rode a wave of optimism to Argentina, given a send-off party from Hampden Park atop an open-topped, double-decker bus, soundtracked by a live performance from Andy Cameron of 'Ally's Tartan Army', singing the song that echoed MacLeod's sentiment that they would 'shake them up, when we win the World Cup'. Scotland's bombastic departure for South America couldn't contrast any more deeply with the Netherlands' back-door departure from Amsterdam.

The journey from Scotland to Argentina in 1978 would be complex, dangerous and exorbitant for Scottish supporters. However, this didn't prevent hundreds from travelling, fuelled by the infectious enthusiasm of their coach. Before the invention of the internet, there was an innocence to wet-behind-the-ears tourists. Spare a thought for the fans who saw an advert in a travel agent's window on Prince's Street, Edinburgh for flights to Port-au-Spain for the World Cup. A quick search online will reveal that Port-au-Spain in Trinidad, leaving the beleaguered Scots with thousands of miles remaining to travel. But travel they did, en masse. Such was the distance and logistical difficulties of this trip in 1978 that many of the Tartan Army took weeks to arrive then weeks to return home safely. Ronnie McDevitt's book *Scotland in the 70s* documents Scottish fans 'clinging to the side of freight trains',[86] crossing mountain ranges and narrowly avoiding bomb attacks on buses, just to arrive in Argentina. There is also the much-repeated tale of Scottish fans enquiring about renting a submarine to travel across continents.

Matchday one in Group 4 kicked off simultaneously, with the Netherlands facing Iran in Mendoza, in the west of the country near the Chilean border, while Scotland faced Peru over 600 kilometres to the north-east in Córdoba.

Netherlands vs Iran: 3 June 1978 – Estadio Ciudad de Mendoza, Mendoza

In Mendoza, the Netherlands found Iran to be a determined yet ill-disciplined foe. The Dutch control of the football kept their opponents at arm's length but they were unable

---

86   Ronnie McDevitt. 2019. *Scotland in the 70s: The definitive account of the Scotland team 1970–79*. Pitch Publishing.

to find a decisive pass to penetrate Iran's defence. Iran made clear their intentions to counter-attack and created the first noteworthy chance of the match. Forward Hossein Faraki sprung an attack on the favourites, with a fierce drive across the face of Jan Jongbloed's goal. The keeper's fingertips pushed the ball across the mouth of the six-yard box. Fortuitously for the Dutch the ball somehow spun to safety as it evaded Iranian attackers and the Dutch defenders, who could have easily diverted it into their own net.

Iran would be made to pay for this missed opportunity just before half-time. René Van de Kerkhof drew defender Nasrollah Abdollahi towards him at the edge of the box. Van de Kerkhof, anticipating contact, shifted the ball to his right as the defender clumsily brought down his man. The awkward, two-footed challenge wasn't out of the ordinary for the time and he escaped without a yellow card. However, the fall caused Van de Kerkhof to injure his wrist, which would require support from a lightweight cast that he would wear all the way to the final. This completely unremarkable piece of protective equipment would be completely ignored until the moments before kick-off in the final, when it would be the source of an enormous furore between players and officials.

Rob Rensenbrink dispatched the subsequent penalty, calmly side-footing the ball into the bottom-left corner as the goalkeeper Nasser Hejazi took a step in the wrong direction. The timing of the goal was vital, as a relaxed Dutch team emerged for the second half in full control. Despite a largely composed first 45 minutes, Iran wilted under pressure in the second half. Rensenbrink added to his tally with a header on the hour, as Van de Kerkhof was again the architect. His superb cross from the right split the static Iranian defenders and was met with Rensenbrink's head. The header gave the goalkeeper no chance from six yards out and the Dutch had secured the win.

Further polish was added with ten minutes remaining as Johnny Rep set off on a dazzling run towards the Iranian box. With a touch to get the ball out from under his feet, he outpaced defender Andranik Eskandarian before weaving between Nayebagha and Sadeghi. Eskandarian had been caught in Rep's slipstream as he weaved around the defenders as if they were traffic cones. He caught up with Rep in the penalty box, only to upend the Dutch wizard. The referee pointed to the spot and issued a yellow card to the defender, whose frustration had reached boiling point. Rensenbrink stood over the penalty spot to complete his hat-trick and, as the goalkeeper dived to the spot where he had placed his first penalty, the Dutchman fired the ball into the opposite top corner, via the woodwork.

Despite their spirited defiance in the first half, the total football of their opponents had exhausted the Iranians, the old adage proving that the ball moves faster than the man.

Peru vs Scotland: 3 June 1978 – Estadio Chateau Carreras, Córdoba

Simultaneously, in Córdoba, Scotland were beginning their campaign. Scotland had toured South America the previous year, acquitting themselves well, drawing 1-1 against Argentina and losing 2-0 to Brazil. They defeated Chile

4-2 in a heavily criticised match, which was condemned by Labour MP Ian Mikardo who commented that as a football fan he didn't want to see Scotland play on waterlogged pitches, but he also didn't want to see them play on 'blood-soaked pitches'.[87] Mikardo was referencing Chile's Estadio Nacional that doubled as a makeshift torture camp during General Pinochet's dictatorship. Similar to the posters from France and Germany encouraging a boycott of the 1978 World Cup, *Chile Fight* magazine created a poster with the slogan 'Don't play ball with fascists', depicting a pair of football boots in a pool of blood.

Despite the similarities in the dictatorships between Chile and Argentina, Scotland's participation in the 1978 World Cup didn't garner the same protestations. Whether that's down to the paucity of information available at the time about the Argentinian regime or due to the fact that participation in the World Cup is clearly of greater importance than a summer tour is unclear. In purely football terms, many in Scotland expected them to dispatch Peru with aplomb. Although they hadn't defeated Argentina or Brazil in 1977, the 4-2 win against Chile proved they could beat South American opposition, particularly the perceived second tier of South America. What Scotland fans hadn't factored in was the atmosphere behind the scenes.

The Scottish squad were situated in the Sierras Hotel in Alta Gracia, 40 kilometres away from Córdoba, the capital city of the province, where they would play their first two matches. The remote location of the training camp

---

87 'The Scotland v Chile friendly labelled the "match of shame". *The Scotsman*, 2018.

would play a crucial role in the slow erosion of Scotland's confidence and spirit. When Ally MacLeod took the Scotland manager's job, he took his Aberdeen team on an end-of-season tour to Dubrovnik, as a send-off. The boozy Brits abroad tour helped smooth over any bitterness the players may have felt about him leaving. Scotland camps were the antithesis to this, as a pre-departure camp in Dunblane and Córdoba's Alta Gracia were infamous for their monotony.

MacLeod was criticised by some of the experienced players who plied their trade in England for repetitive training sessions and no consideration of what players should do during their downtime. The resort's swimming pool was out of commission during the entirety of their stay so Scotland's players spent their time playing cards, watching videos or, to the detriment of the harmony of the squad, arguing about bonuses. These payments for their participation in the tournament had yet to be agreed with the Scottish Football Association (SFA) as Scotland touched down in Argentina and would be a dark cloud hanging over the squad. Some of the older, more savvy players such as Lou Macari and Kenny Dalglish – who represented giants Manchester United and Liverpool, respectively – were concerned about the lack of clarity around bonuses and whether they would have to pay tax on earnings in Argentina. Macari in particular was accused of being money-orientated, comparing his earnings with his club to that of his national team. The issues of bonuses, poor facilities and disharmony in the camp hung heavy in the air as Scotland prepared to face Peru in Córdoba.

Scotland coach Ally MacLeod faced a selection dilemma in midfield, opting for the tried-and-tested Derby County duo of Bruce Rioch and Don Masson, as 25-year-old sensation Graeme Souness was unfortunate not to make the bench for the match. Souness had joined Liverpool in January and, as a lynchpin in midfield, guided them to their second successive European Cup, mixing toughness with artistry. Souness could pick a pass, as proven in the final when supplying Dalglish to score the winning goal, and could handle himself in the midfield boiler room. Reports suggest that MacLeod felt that Peru were no match for Scotland physically and saw no need for an enforcer in the middle of the park.

The match began positively for Scotland and within 15 minutes they took the lead. A fine one-touch move began outside the left-hand side of Peru's 18-yard box as Dalglish came out to meet Willie Johnston's pass. As Dalglish was Scotland's most talented player, he naturally drew two Peruvian defenders towards him. He smartly shifted the ball back inside to Asa Hartford, whose delicate tap forward found captain Bruce Rioch. He spotted that the defenders preoccupied by Dalglish had vacated enough space for a first-time, left-footed strike. It was shot straight at goalkeeper Ramón Quiroga but the pace of the shot and fact that Quiroga had come rushing out to the six-yard line to narrow the angle, meant that he could only divert the ball to his left.

The most alert player in the penalty box was Joe Jordan, who gambled on the goalkeeping error and gleefully raced on to the spilled ball. Jordan fired the ball back in the direction of the goal, placing it under Quiroga's body and into the net.

MacLeod's midfield selection looked to have paid off as Scotland played through their Peruvian counterparts for the opening part of the first half. After the shock of conceding, Peru sought to get a foothold in the match and exchanged goalscoring chances with their European counterparts. Talisman Cubillas, playing a clever one-two with compatriot La Rosa in the penalty box, forced a save from Scotland's keeper Alan Rough. For the remainder of the half Scotland struggled to find the flowing football of the opening 15 minutes and resorted to competing for second balls from Joe Jordan knockdowns.

Scotland's early exuberance soon dissipated, along with their lead. Cubillas played a short ball inside to midfielder José Velásquez, under pressure from both Dalglish and Jordan. A shrewd swerve and quick feet sent Dalglish in the wrong direction. As Velásquez attempted to get the ball from under his feet, he came shoulder to shoulder with Jordan, the Peruvian sending the Scot to the ground, collecting the ball and continuing his charge. The Scots seemed to freeze momentarily, in disbelief at their self-styled hardman being sent sprawling to the Córdobese turf. The British press had regarded the Peruvians as technically and physically inferior to their European opponents, yet this perception was being torn up like ticker tape on the pitch. In truth the Peruvian team wasn't particularly old, but the elder statesmen of the team, Cubillas and Sotil were more recognisable to a European audience than their younger team-mates. Velásquez laid the ball off and it ricocheted off the chest of César Cueto, giving him an opportunity in the box. Cueto kept his composure to slot the ball into the corner of the goal, past the onrushing Alan Rough. Peru were level and left the field at the end of the first half in the ascendancy. They had established midfield dominance, powerful charges from Velásquez and Cubillas frequently bypassing Scotland's midfield duo, making Souness's omission from the matchday squad seem like an even worse oversight.

The second half simmered until the hour mark, when Scotland were awarded an opportunity to restore their lead. Another cross was pumped towards the head of Joe Jordan, who, despite losing the header, applied enough pressure on the Peruvian defender that he headed the ball dangerously into space at the edge of the penalty area. Captain Bruce Rioch reacted first, driving into the box, controlling the ball on his chest and inviting a rash challenge from opposing captain Héctor Chumpitaz. The referee pointed to the spot without hesitation.

Don Masson stood on the spot for an age, as Peru's coach Marcos Calderón used the break in play to replace La Rosa with Hugo Sotil. If the timing of the substitution was a cynical ploy to increase pressure on the penalty taker, it was successful. A fabulous dive from Quiroga allowed him to steer Masson's penalty around the corner of the post, to the delight of his team-mates.

Scotland were made to pay for their missed opportunity within ten minutes as Cubillas scored one of the tournament's most memorable goals. Receiving the ball from Cueto, he steered the ball to his left, 25–30 yards from goal. Although the defence offered the Peruvian far too much space, he seemed to be drifting on to his left foot. Another touch and a half-step caught the defence cold. As he shifted the ball to his right, Cubillas found space to unleash an unorthodox, bullet of a strike, somewhere between a toe punt and an outside of the boot shot. Rather than flying to the opposite corner, the ball whipped past Alan Rough's inside post into the top corner. Rough seemed to only realise the direction of the ball as it flew over his right shoulder. The body language of the Scottish keeper portrayed a sense of utter confusion, echoed by the defenders who stood hands on hips, amid the jubilant Peruvians.

It was a strike worthy of winning any match but Cubillas would repeat the trick a few minutes later with a remarkably similar finish. A sumptuous, left-footed pass from opening goalscorer Cueto from within his own half found forward Juan Oblitas. The striker was scythed down by Stuart Kennedy, who had been left exposed by the quality of pass and pace of the player. After a brilliant first touch, Oblitas found himself in a heap on the turf, courtesy of a cynical challenge that would have undoubtably resulted in a red card in the modern game. However, Oblitas displayed great resilience in immediately springing to his feet, attempting to regain possession, before the referee awarded a free kick.

Any Peruvians who may have felt they had been robbed of a spectacular match-sealing goal by Oblitas were placated by what came next. The placement of the free kick suited a curling effort, and everyone in the Scottish wall expected Juan Muñante to take the kick. However, as Muñante dummied, Cubillas ran on to the ball in a straight line. Replicating his earlier strike, his outside of the boot/ toe punt hybrid strike flew past the Scottish wall and into the same top corner of Rough's goal. The strike sealed a deserved 3-1 win for Peru, who saw out the remaining ten minutes with little incident. The South Americans had recorded a hard-fought win high on quality and spirit.

A humbled Scotland trudged off the pitch to the soundtrack of jeers from the Tartan Army. Their 12,000-mile journey had begun with an unexpected loss, but things were to become much worse for them. Dalglish and substitute Archie Gemmill were selected for random drug testing but, as Gemmill was too dehydrated to provide a sample, Willie Johnston took his place. Johnston returned a positive sample for a drug known as fencamfamin, a stimulant present in the Reactivan tablets he took that day. He would later tell ITN reporter Jeffrey Archer that he took two tablets prior to the match to clear a head cold he had been suffering with since arriving in Argentina. Johnston had self-prescribed the drug and there were no suggestions that there were any nefarious motives, simply an error on his part. However, a failed drugs test could result in the offending nation being expelled from the tournament. Furthermore, there was speculation that other members of the squad may have taken the same drug.

In his book *'78 – How a Nation Lost the World Cup'*, Graham McColl states that Don Masson, Johnston's team-mate '(casually strolled) up to MacLeod, to let him know he had also taken Reactivan'.[88] Although Masson would later retract this statement, the Scottish camp had now descended into a state of panic. Johnston was later sent home, banned from European club competitions and informed by the SFA that his Scotland career was over. Masson's admission to MacLeod spelled the end of his World Cup and Scotland career also.

Russell Isaac, working as a runner at the time with ITV's *World of Sport*, says, 'The Scottish FA didn't protect him [Johnston], he was hung out to dry.' It was a young Trevor McDonald who broke the news to Johnston, much to the chagrin of those in charge of the team, annoyed that the message came from a reporter and not an official. The story broke after office hours and, as the only Spanish speaker on the crew, Isaac managed to book the satellite lines for the story to go out on *News at Ten* in the UK. At this point the relationship between the press and the Scottish camp was irreparable and the SFA was keen to circle the wagons around the camp to protect the rest of the squad. The ostracised Johnston was bundled out of the back doors of Alta Gracia under a blanket and sent home to face the press alone. On the long journey back to Britain via Paris, Johnston was interrogated by ITN journalist Archer. Johnston insisted he just wanted to be left alone and felt sick about the entire incident.

The atmosphere in the Scotland camp would continue to be a source of intrigue for the media, who were enthralled by rumours of drunken visits into Córdoba by players and

88 Graham McColl. 2006. *'78 – How a Nation Lost the World Cup*. Headline.

staff. In truth, the hedonistic image was wide of the mark. Most accounts describe the squad as bored, paranoid and at each others' throats. And they were still lacking a functioning swimming pool.

Netherlands vs Peru: 7 June 1978 – Estadio Ciudad de Mendoza, Mendoza

Matchday two would see the victors of matchday one, Netherlands and Peru, face off in Mendoza. Either could secure a place in the second round with a win but both would have realised that a draw would put them in a very strong position going into the final fixture. Peru's final match would be against supposed minnows Iran, so perhaps a draw would be a better result for them. Nevertheless, with neither team desperate for a win, and the Netherlands without Cruyff, only 28,000 spectators attended.

Despite tormenting the Iranian defence with his speed and trickery, wide-man Johnny Rep was named among the substitutes as Netherlands coach Ernst Happel named a four-man midfield. In the opening half, the Dutch midfield controlled the ball well but offered little dynamism in attack. A lofted pass from skipper Rudi Krol found Van de Kerkhof in the Peruvian box but, pushed wide to a difficult angle, he could only scoop the ball tamely over Quiroga's bar. Quiroga was only challenged twice in the first half, the first a moment of panic purely of 'El Loco's' own creation as he dropped a tame cross at the feet of Rensenbrink. Quiroga scrambled to regain the ball and managed to block Rensenbrink's shot on the spin before collecting the ball. The Dutchman would warm the Peruvian's hands once more as a long-distance free kick was pushed behind the post by Quiroga.

Rep's introduction at half-time signalled a change in approach from the men in orange. They attacked with more purpose, showcasing their total football as defender Wim Rijsbergen exchanged a one-two at the edge of the box and sent a low drive past the post. A further chance then arrived for Rensenbrink, whose half-volley through a crowded box was saved well by Quiroga.

As time drifted towards the 90th minute, the Dutch had created little else and appeared resigned to leave Mendoza level with Peru and unscathed, aside from a late injury to Johan Neeskens, who would only feature for another ten minutes in the opening round. Peru had offered nothing in an attacking sense yet were rarely troubled in defence and were satisfied to top the group going into the final match against Iran.

Scotland vs Iran: 7 June 1978 – Estadio Chateau Carreras, Córdoba

The match in Córdoba pitted the two losers from the first round of fixtures against one another. With chaos and controversy in their camp, and the bitter taste of defeat versus Peru still fresh in their mouths, Scotland may have considered minnows Iran as the perfect palate-cleanser. However, Iran were intent on piling further misery on the Tartan Army.

Iran and Scotland's proximity in Córdoba meant that they shared the stadium's training ground. Surprisingly, Scotland declined the opportunity to scout their opponents' training sessions, deciding instead to focus on themselves. Lightning would strike twice as Scotland would again be accused of underestimating their opponents. MacLeod made a handful of changes for this match, due to Johnston's ban, his mistrust of Masson and an injury to captain Rioch. Souness again found himself out of the team, with Archie Gemmill and Lou Macari selected.

A dour first half passed without incident until a moment of calamity before half-time. A hopeful ball into the box confused goalkeeper Hejazi and defender Eskandarian. As the keeper rushed out to claim the ball, Eskandarian slowed to block the run of Joe Jordan. The goalkeeper punched the ball into his defender's chest and, as all three players fell to the deck, Eskandarian swung his left foot, directing a half-volley into his own net. The Iranian had added an own goal to his World Cup misery, four days after conceding a penalty against the Dutch. The Tartan Army exchanged bemused glances and smiles among the crowd of 7,938.

The Córdobese public's lack of interest in the fixture had been vindicated by the poor quality of football in the opening half. The first moment of quality arrived from the champions of Asia on the hour mark, as a cross from Ghasempour found Faraki in the penalty area. Under pressure, Faraki held possession and weaved away from the area, gliding past defenders who could not commit to tackles for fear of conceding a penalty. Faraki returned the ball to Ghasempour, whose second cross found a Scottish head at the back post. The header cleared as far as Danaeifard at the edge of the box, who, from a standing start, shifted the

145

ball to his right before powering past Gemmill's challenge. The Iranian struck his shot early, before the goalkeeper was set, the ball taking a slight deflection into the net. Iran had drawn level against their illustrious opponents. The camera panned to coach Ally MacLeod as the BBC commentator lamented, 'It can't get any worse, surely?' In truth it didn't get any better for Scotland in Córdoba as the match wound to a close with both teams on one point and edging closer to elimination, next facing the two undefeated teams in the group.

The Scots trudged off the pitch past their compatriots in the stands. The mood of the spectators spanned a spectrum of disappointment, from melancholia to rage. For some the anger overspilled, confronting the team as they left the pitch. A spectator threw his jersey to the floor in front of them and others hurled abuse, threatening to boycott their final fixture in Mendoza. The rumours of a squad arguing about money had reached the fans and, understandably, those who had made such financial sacrifices to attend the tournament were less than pleased. The team bus was prevented from leaving for ten minutes as the fans vented their anger at the Scotland squad, while shaking and beating the vehicle.

Peru vs Iran: 11 June 1978 – Estadio Chateau Carreras, Córdoba

The final group match in Córdoba saw Peru punish a hapless Iran and power their way into the second round. Peru's guile and creativity was too much for the Iranians, who would exit the tournament rooted to the bottom of their group. Once again, Iran bemoaned poor discipline and naivety as they conceded two penalties.

Peru took the lead within two minutes as Jose Velásquez rose highest in the box to dispatch Juan Muñante's corner. Velásquez faced no resistance and he strolled into the box and sent a thumping header low into the net. The Peruvians were outnumbered seven to two by Iranians in the box, including two defenders on Iran's goal line, intimating that perhaps their mere presence didn't equate to the desire required to prevent the goal.

Two moments of ill-discipline marked the final nails in the coffin of Iran's World Cup dream. On the half hour, in a challenge very similar to their match against the Netherlands, Peru were awarded a penalty. The shoulder barge on a passing Peruvian attacker prompted the Polish referee Alojzy Jarguz to point to the spot.

The awarding of the penalty may have seemed a little harsh, particularly due to the agricultural nature of some of the challenges in the tournament and the suggestion that the foul may have taken place outside the box, but, nonetheless, this was another black mark against the disciplinary record of the Iranians. Cubillas strode up and fired the ball high into the net, beyond the lame dive of Hejazi. Minutes later Cubillas rounded Hejazi again, with the goal at his mercy, only for the despairing goalkeeper to hook his leg and bring him to the ground. Cubillas rose to his feet and scored his second penalty of the match, this time striking the ball low into the corner of the goal.

Iran finished the first half with their own moment of quality. A left-footed cross from Iraj Danaeifard was redirected into the path of striker Hassan Rowshan via a Peruvian head. From 12 yards, Rowshan expertly side-footed a volley into the bottom right-hand corner of the goal. Iran's celebrations were short-lived, though, as Peru restored their three-goal lead with ten minutes remaining. Cubillas played a one-two against an Iranian defender in the box, his attempted through ball fortuitously ricocheting back to him, leaving him one on one with the keeper from six yards. Unsurprisingly, the forward, who was in scintillating form, made no mistake, beating the keeper with an outside-of-the-foot finish. This finish was becoming a trademark for Cubillas, as he completed his hat-trick to bring his tally to five goals in the group stages, making him the player of the opening stage.

Iran's World Cup was over and they would return to their home country humbled, bemoaning poor discipline and perceived poor treatment by officials. Manager Heshmat Mohajerani was less than enamoured with the officiating in Argentina, declaring, 'We have had four penalties given against us, is this justice? We lost the game but mainly we lost it to the referee. FIFA should have protected us.'

A buoyant Peru topped the group and made it to the second group stage in fine form. In Mendoza the other two teams would compete to see who would secure the second qualification spot. Scotland required an unlikely win by a three-goal margin to leapfrog the Netherlands into second place.

Scotland vs Netherlands: 11 June 1978 – Estadio Ciudad de Mendoza, Mendoza

Despite needing goals, MacLeod sacrificed a striker for an extra midfielder to compete with a Dutch team blessed with gifted footballers, confident in possession. Souness replaced Lou Macari in the starting line-up, with Joe Jordan trusted to lead the line alone. Souness's presence was attributed by many to be due to Macari's ill-timed ITV interview, where he criticised the SFA, rather than a change in philosophy from MacLeod. Nonetheless, the Scottish selection for the trip to Mendoza saw fresh faces in the line-up.

Despite the protestations of the Scottish fans in Córdoba, Estadio Ciudad de Mendoza boasted a much healthier attendance of 35,000-plus, including General Jorge Videla, as the two teams sought to qualify for the second stage. The crowd quickly witnessed what newcomer Souness had to offer as the Liverpool midfielder picked up a quickly taken free kick. Souness feinted to cross twice, before floating the ball on to the head of captain Rioch, whose header cannoned back off the angle of post and crossbar.

Scotland had a clear urge to score and had begun the match with more urgency and quality on the ball than their counterparts, as the Dutch fluency was further hampered by an injury to Neeskens on ten minutes. Dalglish saw a goal ruled out for a foul in the build-up, before Scotland's promising beginning was thwarted by a moment of self-destruction. Just after the half hour, full-back Stuart Kennedy's weak back-pass was seized upon by Johnny

Rep, who drove into the penalty area. Attempting to make amends, Kennedy compounded his error by fouling Rep and conceding the penalty. Rensenbrink converted the kick, his third of the group stages, to leave Scotland with a mountain to climb. They now needed four goals without reply.

The first of these arrived shortly before the interval, as an unorthodox, hooked cross from Souness found Joe Jordan, who nodded the ball down to Dalglish. Dalglish struck the ball on the half-volley into the roof of the net to give parity to Scotland. The remaining 90 seconds of the half continued at breakneck speed as Scotland chased further goals. This approach almost led to their downfall as Rep spurned a chance when he mis-controlled the ball on his chest as he burst into the Scottish penalty area, unmarked, with only the goalkeeper to beat. Without further incident, the referee blew the half-time whistle.

The match was even but Scotland were in the ascendancy, with 45 minutes remaining to secure the unlikeliest of passages to the second round. They took another huge step towards this in the first minute of the second half as Willy van de Kerkhof blocked Souness in the penalty area. Gemmill stepped up and fired the ball into the bottom corner, meaning the Scots were now halfway there.

As the game approached the final quarter, the Scottish influence on the midfield battle was beginning to wane. Souness, who had been imperious for an hour, had been flogged to death, playing his first passage of competitive football since the European Cup Final a month before.

Barry Davies on commentary for BBC underlined the dilemma MacLeod faced when he said, 'These Scottish boys have gone through an awful lot. The question of substitutions must be on MacLeod's mind. But the team have found rhythm. It's a terribly difficult decision to make.'

MacLeod opted to leave the team unchanged. In the 68th minute Archie Gemmill repaid MacLeod's faith and wrote himself into World Cup folklore. The man from Paisley seized upon a loose ball on the edge of the penalty area, following a crunching tackle on his captain. Gemmill evaded a wild lunge from Wim Jansen, his deft touch taking him into the path of Dutch captain Ruud Krol. Gemmill anticipated the heavy challenge from Krol and displayed incredible balance to glide past the flying Dutchman. A further touch saw him slalom past Rob Rensenbrink, now leaving three defenders in a heap on the floor. As desperate defenders swirled around him, like debris in a hurricane, Gemmill was serene in the eye of the storm. He carefully steadied himself as the goalkeeper rushed out, opened his body and lofted the ball over the despairing Dutchman. It was a goal of pure, individual brilliance. The contrast of Gemmill's balletic poise as he shifted the ball past the erratic Dutch players is jarring, as the Dutch players were selected due to their technical ability. There were no Oranje players uncomfortable on the ball, due to their philosophy of total football, therefore it's utterly absurd to see them lunging at the graceful Gemmill en route to the goal. As the Scottish players ran away celebrating, Souness gesticulated to the bench with one finger raised, proclaiming 'one more'.

The incredible goal offered short-lived respite for Scotland's exhausted bodies and minds. A minute later, they almost conceded a second. A deep cross into the box was missed by Rep, but Kennedy drove an attempted clearing header into the ground, narrowly missing his own goal, as the ball bounced out for a corner kick. But Johnny Rep wouldn't be denied a minute later as he ensured Scotland's World Cup journey would end in Mendoza. In a moment that underlined the Dutch quality and commitment to total football, Krol carried the ball out of his centre-half position. Tired Scotland forwards were unable to press him as he brought the ball to the centre circle, before finding Rep on the right wing. Rep exchanged passes with his skipper, who had now picked up a position in central midfield, before striking a 25-yard shot into the top corner. It was a goal born out of Krol's ambition and Rep's artistry and finished with aplomb. The goal sent the Netherlands as group runners-up into Group A of the second stage. There they would face Italy, reigning champions and arch-nemesis West Germany and Austria. Crucially, they would avoid hosts Argentina, and Brazil and Poland.

Some cynics suggest that the Oranje's loss afforded them an easier route and that they played the game against Scotland purposely in second gear. The change in mindset following Gemmill's goal, which put the Dutch on the precipice of elimination, was evident. Krol in particular displayed uncharacteristic haste in diving into the challenge and, just three minutes later when his team needed clarity of thought, he was back to the ball-playing, confident centre-half that the world recognised.

As the pendulum of momentum swung back to the Netherlands they didn't look back. The Oranje total football machine was on its way to the second round, where they would underline their credentials as the best football team in the tournament, and thrill spectators along the way.

The Second Round – Group A: Austria, Italy, Netherlands and West Germany

AFTER AN emotional and eventful opening ten days, eight teams had been eliminated and eight remained in Argentina. The eight survivors split into two groups of four, with Group A bunching the European rivals together. The hosts' surprising defeat to Italy meant the Azzurri took their place in Group A, in which the matches would be played in the country's two biggest cities of Buenos Aires and Córdoba.

Similarly to Argentina, Brazil had laboured into the second stage, with Austria taking their expected place in Group A, emerging from the quagmire of Mar del Plata with more credit in the bank than the South Americans. The group was completed by 1974 World Cup finalists Netherlands and reigning champions West Germany, who surprisingly finished second in their first-round groups. Whoever topped Group A would be rewarded with a place in the World Cup Final.

Austria vs Netherlands: 14 June 1978 – Estadio Chateau Carreras, Córdoba

Following their stop-start performances in the opening round, the Netherlands arrived in the second round with a clean slate and a point to prove. Coach Ernst Happel, an Austrian who spoke only German, was drafted in with the sole purpose of winning the 1978 World Cup. Happel had won the European Cup in 1970 with Feyenoord, the first Dutch team to ever lift Europe's premiere trophy. The Austrian followed this up in 1971 with the Inter-Continental Cup, making Feyenoord de facto champions of the world. To repeat the trick, this time at international level, Happel would have to go one better than his great rival and coach of the Oranje at the previous World Cup, Rinus Michels.

Happel's coaching career began in The Hague with ADO (now known as ADO Den Haag) and it was here that he made his name as a tactician. In 1968 ADO triumphed over Michels' Ajax to win the KNVB Cup, switching from a traditional 4-2-4 formation to the dynamic 4-3-3 now synonymous with Dutch football. The cup win earned Happel the keys to De Kuip at Feyenoord. Happel's Feyenoord faced Celtic in the 1970 European Cup Final, where history repeated itself as Happel outwitted the great Jock Stein, his 4-3-3 system once again triumphant over the opponents' 4-2-4. Following the loss, Stein declared, 'Celtic has not lost to Feyenoord, I have lost to Happel.'[89]

---

89 Priya Ramesh. 2019. 'Ernst Happel: The Feyenoord years'. *These Football Times*.

Gary Thacker, author of *Beautiful Bridesmaids Dressed in Oranje: The Unfulfilled Glory of Dutch Football*, describes the job of coaching the Dutch national team as a 'game of pass the parcel' during the 1970s.[90] After Rinus Michels' team narrowly missed out on glory at the 1974 World Cup, the KNVB appointed George Knobel, who steered them to a third-place finish at the 1976 European Championship in Yugoslavia, only to be ousted following a fractious relationship with the KNVB and accusations of player power. Jan Zwartkruis was the man in the hot seat for the 1978 World Cup qualification campaign but the KNVB, in true Dutch fashion, opted to shuffle the pack for the tournament proper, installing Club Brugge coach Happel as the man in the dugout, demoting Zwartkruis to a place among the coaching staff. This decision fuelled an already combustible atmosphere, pitting the two coaches against each other in a cold war for control of the team.

Perhaps due to the Dutch national team's propensity for conflict, it was advantageous for Happel that he was famously a man of few words. Despite his penchant for brevity (his speech prior to the final was reportedly only one sentence long), Happel was a man of principle and courage. During his time at Rapid Wien's youth team, Happel was expelled from team gatherings based on his refusal to sing Hitler Youth songs. The Austrian was only 13 in 1938 and vehemently opposed the Nazi regime.[91]

---

90 Interview with Gary Thacker 2021, author of *Beautiful Bridesmaids Dressed in Oranje: The Unfulfilled Glory of Dutch Football*.

91 'Ernst Happel: The "weird man" who conquered European football and helped shape the modern game'. 90 min, www.si.com, 2019.

Prior to taking on the Dutch national role, Happel had won three Belgian titles and had led Club Brugge to a European Cup Final. After winning the same title with Dutch giants Feyenoord eight years earlier, this time Happel came up short, losing Europe's showpiece final 1-0 to Liverpool. Despite this, KNVB officials were sufficiently impressed to draft the Austrian in, pushing Zwartkruis to the fringes.

The KNVB faced a considerable dilemma in the lead-up to the World Cup, as the Netherlands still had to overcome a challenging qualifying group that featured Belgium and Northern Ireland. In Zwartkruis they had a coach that they knew wouldn't lead them to the tournament and Happel, the incumbent coach, was still under contract with Club Brugge, meaning he would be preoccupied with the small matter of the European Cup Final less than a month before the Dutch would depart for Argentina.

In the hinterland between qualification and the tournament itself, it seemed as if the Oranje had a foot in the past and a foot in the present. Johan Cruyff was still captain of the squad and played a crucial role in the two final qualifiers, for a tournament he had no intention of playing in. Cruyff had yet to disclose the true reason to Happel for his refusal to travel to Argentina, for fear of reprisal from the armed gangs that kidnapped famous people in Barcelona. With the biggest tournament in football on the horizon and a World Cup winners' medal missing from Cruyff's trophy cabinet, Happel believed he could convince Cruyff to change his mind. Regarding his insistence to Happel that he wouldn't reverse his decision,

Cruyff admitted, 'I don't think he was convinced. A great sportsman like Happel felt that to miss such an opportunity wasn't right, but I couldn't give him the whole story.'[92]

It was perhaps no surprise that such disjointed preparations for the World Cup played a part in the Netherlands' sluggish performance in the first three matches. However, in Córdoba they found their form and, for the first time in the competition, showcase, the total football they were famous for. As they matured into the tournament, they also found a solution for their most obvious problem: how to fill the huge gap left by Cruyff.

As the new man in the job and with his predecessor still in the camp, Happel may have been tempted to rip up the playbook and assert his authority on the squad. However, the Austrian was a pragmatic character who appreciated that the brief period he had to prepare the national team following his departure from Bruges meant that he wasn't blessed with enough time to completely reinvent the wheel. In addition to this, he had also inherited a headstrong team that wasn't short on self-confidence. Happel had to manage egos as well as a team.

Happel turned to his predecessor for an answer to the Cruyff dilemma. Zwartkruis's solution was a simple one: deploy the accomplished Rob Rensenbrink in Cruyff's role, rather than revamp the entire team.[93] In Cruyff's absence, Rensenbrink thrived on the responsibility. The Anderlecht forward began the tournament in fine fashion, registering

---

92 Johan Cruyff. 2016. *My Turn*. Pan Macmillan.
93 Gary Thacker. 2021. *Beautiful Bridesmaids Dressed in Oranje: The Unfulfilled Glory of Dutch Football*. Pitch Publishing.

a hat-trick including two penalties in the opening match. Scoring penalties was a hallmark of his game, and he went an entire career only missing twice from the spot. Clearly the man from Amsterdam was used to performing under pressure.

The Dutch would feel the weight of expectation once again as they faced underdogs Austria in their opening second round group match. The Austrians had surprised the world in qualifying from a group that contained Brazil and Spain and the Austrian football federation had a treat in store for the squad. To commend them on their qualification for the second stage, the federation allowed the wives of the players to join them in Argentina. In his book *World Cup: The Argentina Story*, author David Miller called it an 'odd concession to domestic life' and suggests it may have had unfavourable implications on the result.[94]

The Dutch, by contrast, lived in monastic conditions in rural Mendoza, at the foothills of the Andes, for the first group stage. They hadn't forgotten having their fingers burned prior to the 1974 World Cup Final, where it was alleged that German publication *Bild* organised a sting operation, infiltrating the Dutch camp and reporting that the players had spent the night in a hot tub with naked models. Legend has it that the Dutch players spent the eve of the World Cup Final on the phone, explaining themselves to their enraged spouses. The KNVB sought to avoid any such embarrassments four years later, with

---

94 David Miller. 1978. *World Cup: The Argentina Story*. Frederick Warne Publishers.

the Dutch players' only source of morbid entertainment being the awkward power struggle between their former and current coach.

On the day of the match, Estadio Chateau Carreras served as a perfect escape from the tension of the Netherlands' training ground, as the players let down their hair and played with a *joie de vivre* against the Austrians. A weight was lifted off Dutch shoulders within the opening minutes as an unlikely goalscorer got them off the mark. Standing square-on over a free kick at the edge of the box, on the right-hand side, Arie Haan resembled a man casually waiting for a train. After a few nonchalant strides, he clipped a sand wedge of a lob into the box with the outside of his boot. Perhaps fooled by his casual body language, the Austrian defenders seemed surprised that the ball dropped serenely into the six-yard box with perfect accuracy to find unmarked defender Ernie Brandts. His header found the bottom corner of the net and the Dutch were a goal up with just six minutes on the clock.

The heavens had opened in Córdoba leading up to kick-off, meaning that once the Netherlands took the lead they were able to zip the ball around quickly on the wet surface, while Austria slipped and slid clumsily around them. Half an hour later, the Dutch consolidated their lead. Having beaten one man, Wim Jansen drew the tackle of defender Gerhard Breitenberger. The Austrian defender was second to the ball and clumsily stepped across Jansen into the space where he expected the ball to be. Jansen had braced for the defender's mistake and flicked the ball past him, drawing the contact and the penalty. From 12

General Jorge Videla casts a watchful eye over the World Cup trophy.

Colleagues and rivals Ernst Happel and Jan Zwartkruis observe their Netherlands team from the sidelines.

Dino Zoff watches Nelinho's wonder strike fly past him in the third-place play-off match between Italy and Brazil.

El Monumental during the opening ceremony of the 1978 World Cup.

Angry Scotland fans show their frustrations towards the players, after their 1-1 draw with Iran in Córdoba.

A lone Brazilian fan in Rosario cheers on his team against the hosts.

*Argentina fans carry their
World Cup winners aloft
around El Monumental,
following their World Cup
victory.*

César Luis Menotti, coach of Argentina. Trademark cigarette hand.

'El Matador' Mario Kempes fires Argentina ahead in the World Cup Final.

Members of COBA march through Paris, protesting the staging of the World Cup in Argentina.

Text on signs and boxes in the image:

- Laat de leeuw niet in z'n hempie staan
- Bloed aan de paal
- Argentina '78
- Argentina '78 VOETBAL en FOLTERING

Bram Vermeulen and Freek De Jonge of Neerlands Hoop stage a demonstration in the Netherlands, protesting the staging of the tournament.

yards Rensenbrink performed his parlour trick, scoring his third penalty of the tournament. The left-footer found the top corner of the net, firing over the despairing dive of Friedrich Koncilia.

Within 60 seconds the Netherlands had scored their third and confirmed their win. Buoyed by his goal and brimming with confidence, Rensenbrink ran on to the ball on the left wing. With one touch, he threaded an inch-perfect cross between Austrian defenders that found Johnny Rep alone at the edge of the 18-yard box. Rep had slightly mistimed his run and arrived at the spot a fraction too early. A heavier than necessary first touch caused the ball to bobble up awkwardly to his midriff, forcing Rep to check his run. The brief pause allowed him to check his surroundings, before executing a precise lob over the onrushing goalkeeper.

The interval appeared to do no favours for Austria, as they were undone by a familiar combination early in the second half. Schrijvers's straightforward goal kick split the disorganised Austrian defence, allowing Rensenbrink to control the ball in his stride and drive past the last man. Rensenbrink rode the challenge, having every right to go down and surely convert another penalty. He instead guided the ball past the onrushing goalkeeper. The cross-shot hybrid didn't have the legs or direction to reach the goal but it rolled into the path of Johnny Rep, who tapped into an empty net.

Erich Obermayer scored a consolation goal for Austria, following a mix-up in the Dutch defence, before the Netherlands restored their four-goal cushion. Rensenbrink was yet again the architect of Oranje brilliance as he received the ball on the halfway line. Driving into the Austrian half, he weaved inside and outside of Austrian goalscorer Obermayer, drawing another Austrian defender towards him as he reached the box. Outnumbered, Rensenbrink squared the ball into the space vacated by the defender and found Willy van de Kerkhof, who gleefully dispatched the ball into the Austrian net.

The Dutch total football machine had arrived in Argentina and, in the absence of Cruyff, Rob Rensenbrink slotted into the role of steering the machine. In truth, many believe that the absence of Cruyff alleviated some of the pressure on the Dutch. Author of *Fierce Genius: Cruyff's Year at Feyenoord* Andy Bollen states: 'Many believe that without Cruyff's controlling and overbearing influence on the team's shape they played without tension, were more relaxed.'[95] The performance against Austria certainly bore the hallmarks of a relaxed team with nothing to prove. In their most complete performance of the tournament, the Netherlands had put Austria to the sword, their players switching positions seamlessly as they led the Austrians around the Córdobese turf, like lost puppies trailing in their wake.

The 25,000-plus in attendance may have believed that they were witnessing the final evolution of the Dutch *totaalvoetbal* on that damp June afternoon in Córdoba. From its embryonic form in the early 70s teams of Feyenoord and Ajax, to Michels' 1974 Oranje vintage, it's

---

95 Interview with Andy Bollen, author of *Fierce Genius: Cruyff's Year at Feyenoord*.

poetic that Happel was the man at the helm for this point in Dutch footballing history. The *totaalvoetbal* blueprint didn't belong to one man or to one team; however, Happel's contribution to the Dutch footballing philosophy can never be dismissed. Priya Ramesh writes: 'Did Happel invent Total Football? That is a question that will never receive a conclusive answer. Did Happel, however, play a crucial role in its development? That is unquestionable. He brought the Austrian philosophy, marrying it with the Dutch way of playing. The significance of Happel's stint at Feyenoord in the history of Dutch football cannot be understated.'[96]

A crucial component of the total football manual was selection of players who were adaptable and able to fill in all manner of positions on the pitch. As fluidity was key to this model, players would often find themselves in unfamiliar positions covering for team-mates who had marauded elsewhere. Vitally, they needed the quality on the ball to be able to do this. This philosophy has the handprint of Happel all over it as the Austrian was famous for his adaptability. Former left-back Theo van Duivenbode represented both Ajax and Feyenoord, winning the European Cup with the latter under Happel's stewardship. On both coaches he said, 'Michels was great in developing a tactical plan at the start of a game. Happel was capable of seeing things that didn't work in a match and tweak it while we were playing. I think Happel read the game better.'[97]

96 Priya Ramesh. 2019. 'Ernst Happel: The Feyenoord years'. *These Football Times.*

97 '50 years ago: Ernst Happel invents total football'. dutchsoccersite.org, January 2020.

Happel's reputation for being able to adapt to ever-changing situations meant he was the right man to lead the Oranje in Argentina, following the loss of Cruyff. Equally, Rinus Michels' ability to develop a tactical plan was crucial in laying the foundations in 1974 for Happel to build upon. Dutch football will forever owe a debt of gratitude to both great coaches.

Italy vs West Germany: 14 June 1978 – Estadio Monumental, Buenos Aires

While the Netherlands dispatched overmatched Austria in Córdoba, Italy and West Germany were adding another chapter to their storied rivalry in the capital. Eight years earlier at the 1970 World Cup the two nations contested a seven-goal thriller dubbed 'the match of the century'. Five of the goals were scored in extra time after West Germany had netted a last-minute equaliser to force the additional 30 minutes. After the match, a plaque was placed on Mexico City's Estadio Azteca commemorating Italy's 4-3 win. Engraved on the plaque is 'Partido del Siglo' (Match of the Century).

The 1978 clash unfortunately didn't live up to its predecessor. Following their disappointing 0-0 draw with Tunisia, West Germany made changes to their line-up as Hansi Müller and namesake Dieter were dropped from their starting XI. Coach Helmut Schön faced scathing criticism in the German press and a near-mutiny in the camp. The slow drip of information regarding disharmony in the squad was now a steady stream. Rumours persisted that senior members of the squad were leaning on Schön to have their say in matters of selection. International veterans and stalwarts of the team, Sepp Maier and Rainer Bonhof, were reported to be two of the senior players in the ear of Schön. Bonhof was reportedly unhappy with the performance of Hansi Müller, claiming he was lightweight defensively, leaving the West Germans vulnerable without the ball. Maier was now representing West Germany in his third World Cup and 'fancied himself to take over the role of Franz Beckenbauer as unofficial player-selector',[98] according to journalist David Miller.

There was no such discord in the Italian camp, as they approached the second round in fine form, boasting a 100 per cent record and the scalp of the hosts, following their triumph in the same stadium four days earlier.

The lack of clarity in the West German hierarchy was mirrored by a thick fog that had descended on Buenos Aires that afternoon. Blowing in from the Río de la Plata, the fog sat low and thick in the Buenos Aires sky, resulting in poor visibility for the opening half hour. Klaus Fischer almost benefited from an unsighted Italian defence as he rose highest to meet Bonhof's corner, nodding the ball just over the bar. Hölzenbein briefly permeated the thick fog with a bullet volley that Zoff saved incredibly well. The Eintracht Frankfurt midfielder controlled a wayward shot on his left thigh with his back to goal, pirouetted 180 degrees and launched a right-footed volley towards Zoff's goal. Zoff, however, was equal to the shot and clawed the ball safely into his grasp at the second attempt.

---

98 David Miller. 1978. *World Cup: The Argentina Story*. Frederick Warne Publishers.

As the first half continued, conditions and visibility improved. The spectators would have been pleased with the timing, as they witnessed what could have been the best goal of the tournament. Roberto Bettega collected the ball just inside the West German half and played the ball forward to Paolo Rossi, whose heel flick drew away his marker. As the defence stood rooted, as if admiring Rossi's piece of skill, Bettega ran on to the ball and slalomed past three West German lunges. The Juventus striker calmly rounded Maier in goal before placing a low shot goalward. Unfortunately for Bettega, Manfred Kaltz had tracked back gallantly as his keeper was rounded and put himself between Bettega and the goal. Kaltz flung himself at the shot and cleared the ball to safety with a last-ditch back-heel, denying the Italian striker a memorable goal.

Italy's next chance was an homage to the total football of their Dutch counterparts playing at the same time in Córdoba. Those watching on black-and-white television in Argentina would have been forgiven for mistaking Italy's blue shirts for orange ones. Gaetano Scirea, operating in his usual sweeper role, somehow found himself in the uncharted area of the left wing. The Juventus legend wrong-footed the full-back with a sway of the hips and floated an inch-perfect cross into the box. The ball sailed over the heads of the defenders and found Bettega, who controlled it perfectly on his chest. Bettega had time to steady himself as Maier rushed out of goal, but under pressure he stabbed the ball agonisingly wide of the near post, much to the disappointment of Scirea, whose journey from sweeper to left-winger had been in vain.

Italy took the ascendancy in the second half, encouraged by their near misses in the opening 45 minutes. They were denied a penalty by the Yugoslavian referee as Kaltz once again cleared a Bettega shot off his line, the Italian striker adamant that Kaltz had used his hands to spare Maier's blushes. The European giants exchanged goalscoring chances for the rest of the half without either threatening to run away with the match. Both teams would have been pleased with a point, despite criticisms from Italy of West Germany's defensive display. Franco Causio declared, 'Germany rebuilt the Berlin wall in Argentina.'[99] The man from Lecce was clearly unimpressed that West Germany's approach meant a repeat of the match of the century was never a possibility.

Italy vs Austria: 18 June 1978 – Estadio Monumental, Buenos Aires

The Italians remained in Buenos Aires for their second match of the group, where they welcomed an Austrian team reeling from their humiliation in Córdoba. Walter Schachner's attempted overhead kick in the early stages suggested that the Austrians were ready to blow away the cobwebs and challenge the Italians from the first whistle. However, within a quarter of an hour Austria were staring down the barrel of another defeat as Italy took the lead. Causio found Rossi in the middle of the park, who repeated his back-heel trick from the previous match. This time Causio collected the ball and returned it to Rossi, who

---

99   David Miller. 1978. *World Cup: The Argentina Story.* Frederick Warne Publishers.

rolled the ball past the keeper and into the net. 1-0 Italy. The Austrian defender actually assisted the final ball into the path of Rossi, helpfully toeing the ball along, when the situation required him to kick the ball off the park. The defender was Heinrich Strasser, who had been selected to strengthen the defence in the wake of their pummelling by the Netherlands. Unfortunately, it was a case of more of the same for Austria.

Carrying the scars of their chastening defeat by the Dutch, Austria may have feared that conceding an early goal would open the floodgates. However, Italy were unable or unwilling to punish them in such fashion. The crowd steadily grew tired of the lack of penetration from either team. Italy, the brunt of their frustration, were frequently booed for lack of ambition to add to their tally. The local supporters seemed particularly vexed by the notion that Italy had taken Argentina's place in this match. Estadio Monumental was meant to be the venue for all Argentina's fixtures; however, their defeat to Italy in the first round meant the Azzurri had usurped them and sent them to Rosario. That evening Argentina played Brazil in a match dubbed 'the battle of Rosario', but there were no suggestions that this match would amount to anything more than a light sparring session, much to the annoyance of the crowd.

Finally, as the match approached its conclusion, Italy began to cause Austria problems on the counter-attack. Austria, needing something out of the match, began to commit more numbers to their attack, allowing Italy opportunities when they lost the ball. Substitute Cuccureddu of Juventus, a defender brought on to see out the match, almost scored the second for Italy. Presented with a pass from fellow substitute Francesco Graziani, Cuccureddu feinted to shoot from outside of the box. The movement fooled defender Obermayer, who threw himself into a block. Anticipating the leap of the Austrian, Cuccureddu dummied the shot, tapped the ball past him and collected it in the 18-yard area. After showing such nuance with his deft touch, Cuccureddu inexplicably put his laces through the ball and blasted the Adidas Tango size 5 into the darkening night sky.

However, there was still time for Italy to add another near miss as Graziani reacted first to a mix-up in the box, controlling the ball before stabbing it past the post. The match finished 1-0, sending Austria out of the tournament and putting Italy in pole position for the final, maintaining their undefeated record.

Netherlands vs West Germany: 18 June 1978 – Estadio Chateau Carreras, Córdoba

A repeat of the previous World Cup Final, a shot at redemption for the Dutch and a match four years in the making. To understand the importance of this fixture, we have to rewind the clock four years to 7 July 1974. The venue: Munich's Olympiastadion.

The Dutch team of 1974, under the guidance of Rinus Michels, had swaggered into the final. In their wake lay Uruguay, the first nation to ever be crowned champions of the world, current champions Brazil and an Argentina team beaten so badly that it led to a period of soul searching in the Argentinian game. The manner in which the

Dutch dispatched their South American foes suggested a power switch in the game, their total football philosophy seemingly light years ahead of the Americas.

All that stood in the way of Dutch dominance was the stubborn resistance of the home nation. West Germany had stuttered to the final, losing to East Germany in the opening round in a match dubbed *ein kampf zwischen bruden* (a struggle between brothers). The humiliating 1-0 loss to their neighbours from the east was politically damaging and crushing to their confidence. The fixture was described as 'a touchpoint, a nexus, between the divided country and, more pertinently, the divided people', such was the scarcity of meetings between the teams either side of the wall.[100] It was a loss that the hosts would never avenge, as the nations didn't meet again before the reunification of the country.

The match was particularly poignant for coach Helmut Schön, who was born in the city of Dresden, in the east of the country prior to the partition. He represented Dresdener SC and Hertha BSC in the east before defecting west at the beginning of his coaching career. In fact, the East German victory was hugely significant on both sides of the Berlin Wall. Goalscorer Jürgen Sparwasser reflected: 'If one day my gravestone simply says "Hamburg 74" everybody will still know who is lying below.'[101] The victory sent the brothers, divided by a wall, down very different paths. Group winners East Germany's reward was a place

---

100 Gary Thacker, 2018. 'The most politically-charged match in history: when East Germany met West in 1974'. thesefootballtimes.com

101 Nick Miller. 'World Cup's biggest upsets: United States stun England, Brazil's Maracanazo woe'. ESPN.com

in the second round alongside Argentina, Brazil and the seemingly unstoppable Dutch.

Fortuitously, West Germany's second-place finish meant they would play Poland, Sweden and Yugoslavia in the second round. After two wins, a place in the final would be assured should they beat Poland. The Polish team of 1974 was much admired for its attacking prowess, boasting Grzegorz Lato as the tournament's top scorer. However, torrential rainfall on Frankfurt on the day of the match compromised the pitch surface, littering it with puddles as deep as ten centimetres in some places. West Germany triumphed 1-0 in a sodden Waldstadion, booking their place in the final, where they would, of course, face Michels' Netherlands.

The Netherlands had swept aside all challenges on their route to the final, whereas West Germany were commonly regarded as lucky to be there. The Netherlands were, therefore, unquestionably the favourites for the 1974 World Cup Final. The confidence of the public was eclipsed only by the confidence of the players themselves, Cruyff famously quipping, 'We knew that we were better.' To some, this mindset can seem inherently arrogant but the extreme self-confidence was crucial to the Dutch football identity. Total football simply isn't possible without an air of arrogance on the ball; a left-back picking up the ball in a No.10 position must have confidence in his ability, otherwise he has no business being there.

Another obvious factor in the significance of this fixture was the Second World War, as less than 30 years before this tournament the Netherlands had been occupied by Nazi Germany. The nature of international tournaments means that nations who have a history of conflict with one another often meet on the field of play. The shadow of war looms heavily over these occasions but the general rule is that they're downplayed by the competitors or sometimes become unspoken elephants in the room. The 1974 World Cup Final was a notable exception and fuelled the Dutch approach to the game. Midfielder Wim van Hanegem confessed, 'I don't like the Germans. Every time I played against Germans, I had a problem because of the war. They murdered my father, sister and two brothers. I am full of angst. I hate them.'[102]

The stage was set for the Dutch to take their spot upon the throne of international football, and they began the match in the perfect fashion. The Netherlands kicked off and exchanged a few simple passes, then, before even a minute had been played, Johan Cruyff elected to up the tempo of play. The world's greatest player drove towards the West German box, accelerating past Schwarzenbeck, before Bertie Vogts hacked him down inside the area. Neeskens stepped up and blasted the Netherlands into the lead. Within 60 seconds of the start the Dutch had one hand on the trophy and the Germans had yet to touch the ball. The ease with which Cruyff powered through the defence from a standing start suggested that the Oranje could penetrate the West German defence at will.

Following their goal, the Netherlands sought to maintain possession and tire their opponents as they

———
102 Peter Seddon. 2005. *The World Cup's Strangest Moments*. Robson Books.

chased shadows. If the first 60 seconds were to be believed, the quality of the Dutch meant that they would be able to keep West Germany at arm's length and protect the ball for 90 minutes if they so wished. There was also the impression that the Netherlands sought to humiliate their opponents as they passed the ball around them. Johnny Rep recalled, 'We wanted to make fun of the Germans. We didn't think about it, but we did it, passing the ball around and around.'[103]

For the next 25 minutes, the Netherlands taunted West Germany like a matador torturing an exasperated bull. Their 'death by a thousand passes' strategy drew the ire of their opponents but the Dutch never dealt them a killer blow. Rep added that the Dutch 'forgot to score the second goal'.[104] Ultimately, the Netherlands would pay the price for their self-indulgence, like Narcissus, who met his demise admiring his own reflection. On 25 minutes West Germany were awarded a questionable penalty and, with a stroke of Paul Breitner's boot, they were level. For all their technical superiority, the Netherlands couldn't be separated from their opponents on the scoreboard.

Momentum is one of sport's most powerful forces and total football was no match for this phenomenon as Gerd Müller scored West Germany's second goal before half-time. West Germany were able to hang on for the win. Desperate for a route back into the match, Michels' total football machine ended up pumping high balls into the box, desperate to feed off scraps.

---

103 David Winner. 2000. *Brilliant Orange*. Bloomsbury.
104 *Ibid.*

The Netherlands' arrogance had conspired for them to snatch defeat from the jaws of victory. They left Munich humbled but came to Argentina steadfastly loyal to their total football philosophy, this time with Ernst Happel at the wheel. Four years later in Córdoba, the Netherlands were offered an opportunity at redemption. A win against West Germany would see them consolidate their position at the top of the group and leave them 90 minutes away from a World Cup Final.

Following their draw against Italy, West Germany switched to four at the back and a more progressive 4-3-3, partially due to necessity following injuries to Flohe and Zimmermann. The Netherlands were unchanged, with Piet Schrijvers again selected in goal, preferred to Jan Jongbloed, who had started the three first phase matches. Happel selected five Dutch players who played in the 1974 World Cup Final, to West Germany's four. Curiously, all three 1974 goalscorers were absent, following Müller's retirement, Breitner's sabbatical and Neeskens's injury.

The match began in a similar way to the previous World Cup Final but this time roles were reversed as West Germany took the early lead. Bonhof stood over a free kick at the edge of the box. The token Dutch wall was no obstruction for Bonhof, whose thunderous strike was too hot for Schrijvers to handle. The Dutch goalkeeper's block sent the ball into the path of Rüdiger Abramczik, whose stooped header found the bottom corner. West Germany were ahead with barely two minutes played.

Following their goal, West Germany fell into a similar trap to their opponents four years before and surrendered the momentum. This time the champions sought to protect their lead rather than add to their tally and their 4-3-3 began to resemble more of a 4-5-1, with striker Dieter Müller increasingly isolated. Arie Haan punished their hesitancy when he was allowed to drive through their half unopposed. He carried the ball to within 35 yards of the goal, before powering his boot through the ball with a ferocious whip of the right leg. The ball seemed to gather pace, reaching terminal velocity as it flew inside the right-hand post and into the net. Goalkeeper Maier appeared to misread the flight as he laboured across his goal, surprised to discover the ball in the net. He would never have made the save, even had he dived to his right. However, the Bayern Munich stalwart looked all his 34 years as he stumbled across the goal, placing his hands on his hips, incredulous that the ball had sailed his side of the post.

West Germany were almost made to pay a further price as Johnny Rep sent a free header narrowly wide. This time Maier was relieved to see the ball bounce up off the Córdobese turf and land the other side of the post. The teams left the field level at the end of the first half with the Dutch unquestionably in the ascendancy, frustrated that they hadn't been able to take a lead into the dressing room.

West Germany offered more at the beginning of the second half, aware that another draw would leave them behind the Netherlands and, most likely, Italy, who were playing a deflated Austria at the same time. However, a lightning-quick counter-attack, orchestrated by Rensenbrink and Rep, prompted defender Manfred Kaltz to flatten the latter in the West German half. Kaltz's shoulder to the chest would be a straight red card in modern rugby union but went unpunished by the referee.

West Germany then took the lead on 70 minutes, thanks to a Dieter Müller header. Erich Beer's cross found the FC Köln striker in between three Dutch defenders on the penalty spot and Müller powered his header into the turf, the ball bouncing past Schrijvers in goal. The defenders had been caught on the back foot following a quickly taken free kick and, similarly to four years earlier, the Dutch were 2-1 behind despite their dominance on the ball. Having weathered the early Dutch storm, West Germany now had something to hold on to. Naturally, the Netherlands were now pushing harder for the goal but both teams still possessed a threat. Both goalkeepers stood relieved under shaking crossbars as first Rep's deflected shot hit the bar and then Beer's cross almost bewitched Schrijvers, bouncing off the bar to safety.

With ten minutes remaining Happel sacrificed defender Piet Wildschut to add another player to the Netherlands attack in Dick Nanninga. Happel's desperation paid dividends as the Netherlands scored a goal born out of sheer will and crafted in Eindhoven. PSV left-back Poortvliet competed for a ball in central midfield, winning his sliding challenge and collecting the ball following another challenge in midfield. Poortvliet spotted the run of PSV team-mate René van de Kerkhof, who had found space on the left. Van de Kerkhof had benefited from Nanninga's run, which drew German defenders into the centre of the box. The PSV midfielder shaped to shoot with his left foot, prompting desperate lunges from German defenders. As they slid past, the Dutchman shifted his weight, switched the ball to his right foot and curled the ball past Maier in goal. Defender Rolf Rüssmann showed more awareness than his goalkeeper did for the first goal, diving at the ball and attempting to claw it out of the net, but he could only help it along its way, punching the ball into the bottom corner. Despite Dutch devotion to all things aesthetically beautiful in the game, they weren't perturbed by Rüssmann robbing Van de Kerkhof of a top-corner finish as they embraced wildly, celebrating the goal.

Ten minutes remained for the Netherlands to complete their comeback; however, a moment of ill disciple saw the momentum swing away from them as quickly as it had come. Following a clash with Hölzenbein, the man felled for the penalty four years earlier, Nanninga was shown a second yellow card for dissent. David Miller reported, 'He reacted with that slightly superior, amused attitude with which the Dutch tend to view authority.'[105] Now the Netherlands had to negotiate the final minutes with ten men. Nanninga had only been on the pitch ten minutes yet found himself the first man back in the Dutch dressing room following his red card.

Perhaps exhausted by the endless swings of the momentum pendulum, West Germany were unable to create another chance and the match finally petered out to a 2-2 draw. The Córdobese crowd had been treated to one of the matches of the tournament. However, the draw suited the Netherlands far more than West Germany,

---

105 David Miller. 1978. *World Cup: The Argentina Story*. Frederick Warne Publishers.

following their 5-1 demolition of Austria in the first match. The final matchday just three days later would be interestingly poised. Austria's two losses meant they wouldn't make it any further, while West Germany had an outside chance of making the final, depending on the result of the other match. The Italy vs Netherlands match would be a de facto semi-final as the winners would be assured of a place in the final. The Dutch could even afford a draw, due to their superior goal difference, as long as West Germany didn't defeat Austria by more than five goals.

Austria vs West Germany: 21 June 1978 – Estadio Chateau Carreras, Córdoba

Still harbouring faint hopes of finishing top of the group, West Germany welcomed neighbours Austria to Córdoba. Austria, having lost their opening two group matches, were out of the running for the final and had only pride to play for. West Germany had yet to register a win in the group and required a victory of similar margin to that of the Netherlands when they had faced the Austrians. They were also relying on the result of the other match going their way. What followed was a historic occasion and immortalised by the title 'The miracle of Córdoba' or 'The disgrace of Córdoba', depending on which side of the border you hear the story.

Austria's humbling defeat to the Netherlands had somewhat taken the shine off what was a strong showing. They had come into the tournament undefeated in qualifying and in Argentina topped a group where they were considered outsiders behind Spain and Brazil. The unheralded Austrians were stung by being dismissed as no-hopers, making their first World Cup appearance for 20 years, written off before a ball had been kicked in anger. Legendary goalscorer Hans Krankl recalls with satisfaction, 'Our opponents thought that they'd walk all over us and win easily, but it turned out very different.'[106]

Although unable to progress any further, Austria still had the opportunity to end the tournament on a high by defeating their West German neighbours. To do this, however, they would have to reverse the tide of history and record their first win in the fixture since 1931. On that occasion, Hugo Meisl's Austrian 'wunderteam' defeated Germany 5-0 in Vienna. Helmut Senekowitsch's 1978 vintage represented the best Austrian team in 50 years and, on a chilly Córdobese afternoon, took to the field to defeat their 'big brother. The big brother that looked down on us.'[107]

West Germany by contrast were not fielding their strongest team in a generation. The public was becoming aware of growing tensions among the squad and there was simmering resentment from the fans, who chanted 'Bonhof out' during the match. Bonhof had been made a scapegoat by the fans, angry at his perceived role at ostracising young midfielder Hansi Müller from the team, when Bonhof himself was delivering below-par performances in the middle of the park. Of course, much

---

106 'Krankl and Austria's "World Cup miracle"'. FIFA TV.
107 *Ibid.*

of the fans' information was based on rumour and hearsay but Bonhof's image wasn't helped by coach Schön's brutal assessment that 'this tournament would have been better if Bonhof had played as he did in 74'.[108] That statement could be levelled at the whole West German squad, which hadn't performed anywhere near the level of the 1974 champions.

Nevertheless, despite Schön's mournful glances towards the past, West Germany began the match against Austria well. A crisp exchange of passes between Karl-Heinze Rummenigge in central midfield and Dieter Müller, who had taken up a position on the right wing, cut through the Austrian defence. Bringing the ball from deep, Rummenigge played two consecutive one-twos with Müller before driving into the penalty box and calmly slotting the ball under the advancing goalkeeper. West Germany had taken the lead on 19 minutes and sought to increase the pressure on their opponents, hoping to force a similar first-half collapse by Austria that they had shown against the Netherlands. Determined not to suffer this same fate, Austria held firm and made it to half-time only one goal in arrears. As things stood, due to events in the other match, West Germany were heading for the third-place play-off.

On the hour mark, the complexion changed for the reigning champions. Austrian winger Eduard Kreiger's whipped cross from the right caused chaos in the box, culminating in captain Vogts diverting the ball into his

---

108 David Miller. 1978. *World Cup: The Argentina Story.* Frederick Warne Publishers.

own net via a wayward knee. Austria's celebrations had barely cooled when they scored their second and took the lead. Kreiger, becoming more and more influential in the match, appeared this time on the left wing. He clipped a left-footed cross with a low trajectory across the West German defenders. The flight of the ball caused the defence to fall back a half-step, allowing Hans Krankl space in the box. The striker cushioned the ball with the inside of his foot and, in one movement, unleashed a volley into the top corner, whistling past Maier in goal. The strike was a moment of true quality from a top-class centre-forward. The finish was Krankl's finest in the red shirt of his nation and would have drawn admiring glances from his future employers at Barcelona, who were poised to sign the striker at the end of the tournament.

On the brink of a humiliating exit, West Germany's response was swift and decisive as Hölzenbein headed a Bonhof free kick into the Austrian net. West Germany had once again forced their way into the third-place play-off fixture. The reigning champions now had 20 minutes remaining to navigate.

However, there was another dramatic twist in the dying embers of the match. Hans Krankl stood underneath a booming cross-field up-and-under, the Austrian having no chance to win the header as Rolf Rüssmann rose highest. Krankl, showing football intellect that would have impressed the Barcelona officials in attendance, gambled on the German missing the ball. Rüssmann appeared to mistime his header, jumping underneath the ball. Krankl nodded forward, controlled the ball on his knee and weaved into the penalty area. Leaving despairing defenders lunging after him, Krankl calmly slotted the ball underneath Maier, securing a 3-2 victory for Austria.

The Miracle of Córdoba was complete and Austria had concluded their campaign with a legendary victory over their illustrious neighbour, eliminating the reigning champions. Krankl's goal prompted a now legendary cry from Austrian commentator Eduard Finger: 'Here comes Krankl ... in space, he shoots ... Goooal! Goooal! Goooal! Goooal! Goooal! Goooal! I am going bonkers! Krankl has scored – 3-2 for Austria! Ladies and gentlemen, we are hugging each other here. Rippel, my colleague, graduate engineer Posch, we're kissing each other ... 3-2 for Austria, by our Krankl's magnificent goal.'[109]

The Miracle of Córdoba enhanced the reputation of Austrian football. Krankl's transfer to Barcelona was extremely successful as he won the UEFA Cup Winners' Cup the following season, scoring in the final. The trophy topped a fantastic first season in which he also won the Pichichi trophy for top goalscorer in La Liga.

The 'Disgrace of Córdoba', as it became known in Germany, left a darker legacy. Schön departed his role as West German manager, unable to reach the heights of 1974. In his final press conference the coach fired a barb at the West German press, who had criticised his team throughout the tournament, suggesting that the squad were at loggerheads and Schön didn't know his best team. Schön said, 'I thank the press for their suggestions, but it is my

---

109 Sam Bettany. 'Remembering the miracle of Córdoba: Austria 3-2 West Germany'. byfarthegreatestteam.com

belief that we would not have achieved better results by changing the players.'[110]

Italy vs Netherlands: 21 June 1978 – Estadio Monumental, Buenos Aires

West Germany and Austria were now eliminated, so all that was left to settle was who would top the group and take their place in the World Cup Final. The clash between Europe's best teams drew a crowd of 67,000 to Estadio Monumental. Fernando Spannaus, who was in attendance, recalls that home interest was particularly high: 'That Saturday we said, guys we have to go, there must be tickets. We had some choripán, a few glasses of wine, started to get drunk and queued up to go in. Unthinkable now. From Spain in 82, everything was different and more organised.'[111] The 1978 World Cup was the last of its kind, where curious fans could stumble up to the ground and witness the world's greatest players, without worrying about buying tickets in advance.

For all the youthful exuberance and excitement in the stands, the stadiums were not off limits for military operations during the tournament. Rubbing shoulders with regular match-goers, military officials used the matches as surveillance missions. They would often release political prisoners briefly, chaperoning them to the matches to see who they spoke to and fraternised with. The prisoners were effectively honey traps, put in place to draw in more people

---

110 David Miller. 1978. *World Cup: The Argentina Story*. Frederick Warne Publishers.

111 Interview with Fernando Spannaus, 2021.

perceived as subversive by the military. Dutch journalist Frits Barend noted the military presence at the Netherlands vs Italy match, reporting, 'I didn't go to the stadium [El Monumental]. I went to Plaza de Mayo. My seat was empty half an hour before the game had started and an army officer asked my colleague where I was. He said, "Frits Barend is stated to be here." He sat down in my seat and started interrogating my colleague about me.'[112]

The Netherlands were boosted by the return of talismanic Johan Neeskens, who hadn't featured since his early departure from the Scotland match but was sufficiently fit to play from the start against Italy. Perhaps not regarded in the same esteem as his namesake Cruyff, Johan Segon (Johan the second), as he was known in Catalunya, was the physical embodiment of *totaalvoetbal*. Neeskens had won three consecutive European Cups with Ajax, the first of which saw Rinus Michels select him at right-back. Neeskens's industry and natural fitness allowed him to adapt well to his new-found central-midfield role the following season, and his artistry was eclipsed only by Cruyff himself. Neeskens's incredible stamina also meant that he set an imperious example without the ball. Football writer Priya Ramesh remarked that, following his move into midfield, Neeskens's 'instinctive harrying of opponents could be a trigger for the entire team to move upfield with him and capitalising on a key Dutch concept in space'.[113]

---

112 *A Dirty Game*. Documentary dir. Jaap Verdenius and Kay Mastenbroek, 2002.
113 Priya Ramesh. 2018. 'Johan Neeskens: more than just the other Johan'. thesefootballtimes.com

In the absence of Cruyff, Neeskens's return to the starting XI, although harsh on Wim Jansen, was a massive relief to his team-mates. Rensenbrink, the Van de Kerkhof brothers and Arie Haan were assisted by another hard-working but equally creative body in the middle of the park. Upon his return, Neeskens underlined the challenges he faced to get back up to speed and the challenges the Dutch side faced against the undefeated Italians: 'Italy have everything – technique, finishing power, strength, experience.'[114]

To their credit, Italy began the match every inch the accomplished outfit that Neeskens had predicted. The power in attack that the Dutch midfielder had warned of came to pass as the Dutch defence struggled to contain the rampaging Roberto Bettega, one of nine Juventus players in the Italian starting XI. The familiarity and fluidity of the Italians made the Dutch players looked like strangers in comparison, as another forage forward from Bettega presented an open goal for Causio, who was adjudged to be offside.

This would be a precursor for what would follow a minute later as Italy took the lead. Passing in triangles around an uncharacteristically pedestrian Dutch defence, Bettega exchanged passes with Benetti before bracing himself to slot past Schrijvers. In his desperation to make the tackle, PSV's Ernie Brandts pushed the ball past his goalkeeper and into the net. To add injury to insult, the Dutchmen collided, causing Schrijvers to depart the pitch.

---

114 David Miller. 1978. *World Cup: The Argentina Story*. Frederick Warne Publishers.

Jan Jongbloed came on as substitute, making his first appearance since the 3-2 loss to Scotland in the first round.

Jongbloed's international career is one of the most unique in Dutch history. He made his debut in 1962, playing five minutes in a 4-1 loss to Denmark, conceding the final goal. Twelve years later, on the eve of the 1974 World Cup, Rinus Michels plucked Jongbloed from the international wilderness, making him his first-choice goalkeeper for the tournament. Jongbloed was goalkeeper for FC Amsterdam at the time and nobody would have predicted that he would be selected over Piet Schrijvers in goal. However, Jongbloed's ability with the ball at his feet, due in part to him playing as a forward in his youth, meant that he was an attractive proposition for Michels and, crucially, Cruyff.[115] The influence of the captain in 1974 can't be underestimated, and keeping Cruyff happy on the pitch meant that Michels reportedly had to make certain concessions in selection. Author Gary Thacker states that the selection of Jongbloed 'demonstrated the unhealthy amount of influence Cruyff could exert'.

Nonetheless, Jongbloed played in every one of the Netherlands fixtures en route to the 1974 World Cup Final. He was also selected for the first round of matches in 1978 but, interestingly, dropped before the second round. Although he had conceded three goals in the final group match against Scotland, Gary Thacker suggests that Jongbloed's omission from the bench for the second round wasn't down to goals conceded. Instead, it was thought to be a key battle in the

---

115 Gary Thacker. 2021. *Beautiful Bridesmaids Dressed in Oranje: The Unfulfilled Glory of Dutch Football*. Pitch Publishing.

developing power struggle between head coach Happel and his predecessor Zwartkruis. A conflict had developed between the two, with suggestions that Zwartkruis was on the verge of staging a coup following the loss to Scotland. Perhaps Happel's concession on the question of goalkeeper was a compromise to maintain overall power.

Zwartkruis had experimented with many goalkeepers during his reign and didn't trust Jongbloed in the way that Happel or Michels did. He disregarded the necessity for a 'footballing' goalkeeper following a tweak in systems and influenced Happel to instead switch to Schrijvers between the sticks. Happel, always willing to listen to the advice of his coaching staff, relented and Schrijvers would surely have held on to the goalkeeper's jersey for the rest of the tournament had his injury not ruled him out. However, following the collision between Schrijvers and Brandts, Jongbloed found himself making that familiar walk out of the wilderness and into the goal of the Oranje. Wearing the No.8 jersey, a number now synonymous with central-midfield lynchpins, the goalkeeper famed for his ability with his feet had his hands full keeping out an Italian team hungry for more goals.

Italy's chances were mounting as a moment of confusion in the Netherlands box allowed Bettega to cushion a header from Cabrini's cross into the six-yard area. Rossi arrived as tentative Dutch defenders, including captain Krol, glanced confused looks at one another. Fortunately for the Dutch, the most alert man in the box was the substitute goalkeeper Jongbloed, who managed to claw Rossi's header over the bar to safety. Benetti's volley from the edge of the box shortly after added to the pressure on the man in goal and his shell-shocked defence.

Following a very positive opening 30 minutes where Italy had been more than a match for their much-heralded opponents, they began to sit back, as if the enormity of their situation had dawned on them. As things stood, they were in the World Cup Final and forages into the Dutch danger zone became less frequent as the match approached half-time. The Netherlands had cleared their heads and Johan Neeskens, deployed deeper than usual, began to exert his influence higher up the pitch. At the end of the first half, Italy had the advantage and the satisfaction that they had caused their opponents problems, without much threat to their own goal. However, the Netherlands, who had twice come from behind against West Germany, would surely pose more of a problem in the second half.

The fans in attendance didn't have to wait long for the Dutch rebuttal as, on 49 minutes, a clipped ball from Krol into the Italian box caused a game of head tennis. The ball fell to Ernie Brandts 20 yards from the Italian goal. He trapped the ball before taking a stride forward, striking the ball quickly. Before two Italian defenders lunged at his feet, Brandts sent a bullet of a shot over the shoulder of a diving Zoff. This time the ball found the top corner of the same net in which he had scored an own goal in the first half. The Netherlands had equalised and Brandts, scoring at both ends, now required one more for the match ball. The defender had been upended while striking the ball and now found himself mobbed by ecstatic team-mates, who jumped on him as he lay on the turf, soaking up the sounds of redemption from the stands of El Monumental.

As things stood, it was now the Netherlands who topped the group and were in the driving seat to claim their spot in the final. Italian coach Bearzot had replaced Franco Causio, one of Italy's most effective attacking options, with Claudio Sala. Although on paper not necessarily a defensive move, the removal of Causio blunted Italy's attack. Brandts' goal just after half-time meant that, to reach the final, Italy's attack needed to fire more than ever. However, the precarious position in which Italy found themselves transmitted to the players. The fluidity of their attacks in the first half had dried up and the play became disjointed as both teams conceded fouls and rattled into tackles on one another. In the scrappy 20 minutes after the Dutch equaliser, Italy collected two yellow cards to the Netherlands' one as tempers threatened to boil over.

With 20 minutes remaining, from a quickly taken free kick, captain Krol laid the ball off to Arie Haan, seemingly challenging him to repeat his trick from the previous match, where he had scored from distance against West Germany. The Italian defenders didn't expect Haan to rise to the challenge as they ambled into position. Only captain Zoff was alert as he screamed at his outfield players to close down Haan, before scrambling across his goal as the Dutch midfielder took aim from more than 35 yards out. This strike surpassed Haan's goal against West Germany, taken from further out and struck even sweeter. The ball whistled through the air and into the top corner. Bewitching the eyes, the ball seemed to slalom between the Italian defenders, but on replay it was clear that the strike was unwavering in its path to Zoff's top corner, like a heat-seeking missile. Zoff's agonising dive in vain, clutching at thin air, meant that the goal was even more aesthetically pleasing than Haan's previous one. A truly wonderful finish.

The strike speaks volumes for Haan's confidence in his ability. A lesser player would have thought that their goal in the previous match was a once-in-a-lifetime strike, but as soon as his captain threw down the gauntlet, Haan was willing to oblige in repeating the trick. His sublime strike was the death knell for Italian resistance, as they had no answer to the Oranje's quality. Needing two goals against such technically gifted opposition, with such little time left, was a near-impossible feat and the Italians were now chasing shadows. The goal deflated them, and the Dutch were able to manage the final 15 minutes with ease. Suffering their first loss in the tournament, Italy missed out on the final and had to make do with a third-place play-off against the second-placed team from Group B.

Successive victories from losing positions meant that the Netherlands had showcased the necessary resilience, alongside their undeniable ability, to become world champions. They had booked their place in the final four days later against an as-yet-unknown opponent.

The Netherlands vs Italy game was the first of a de facto semi-final triple-header on 21 June. Next, Brazil would play Poland before Argentina took to the field to play Peru. The scheduling of the final day of fixtures was a dream come true for spectators, who were able to watch three matches of high-stakes football on the same day. However, the scheduling of the final day meant that Argentina took to the field knowing what was required of them to reach the final, following Brazil's match. This poured fuel on the fire for those who considered the hosts to be enjoying advantageous treatment from the organising committee. The rumblings of discontent would turn into a thunderous uproar that evening as Rosario played host to the most controversial match in World Cup history.

The Second Round – Group B: Argentina, Brazil, Peru and Poland

THE RESULTS from the first-round groups, including surprise second-place finishes for Argentina and neighbours Brazil, meant that Group B of the second round had a distinctly South American feel. The matches took place in Mendoza and Rosario, meaning that the host nation were forced to play away from the capital city. However, in Rosario, they would forge a new fortress where a partisan atmosphere fuelled La Albiceleste to discover their mojo, culminating in the tournament's most memorable and controversial match.

Alongside Argentina and Brazil were Peru, who had emerged top from a first-round group including the Netherlands, Scotland and Iran. To meet the Netherlands again, this time in the final, Peru would have to disrupt the traditional hierarchy of Latin American football, which dictated that they were expected to doff their caps to the superior Argentina and Brazil. Writing at the time, David Miller commented that despite winning their group Peru were regarded as 'South America's soft touch'.[116] However, as mentioned previously, this 1978 team were at the apex of Peruvian international football, building on the successful foundations of the 1970 World Cup team and boasting the title of champions of the Americas, following their 1975 Copa América win.

The group could have been a fully Latin American contest had Mexico topped their first-round group, giving the second round inter-continental dimensions. However, this was never likely as Mexico tumbled out of the tournament after losing every single match, with Poland emerging as winners of Group 2 to join the South Americans. Poland were building on a fantastic third-place finish at the previous World Cup, where they defeated Brazil in the third-place play-off.

Peru vs Brazil: 14 June 1978 – Estadio Ciudad de Mendoza, Mendoza

Barely emerging from their first-round group with their reputation intact, an impotent Brazil had their blushes spared by Spain's shock defeat to Austria. The South American samba kings made it out of their group by winning only once and scoring just two goals in the process. However, they would point to the overly officious timekeeping of referee Clive Thomas in scratching a goal and subsequently a win off their record in their opening match.

Brazil were equally unhappy that they had played all of their group matches on the now infamous Mar del Plata

---

116 David Miller. 1978. *World Cup: The Argentina Story*. Frederick Warne Publishers.

pitch. The other teams in the group had the respite of at least 90 minutes on Vélez Sarsfield's far superior surface, but Brazil had to make the most of Estadio José María Minella's energy-sapping cabbage patch. Many voices inside and outside of Brazil's football federation believed this to be a cynical ploy by the hosts to put their great rivals at a physical disadvantage.

If the ploy is to be believed then it must be considered somewhat successful, as Brazil were forced into changes for the second round. Creative spark Zico played the first two matches of the tournament but, after being substituted towards the end of the second match, he wouldn't start the next two. Fatigue, a fall-out with the national coach, or a combination of both factors played a part in his omission. The quick turnaround of fixtures meant that Coutinho had to protect the legs of his players and Zico found himself on the bench, rested for key matches later in the tournament. Reinaldo, likewise, a player plagued by knee injuries, felt the wrath of the Mar del Plata surface. He wouldn't feature again, except for a 45-minute cameo in Brazil's final match, although rumours persisted that his absence was politically motivated, rather than based on fitness. Also absent was Rivellino, nursing an injured ankle, suffered in the opening stages, an injury that saved Coutinho an awkward decision regarding dropping the out-of-form veteran from the starting XI.

Following their misadventures in Mar del Plata, Brazil were keen to start the match against Peru on a good footing. They began positively, with midfielder Batista collecting a throw-in in Peruvian territory, receiving the ball stationary, with the Peruvian defence well set up. However, a drop of the shoulder from Batista and a change of pace allowed him to glide past one tackle and draw another, before sliding a pass through to Roberto Dinamite at the edge of the penalty box. Batista was not exactly famed for his turn of pace, which caught the Peruvian defence off guard. Dinamite's shot was struck low but Quiroga was equal to it, collecting the ball into his grasp. However, the swift movement was a signal of Brazil's intent, keen to show more ambition now that they felt solid turf under their feet for the first time in the tournament.

Peru suffered an early setback as full-back Ruben Diaz had to be replaced within ten minutes, his injury meaning that he would play no further part in the tournament. Peru's misery was compounded within minutes as Brazil took the lead. Toninho stood over a free kick from 30 yards, square on. The defender with a penchant for set pieces took 13 steps back, preparing a huge run-up. His body positioning seemed to pay tribute to his opponent across the field, Cubillas, who had scored a trademark outside-of-the-boot free kick against Scotland in the previous round. The Peruvian wall braced nervously for what would have needed to be a thunderous strike to defeat Quiroga from such range. However, much to the bewilderment of the wall, it was Dirceu, standing just to the left of the ball, who took the free kick. He took two steps and whipped a ferocious left-footed shot into the corner of the net, teasing Quiroga, who desperately tried to grasp at the ball as it spiralled away from him. David Miller described the free kick as 'a wickedly curving shot that, had it not gone in the net, would have curved right back on itself like a boomerang'.[117] It was barely feasible that Dirceu could strike a ball with such power, with such little backlift, as the players in the Peruvian wall stood in awe of the ball curling over their heads.

The goal was Brazil's first moment of quality in the tournament and lifted a tremendous weight off their shoulders. From this moment, the Brazilians played with a new-found swagger, eager to live up to their reputation. Toninho stood over another free kick from a similar distance shortly after. With no Dirceu nearby, the full-back was clearly no decoy. Attempting to emulate his compatriot's moment of genius, Toninho took a 12-yard run-up as goalkeeper Quiroga braced for impact. Toninho's bullet shot was unwavering as it hurtled towards the Peruvian goal. However, Quiroga was equal to the strike and wisely diverted the ball around the post, rather than attempt to hold it.

Perhaps due to the fact they were facing South American opposition for the first time, Brazil played with a freedom that the benched Zico had longed for when he bemoaned his nation's 'systemic' approach. However, Brazil's expansive style allowed Peru opportunities on the counter-attack in the first half. Their best chance came as a perfectly weighted through ball from La Rosa released Oblitas on the left wing. He carried the ball into the penalty area, drawing the attention of defender Oscar. The Peruvian created enough space to fire a low cross across the

---

117 David Miller. 1978. *World Cup: The Argentina Story*. Frederick Warne Publishers.

box, which evaded defenders and attackers until it arrived at the feet of Muñante. With the Brazilian goal at his mercy, Muñante elected to strike the ball with the outside of his right foot, when it was crying out to be struck with his left. His choice of shot allowed the defence a split second to regroup and brace themselves on the line. The human shield of defenders and goalkeeper managed to deflect the shot to safety, safeguarding Brazil's one-goal lead.

On the half hour, Brazil made Peru pay for their wastefulness in front of goal. Dirceu received the ball 20 yards from goal following scrappy play and set his sights. The Peruvian midfield dawdled in closing down the playmaker, who, emboldened by his earlier wonder-strike, took aim from distance. This shot wasn't struck as cleanly as his earlier effort but fizzed along the surface. Emulating his flat-footed defenders, Quiroga reacted far too slowly as the ball squirmed under his body and into the net. The Argentinian-born goalkeeper, known affectionately as 'El Loco', had another unwelcome memory to add to his World Cup archive of mistakes.

Misfortune was beginning to pile up for the Peruvians as the influential Oblitas suffered an injury, forcing coach Marcos Calderón to replace him with Percy Rojas. The loss of Oblitas and Diaz forced the coach to rearrange his team, Calderón later stating, 'These early injuries obliged us to change our whole pattern.'[118] The injuries and goals conceded had forced Peru to rip up their initial game plan and they found it impossible to gain parity with a Brazil

---

118 David Miller. 1978. *World Cup: The Argentina Story*. Frederick Warne Publishers.

clicking in attack for the first time. The match seemed to typify what heavyweight champion Mike Tyson would later say to define boxing: 'Everyone has a plan, until they get punched in the mouth.'

Putting the weary Peruvians out of their misery, Brazil landed the knockout blow on their reeling opponents midway through the second half. Roberto Dinamite controlled a bouncing ball in the box, stabbing it past defender Duarte, who comically tried to get the Brazilian attacker under control by holding on to his shoulder and pulling his shirt as he advanced towards the byline. Dinamite, to his credit, stayed upright, desperately trying to keep the ball in play as Duarte theatrically raised his arms in an attempt to protest his innocence. Dinamite was then upended by another Peruvian defender as they seemed determined to concede a penalty. Zico, who had only been on the field for two minutes, scored the subsequent spot kick. Quiroga's nonchalant hands-on-hips approach to saving the penalty left a lot to be desired as he chose the right corner but couldn't get down quickly enough.

Brazil had recorded their most impressive victory so far in the tournament, repeating their 1970 victory over the same nation. Coutinho was satisfied with the display, stating, 'For the first time we have found our rhythm and collective spirit.'[119] Perhaps the coach's self-effacing reference to 'collective spirit' was a nod to the squad's newly established selection committee that took away the coach's autonomy over the team he fielded.

---

119 *Ibid.*

Argentina vs Poland: 14 June 1978 – Estadio Gigante de Arroyito, Rosario

The tournament organisers' insistence that Argentina always feature in the evening fixture meant that the second match of the group kicked off half an hour after the final whistle of the first one. After Brazil had thrown down the gauntlet with their three-goal defeat of Peru, Poland faced Argentina in Rosario, both teams harbouring serious ambitions of fighting Brazil for the top spot.

Argentina's switch to Rosario, leaving behind the capital comforts of Buenos Aires, meant a return to familiar ground for 'El Matador', Mario Kempes. Before leaving for Valencia, Kempes had called this stadium home, representing Rosario Central with distinction – scoring 85 goals in just 107 appearances. 'In Rosario, it was like my own World Cup. I returned to the Arroyito stadium. My home.'[120] Kempes, despite strong displays that had thrilled spectators, had yet to score a goal in the tournament. Home fans were hopeful that El Matador would be able to call upon muscle memory to find the most familiar of nets.

The fans in attendance didn't have to wait long, as a move that began with Osvaldo Ardiles found Daniel Bertoni on the left wing. Ardiles's perpetual motion in the middle of the park drove La Albiceleste forward. Since his selection in 1975, Ardiles had consistently repaid the faith shown in him by national coach Menotti and relished the responsibility of being the lungs and legs of midfield. From Ardiles's pass, Bertoni found acres of space as the Polish

---

120 *Pele, Argentina and the Dictators.* Goalhanger films. 2020.

defence stood off the attacker. This decision proved fatal as Bertoni expertly clipped a cross deep into the penalty area. The ball seemed to hang in the air for an eternity, as if it was unwilling to drop until it met a worthy recipient. That man waiting to receive the ball was the prodigal son of Rosario, galloping through defenders and brushing others aside, his eyes widening as he saw the perfect pass beckoning. The ball couldn't have been more destined for Kempes had it had his name written on it, and the striker duly obliged in thumping his header past Tomaszewski in goal. El Matador raised both hands in celebration before the ball had even hit the net and, as he raced through the ticker tape that littered the turf, he was a man reborn.

The absence of Leopoldo Luque, who was grieving the death of his brother, posed a headache for Menotti. In the previous match, El Flaco had selected Daniel Bertoni as a lone centre-forward, flanked by Ortiz and Valencia. For all Bertoni's undeniable quality with the football, he didn't possess the physicality of the absent Luque and, as a result, found himself isolated and bullied by Italian defenders. To face Poland, Menotti opted for a front three of Bertoni, Kempes and Houseman, who returned to the starting XI after being demoted to the bench in the previous match. This attack to face Poland had an element of fluidity that was absent when the hosts had faced Italy. Rather than simply replacing one centre-forward with another who didn't possess the same physical attributes, Menotti selected strikers who were able to interchange and pick up each other's positions, like the 'total football' philosophy of the Dutch, which he so admired. This was typified by

Bertoni marauding on the left wing and placing his pinpoint cross on to the head of Mario Kempes, who had charged into the box like an orthodox centre-forward. Menotti's decision to switch the positions of Daniel Valencia and Kempes, the latter pushed further up the field, meant El Matador's attacking prowess was unlocked in the second round. Following his opening goal, the Valencia hitman never looked back.

Trailing by a goal, Poland did exceptionally well not to combust in the cauldron of the Arroyito stadium. In fact, they managed to temporarily silence the crowd following a moment of desperation in the penalty area by the goalscorer Kempes. Poland's captain Kazimierz Deyna clipped in his free kick from the byline and the ball flew over the heads of the defenders and goalkeeper Fillol, who misjudged the flight of the ball. At the back post, Tarantini's attempt to clear the ball to safety merely directed it back into the path of Grzegorz Lato. The 1974 World Cup golden boot winner seemed destined to find the net, only for the diving Kempes to punch the ball off the goal line. Kempes's cynicism forced the referee to point to the spot but the opportunity for Poland to equalise was deemed punishment enough as Kempes escaped a booking. Deyna stood over the ball from 12 yards. The home crowd, paralysed by tension, stood transfixed, while the exasperated Menotti rubbed his forehead and drew from his trademark cigarette.

A ten-year veteran of the national team, captain Deyna was their most experienced player. His tenure in the national shirt defined a golden generation for Polish football. His nine goals at the 1972 Summer Olympics, including a brace in the final versus Hungary, inspired Poland to the gold medal. Two years later, at the 1974 World Cup, Deyna starred as captain of the bronze medallists and would later collect an individual bronze medal, placing third in the European Footballer of the Year awards behind Franz Beckenbauer and Johan Cruyff.[121] He would surely have represented one of Europe's biggest clubs following his heroics at the previous World Cup had Poland's ruling Communist Party not forbidden their players from moving abroad prior to their 30th birthday.

There was nobody more experienced or qualified to take the penalty but the pressure cooker atmosphere of Rosario conspired to stifle even the most confident of men. The weight on Deyna's shoulders was palpable as the captain shuffled towards the spot and almost apologetically passed his penalty into the arms of Fillol. Never had a man of such experience and quality looked less likely to score a spot kick. As he turned away gazing at the ticker tape on the turf, his body language contrasted with his status as Poland's talisman. Fillol barely had to step to his left to drop on to the ball. In truth, he could have bent down and picked the ball up in one motion. The crowd at the Arroyito exploded in an outpouring of joy, tempered heavily with relief as they sensed the pendulum swinging back the way of La Albiceleste.

At half-time, sensing that they needed to press home their advantage and score a second goal to secure the win,

---

121 Yousef Teclab. 2018. 'Kazimierz Deyna: the tragic but brilliant Polish midfielder who defined a Golden Polish era'. thesefootballtimes.com

Menotti turned to Ricardo Villa. The Atlético de Tucumán man was required to inject pace into the Argentina midfield and replaced Valencia, whose race had been run. Valencia was unfortunate to be the man Menotti frequently hauled off when the team required a reshuffle. Villa featured twice off the bench in the second group phase, seen by Menotti as a creative spark who could make things happen on the pitch. Although his game time was limited to two halves, totalling 90 minutes of play, Villa impressed Tottenham Hotspur enough to secure a transfer to England along with Osvaldo Ardiles after the World Cup. Villa would become a cult hero in England for his match-winning performance in the 1981 FA Cup Final replay. 'Ricky', as he was christened at White Hart Lane, later laughingly stated, 'Sometimes it feels like I only played one match, and only ever scored one goal,'[122] referencing his '81 winner, despite being a key figure of the 1978 World Cup-winning squad and someone who Menotti trusted implicitly.

Poland began the second half with renewed vigour, stubbornly refusing to be swept aside by Argentina's gathering momentum. Zbigniew Boniek drove the ball forward, seeing an opportunity to cast himself as the hero, following Deyna's woes from the penalty spot. Boniek weaved through the Argentinian defence on the edge of the 18-yard box, gracefully shifting the ball from right to left, before passing Passarella, who hung out his trailing leg attempting to win the ball. The Pole effortlessly glided past the defenders before rounding Fillol in goal; however, his

---

122 Marcelo Mora y Araujo. 2007. 'Whatever happened to Ricky Villa?' *The Guardian*.

final touch pushed the ball slightly out of his path to the right, preventing him from firing a shot at goal. Rampaging on to the ball was Grzegorz Lato, the striker who would play for his country 100 times in his storied career, scoring 45 goals, placing him third on his nation's all-time top goalscorers' list. Similarly to when Deyna stood on the penalty spot, Poland found themselves with the right man in the right place. However, once again, that man would be unable to convert the chance, as Lato hit the side-netting with his drive, sparing Argentina. Moments later captain Deyna would call Fillol into action, drawing a full-stretch save from a free kick.

However, Argentina extinguished their visitors' final hopes as they broke on a Polish clearance to devastating effect. Goalkeeper Tomaszewski's punt upfield sailed through the Rosario sky so high that Ardiles may have wanted to dust the snow off the ball before trapping it. The midfielder controlled the ball with the touch of a surgeon before getting it out of his feet and charging forward in one fluid motion. The archetypal Ardiles run, which Menotti so valued, took him from the halfway line to the edge of the penalty area. As the Polish midfield parted like the Red Sea, inviting Ardiles to continue, the remaining defenders lunged at his feet, allowing him to slide his pass to the unmarked Kempes. Kempes arrived at the edge of the box at the perfect time, in a move that typified the burgeoning, telepathic relationship between the two. El Matador showed great composure while taking the ball into the box as the final defender zeroed in on the marksman. Untethered from the shackles of pressure following his opening goal, Kempes checked to his left, giving himself a yard of space before firing the ball under the Polish goalkeeper and into the corner of the net. Illustrating his gratitude, the goalscorer raced to embrace Ardiles, who was now on the turf catching his breath following his dash through the Polish half.

The second goal had taken the wind out of the Polish sails, as they now reluctantly accepted that it wouldn't be their day. It's hard to underestimate the significance of Argentina's first victory in Rosario. Humbled by their defeat by Italy, La Albiceleste drew strength from Estadio Arroyito's partisan crowd, away from the gaze of the capital. César Luis Menotti understandably tried to play down this factor, managing expectations when he stated, 'I don't want to dramatise our performance. I am convinced we can play better in the remaining matches.'[123]

As it stood, Argentina claimed two points from their opening victory of the second round and sat behind great rivals Brazil in the table on goal difference. The team and the dictatorship would have been encouraged by a satisfactory opening 90 minutes, although events elsewhere in Mar del Plata soured the occasion for the military. In the centre of the city, between the streets of Santiago del Estero, Alberti and Peralta Ramos, the audio transmission of the match had yet again been interrupted by Los Montoneros. The most high-profile 'subversive' organisation had once again found a way to reach the people of Argentina with their message. This time their communication was more potent,

---

123 David Miller. 1978. *World Cup: The Argentina Story*. Frederick Warne Publishers.

as on some televisions, the audio transmission remained even as Battalón 601 chiefs cut video transmission.[124]

The military and police found it impossible to find the source of the transmission and were instead reduced to patrolling the streets with radio direction finders, left over from the Second World War. It wouldn't be until July that they found the apartment from where Los Montoneros had launched their transmission, once again finding the dwelling adorned with anti-dictatorship messaging, the words 'liberation or dependence' scrawled on the walls.[125]

Poland vs Peru: 18 June 1978 – Estadio Ciudad de Mendoza, Mendoza

The two losers of the opening round of fixtures faced each other in Mendoza, hoping to get their World Cup campaigns back on track. Peru's heavy loss to Brazil left them with a mountain to climb but Poland may have still held a faint glimmer of hope for a place in the third-place play-off, having lost by two to Argentina. They made two changes from their loss to the hosts, the most interesting of which was a change in goal, with Zygmunt Kukla starting between the posts. For Peru, Oblitas had recovered from his knock against Brazil, forcing Percy Rojas to return to his position on the bench.

Peru's full-back Navarro, replacing the injured Diaz, found the match to be a baptism of fire, as he was at fault for the only goal. Intercepting an attempted through

---

124 Nicolas Sagaian. 'Radio Liberacion: Interferences by Montoneros during the 78 World Cup'. papelitos.org
125 *Ibid.*

ball from Boniek on the right wing, Navarro turned back into play. Lato, the intended recipient of Boniek's pass applied pressure on Navarro, snapping at his heels without conceding a foul. The full-back mis-controlled under pressure, nudging the ball to the touchline. Rather than allow the ball to roll out, Navarro stretched to keep the ball in play, before inexplicably playing a short pass straight to the Polish striker. Lato, scarcely believing his luck, gleefully received the ball, before accelerating away from the defender. The renowned goalscorer knew exactly where to put the ball and floated a right-footed cross into the penalty area. Arriving at the penalty spot, Andrzej Szarmach powered his header into the bottom corner. Quiroga in goal was utterly helpless against the Polish attack's precision and power, helped in no small part by Navarro's moment of panic on the touchline.

Mere minutes later, Poland almost doubled their lead. Attacking yet again from the flanks, Deyna pushed his header against a post with Quiroga's goal at his mercy. The ball rebounded to Lato, who would have been disappointed to divert his header back into the hands of Quiroga, although the collision with the post took much of the pace off the ball.

Deyna, Boniek and Lato were linking to great effect, stretching the Peruvian defence to its limits. A length-of-the-field move saw Lato draw a diving save from Quiroga, who pushed his blistering, edge-of-the-box shot wide of the far post. The Europeans enjoyed the majority of the second-half chances as Peru succumbed to their second successive defeat. Poland's win meant they would travel to Mendoza to face Brazil still in contention for at least a third-place play-off match. By contrast, Peru's World Cup was drawing to a close. Having bloodied the noses of the Netherlands, hammered Iran and humbled Scotland, Peru's World Cup campaign had wilted in the second round. Relatively satisfied with their lot, they had done justice to the heroes of 1970 and travelled to Rosario with nothing but pride remaining to play for. Crucially, they would face an Argentine team with everything to play for.

Argentina vs Brazil: 18 June 1978 – Estadio Gigante de Arroyito, Rosario

The second round of fixtures in Group B now featured the two juggernauts of South American football, Argentina and Brazil, on a collision course. The meeting of the two giants, both victorious in their previous matches, would become known in Brazil as 'La Batalha do Rosario' (The Battle of Rosario). Despite both nations boasting enviable squads, blessed with youth and talent, precious little quality football was played in the powder keg atmosphere of Estadio Gigante de Arroyito. At the best of times, the Superclásico de las Américas can be a volatile cocktail. However, under the floodlights in Rosario, the dominant ingredient in the cocktail was aggression.

The rivalry between the two nations dates back to the early days of football on the continent. In post-colonial South America, the growing social phenomenon of football was used as a tool of nation-building, a central pastime that spanned the social classes and stoked the fires of patriotism. While the 1978 World Cup is an explicit example of a dictatorship hijacking a popular pastime to unite a divided people and root out subversives, it's certainly not the first time it has happened. Football was being used as a political tool on the continent when the junta's parents were still in their nappies. Juan Domingo Perón, upon sweeping to power in 1943, 'set aside considerable state funds'[126] to build or refurbish stadiums across the capital, such was the potential of the cultural phenomenon of football to curry favour across the political classes. El Monumental received a refurb, as did Racing Club's 'El Cilindro', which was officially named after the president (said to be a fan of the club). But it was perhaps in the barrio of La Boca, home of River Plate's great rivals, that Perón enjoyed his most vocal support, fans singing 'Boca, Perón, una corazon' (one heart) signifying the bond between the working classes on the terraces and the premier in Casa Rosita.

To understand the rivalry between the footballing nations of Argentina and Brazil, we have to understand the core differences between the people. In Brazil, suffering a hangover from the colonial times, 'idleness was worshipped as a trace of royalty', according to economist Juliana Mello,[127] and as a result the heavy industry relied on slave labour. In Argentina, the indigenous population were exploited, whereas Brazil exploited the burgeoning African slave trade. As time passed, this led to a far more

---

126 Andrew Flint. 'The clockwork of La Maquina, the team that reinvented Argentine football'. thesefootballtimes.com
127 Juliana Mello. 2012. 'The difference between Argentina and Brazil'. thebrazilbusiness.com

diverse population in Brazil than their neighbours. In the 1930s, under the rule of populist leader Getúlio Vargas, Brazil made efforts to integrate the black population into society. Nicknamed the 'father of the poor', Vargas saw the opportunity to use football as a bridge between social and ethnic groups. The samba culture of Brazil's black population was synonymous with athleticism and physicality and would come to define the game in the country. Thus, an identity was born. Brazil's success in building a diverse footballing culture pre-dated Peru, for example, whose integration of black and indigenous people into the national team would have to wait until the 1970s. The birth of 'samba football', blending the culture of its African population with European influence, established a contrasting football identity to Argentina. In early 20th-century Argentina, Porteño culture was the predominant influence on football, placing value on street smarts and individual ingenuity.[128]

The differences in ethnic make-up of the nations led to tension in the press and on the terraces. In the early 20th century an Argentinian publication printed the headline 'los macacos vienen' (the monkeys are coming) prior to a Brazilian tour of Argentina. The story was equipped with a cartoon strip depicting the Brazilian footballers as monkeys. The racial component of the rivalry between nations has unfortunately simmered along throughout the

---

128 Dr Peter Watson (teaching fellow of Latin American studies at the University of Leeds). 2020. *These Football Times* podcast, *Political Football: The Story of the 1978 World Cup: Violence, Protests, Controversy and a Stunning Home Glory.*

generations. As recently as 2022, Boca Juniors fans were condemned for their racist abuse of Corinthians supporters in their Copa Libertadores group match. The fans made monkey gestures at their Brazilian opponents, echoing the century-old cartoon.

Much of the racism directed towards Brazilians stems from the belief among some Argentinians that the country is more refined than its South American neighbours. Argentine writer Jose Luis Borges famously described the country as a 'land of exiles'. This image of Argentina is core to the identity of the nation to many. 'Argentina's most powerful images: the idea that it is a modern country built from scratch through liberal economic and social policies and massive European immigration.'[129] Of course, this theory completely ignored the indigenous population of Argentina, highlighting the attitude towards non-Europeans by some Argentinians.

Although the rivalry sometimes contains an unwelcome racial component, in comparison to so many rivalries between neighbours there is no history of military conflict between the nations. The bragging rights belong solely to what has been achieved on the football pitch, not on the battlefield. In this respect, the rivalry is a pure footballing one, preciously undiluted from bellicose war rhetoric. Prior to the 1978 World Cup, the rivalry was dominated by Brazil. Boasting three World Cup wins to Argentina's zero, Argentina also lagged behind the rest of the continent, as Brazil, Uruguay and even Chile, considered a rung below

---

129 Gabriela Nouzeilles Graciela Montaldo (Eds.). 2002. *The Argentina Reader: History, Culture, Politics.* Duke University Press.

Argentina on the South American football ladder, had hosted the event.

Before his exile, Juan Perón had tried to bring the 1950 World Cup to Argentina but missed out to neighbours and eternal rivals Brazil. Ironically, had there been a World Cup during the 1940s, Argentina would surely have been favourites. A decade before Hungary's Mighty Magyars became the team to define the 1950s, a footballing revolution was taking place in Buenos Aires. The River Plate team of the 1940s are considered by many football historians to be an early inspiration for the Netherlands' philosophy of total football. Spearheaded by five attacking players of such undeniable ability that they could interchange seamlessly, like cogs in a high-performance machine, they became known as 'La Máquina'. Football historian and author of *Angels with Dirty Faces: The Footballing History of Argentina*, Jonathan Wilson, describes the grace and functionality of La Máquina, stating, 'There are two types of machines – there's the rudimentary mill; and then there's the watch, which has real aesthetic beauty to its mechanisms. I guess, that's what we get from La Máquina – the idea that this is a beautifully fragile mechanism, with lots of minute, individual parts which all fit together brilliantly.'[130] The moniker of La Máquina was coined by Uruguayan journalist Ricardo Lorenzo in 1942. Writing for *El Gráfico*, Lorenzo was blown away by the dynamism and telepathic ability of the team, noting that they functioned like clockwork, a

---

130 Srijandeep Das, interview with Jonathan Wilson. 2017. 'From Maradona's "anti-futbol" coach to "La Maquina", busting Argentina's biggest football myths'. Scroll.in

characteristic that earned the Netherlands' 1974 team their 'Clockwork Orange' nickname.

La Máquina, in the guise of the blue-and-white shirts of Argentina, were unfortunately never given the opportunity to play at a World Cup. The war-torn 1940s meant there would be no World Cup in that decade, when Argentina's players were truly in their pomp, then Argentina boycotted the 1950 and 1954 World Cups in Brazil and Switzerland, respectively. Perón perceived FIFA's decision to award Brazil and not Argentina the 1950 World Cup to be a personal snub, and the practice of boycotting international tournaments was in line with Argentina's isolationist policy. Perón's reluctance to send a team to Brazil in 1950, however, suggests that he feared a 'national calamity', should they return defeated.[131]

Argentina would pay the price for their World Cup sabbatical, crushed eight years later in 1958 by Czechoslovakia. Their 6-1 defeat was dubbed 'the disaster in Sweden'. The disaster was further compounded by the fact that the tournament was won by their great rivals Brazil, whose triumph in 1958 heralded the birth of a genius as Pelé dazzled on a global stage for the first time. He would repeat the trick in 1970, inspiring Brazil to their third World Cup. The 1970 vintage was regarded as one of the finest international teams of all time, defeating Italy 4-1 in the final, the performance typified by Carlos Alberto's goal, considered one of the greatest ever scored. For a continent obsessed with the notion of football hierarchy, it was very difficult

---

131 Matt Gault. 2015. 'The politicised history of Argentine football'. thesefootballtimes.com

for Argentines to argue supremacy as their neighbours etched their name into global football's record books.

In 1978, 20 years later, the second-round meeting in Rosario brought the rivalry to boiling point. As mentioned before, Argentina were never meant to end up in Rosario, but their detour away from the capital gave them the opportunity to effectively qualify for the final at the expense of their greatest rivals. A win over Brazil would put them on four points out of four, with the already eliminated Peru waiting for them in the final group match. Brazil, by contrast, were desperate to keep the scores at 3-0 in the World Cups won stakes and prevent Argentina from advancing to a final in Buenos Aires, which at times seemed destined.

What transpired in Rosario was the inevitable result of two teams that had more to lose in defeat than to gain in victory. Brazil's 1970 team and River Plate's La Máquina would have watched through their fingers as neither team sought to play attractive football. Performance was very much relegated to a place behind result in their list of priorities. Brazil's team selection suggested caution, as their most talented playmaker Zico was named among the substitutes. Coutinho once again elected to use the Flamengo starlet from the bench. His place in the starting line-up was instead given to Chicão. Unknown outside his native Brazil, Chicão was an anomaly in the squad, gaining just nine caps in his international career. Seen as a midfield enforcer, ball-winner and safe pair of hands, Chicão didn't possess a fraction of the ability of Zico. However, he was accustomed to the dark arts of midfield trench warfare.

As it transpired, Zico's skill in finding passes and evading tackles would have been superfluous in a match that displayed more collisions than a demolition derby. The selection of Chicão in a three-man midfield with the combative Batista and effervescent Dirceu meant that there was also no place for the veteran Rivellino. Returning to fitness following his ankle injury, Coutinho was reportedly willing to make a concession, selecting Rivellino on the unfamiliar left wing. According to *Daily Express* reporter David Miller, the veteran was disinclined to play anywhere other than the midfield playmaker role, prompting another fracas with his coach. Perhaps Rivellino's status as World Cup winner and Brazil's insistence on democracy in selection gave him the confidence to present his coach with such an ultimatum; however, the result was a place on the bench. Coutinho felt unable to sacrifice any more pace in a midfield that contained Batista and Chicão and needed the legs of Dirceu. It would be remiss to ignore the talent of Dirceu, who had already illuminated the tournament with moments of eye-catching skill. The midfielder, who would go on to represent Atlético de Madrid with distinction, was more than merely an engine and was good value for his place.

Menotti made changes to the Argentina team that defeated Poland, dropping Kempes deeper into a more familiar midfield role, while Ortiz returned alongside Leopoldo Luque, fresh from being granted compassionate leave by his coach. Menotti, secure in the knowledge that he led a squad forged on togetherness, saw fit to fire a barb at the Brazilian camp when quizzed about their midfield selection and the role of Rivellino, stating, 'If he is the same Rivellino I knew in 1974, he is dangerous. If he is the same as we have seen him here, it does not worry me.'[132] Mind games aside, Rivellino needn't have weighed on Menotti's mind, as Coutinho never shot a glance at him on the bench. Cast out into the cold night air of Rosario.

Whether Coutinho's selection of Chicão was a self-fulfilling prophecy that goaded Argentina into a fight is a source of debate. Similar to an ice-hockey team selecting all its enforcers in a line, Brazil's selection suggested that they were ready to fight. Coutinho's men in gold shirts entered the bear pit of Estadio Gigante de Arroyito and declared war. As the battle lines were drawn, returning hero Leopoldo Luque set the tone within the first ten seconds by kicking Batista to the ground a full second after he had released the ball. Returning to the tournament following the death of his brother, Luque could be forgiven for being a little off the pace, but the nature of his challenge suggested it was cynical rather than cumbersome. The Hungarian referee allowed play to continue, sensing perhaps that it was better to let the game flow in the early moments rather than disrupt proceedings with the whistle.

The referee's lenience was punished by the Argentina players, as from the next phase of play Luque and Bertoni combined to sandwich another Brazilian in a gang tackle. Brazil were incensed. The architects of the challenge were targeted by the Brazilians, looking to settle the score as Luque and then Bertoni were fouled in quick succession,

---

132 David Miller. 1978. *World Cup: The Argentina Story.* Frederick Warne Publishers.

the latter upended from behind by an onrushing Oscar, who showed little interest in winning the ball. As Argentina prepared to take the subsequent free kick, Oscar appeared to fire a sly dig into the back of Luque, sending the River Plate man to the Rosario turf, clutching where he had been struck. Ardiles and Passarella remonstrated with the ref, who had been oblivious to the incident, claiming that their team-mate had been assaulted. Understandably the referee was eager for play to recommence as quicky as possible and waved away their claims. The match was only two minutes old and had been stopped on half a dozen occasions already. With precisely zero football played during this time, the match stood on the precipice of descending into farce, and the combustible atmosphere of Rosario weighed heavy on the officials.

The first genuine goalscoring opportunity arrived five minutes in when Luis Galván scythed down Brazil's Dirceu, who had exchanged passes with Batista 35 yards from the Argentinian goal. As was the pattern of the opening exchanges, flair was no match for physicality as Dinamite hit a low free kick lamely into the hands of goalkeeper Fillol. The best chances for either team came in the first half, as Gil's fierce shot was stopped low by Fillol and Ortiz spurned Argentina's best opportunity, spooning his effort wide from near the penalty spot.

When the teams emerged for the second half, their exuberance had been replaced by caution, as a loss for either would have been catastrophic. The occasion seemed to weigh heavily on both teams as the match was played at an incredibly high pace, only to be littered with heavy touches, missed passes and late tackles. The mouth-watering match-up between two coaches whose philosophy was based on risk-taking, high-octane, Dutch-inspired football was failing to live up to expectations. The pressure was stifling any creativity and limited both teams' ability to play ambitious football.

Menotti was reported to be disgusted with Argentina's performance, their limited creative output and reliance on physicality a stark contrast to his own views on the game. He famously detested low-risk, laborious football. Sports broadcaster Tim Vickery claimed that Menotti was furious with his team and wouldn't talk to them afterwards, feeling that he had been let down by how they approached the match. Other commentators pour scorn on this notion, suggesting that such a story is merely part of the myth of Menotti. Although a self-styled 'coffee shop philosopher',[133] Menotti was no fool and understood a nil-nil draw suited Argentina, who would play their final match after Brazil had played theirs. Menotti expertly waved away any suggestions that Argentina held the advantage, however. The Rosario native, on home turf, suggested that Brazil held all the cards and were able to make Argentina very nervous, should they record a good victory over Poland.

Brazil vs Poland: 21 June 1978 – Estadio Ciudad de Mendoza, Mendoza

Level on points on the final day, Brazil and Argentina both had the opportunity to book a place in Sunday's final.

---

133 *Pele, Argentina and the Dictators*. Goalhanger films. 2020.

Separated only by goal difference, the final matchday of Group B represented a shoot-out to establish who could win by the greatest amount. At least that's how it was viewed in South America, as Poland's defeat of Peru had put them two points behind Brazil, with an opportunity to leapfrog them should they win by a two-goal margin.

Requiring a handsome win, prior to Argentina's evening fixture against Peru, Coutinho restored Zico to the starting XI. Following impressive cameos off the bench against Peru and Argentina, Zico was tasked with bringing creativity to a team in need of goals. However, his afternoon was cut short as he was injured within ten minutes. Felled by a heavy challenge from Kasperczak, Brazil's most creative force was replaced by Palmeiras striker Jorge Mendonça.

Zico's absence was quickly forgotten by Brazil, who took the lead from a free kick a quarter of an hour into the match. The ball was placed a yard outside the penalty area, to the left of the goal, much closer than Dirceu's previous free kick goal and not in Toninho territory. Cruzeiro full-back Nelinho stood over the ball. With an audible crack of the right boot, he blasted the ball into Kukla's top corner. The ball deviated slightly, starting level with the post before flying inside it, out of the goalkeeper's reach. The ball was struck with such ferocity that even had Kukla been standing directly in front of it, it would have been impossible for him to react in time. Nelinho's moment of brilliance underlined Brazil's threat from dead-ball situations, blessed as they were with free kick takers gifted with power and grace.

Showcasing further quality from a dead ball, Brazil defender Amaral stood over a free kick on the halfway line. Reminiscent of the Netherlands' 'total football' philosophy requiring every player to be comfortable on the ball, seemingly every Brazilian could strike a dead ball with quality. Amaral switched the focus of play, effortlessly booming a 45-yard, crossfield pass to Roberto Dinamite at the edge of the six-yard box. Underestimating Amaral's ability to find an attacker from so far out, the Brazilian forward was allowed ample space to bring the ball down on his chest. Taking a touch to get the ball out from under his feet, Dinamite then fired a low shot at goal. Showing uncharacteristic tension, the striker snatched at the chance and sliced his effort harmlessly wide.

Much like during their defeat by Argentina, Poland stubbornly refused to play the part of also-rans, as they absorbed Brazilian pressure and forged their own chances. A tame effort from Deyna drew a save from Leão, but the shot did no justice to the move that preceded it. Covering the length of the field, a series of intricate passes found Kasperczak on the right wing, who fired a low ball across the face of the Brazilian box. With all eyes on Boniek, he stepped over the ball, allowing Deyna space for a shot. His scuffed effort was a disappointing end to a move that illustrated the quality possessed by the Poles, who were growing into the match, with captain Deyna at the heart of everything. When not orchestrating moves in the middle of the park, linking up with Boniek, he was taking up positions on the flanks, dropping a shoulder and gliding past full-backs.

In the dying seconds of the first half, Poland produced another moment of fantastic quality and, this time, it was enough to breach the Brazilian defence. The irrepressible Boniek, charging infield from the right wing, exchanged one-twos with first Lato and then Deyna, the latter lofting a through ball into the penalty area. Toninho, sensing the danger, challenged Deyna for the header. The two players collided, causing confusion in the box. The man most alert was inevitably Poland's great goalscorer Lato, who tracked the bouncing ball and fired a low half-volley into the net. 1-1. An opening 45 minutes of pulsating football had been bookended by two moments of brilliance.

Despite their dominance in the early stages, Brazil were never likely to run away with the match against their talented opponents, who were growing into the occasion. Buoyed by the cheers of the crowd, Poland relished their role, creating chaos in the ever-changing climate of Group B. Pushed on by the cheers of the Mendoza faithful at their back, Poland began the second half the way they had ended the first. They advanced into the Brazilian half, Lato taking up dangerous positions, fed by the pivotal Deyna in midfield. The striker whipped a left-footed strike wide of the goal when teed up by his captain, as Poland sought to take the lead, which would draw them level in the group with the blue-shirted Brazilians.

However, the match would sway back in favour of the South Americans thanks to a five-minute period on the hour mark. Toninho, attacking down the left wing, floated a ball into the Polish box, which was cleared only as far as substitute Mendonça. He took the sting off the ball with a smart touch, steadied himself and fired an opportunistic strike against the upright. The sharpest man in the box, and first to react, was Brazil's Roberto Dinamite, who stabbed the rebound past Kukla to give Brazil the lead.

Brazil now sought to cement their dominance and forge their path to the final. At 2-1 they currently enjoyed a three-goal advantage over Argentina on goal difference. With Argentina still to play the already eliminated Peru, Brazil needed a larger cushion to feel comfortable. Moments after taking the lead, a moment of trickery from Dirceu bewildered defender Maculewicz near the 18-yard box. With zero room for manoeuvre between there and the corner flag, Dirceu beckoned a challenge from the physically imposing defender. As Maculewicz advanced, attempting to take man and ball over the line for a goal kick, Dirceu nutmegged him and drove into the penalty area. Dirceu cut the ball back for Mendonça, who squared it to Gil near the penalty spot. Gil's low drive defeated everyone in a crowded box, only to bounce back off the post into the path of Mendonça. The Palmeiras striker crashed his left-footed drive against the crossbar, as Polish defenders lay strewn on the turf, desperately trying to block the ball, which was now cannoning indiscriminately around the penalty box. Poland momentarily cleared their lines, only for the ball to reach Dirceu, 25 yards from goal. His left-footed shot hissed through the air, curving towards the bottom corner. The goalkeeper, again unable to lay a glove on the ball, saw it cannon off the woodwork for the third time in 20 seconds, this time rebounding to Roberto

Dinamite. The striker had again found himself in the right place, and the opportunist ended the game of pinball, crashing the ball into the roof of the net for a 3-1 lead.

Firmly in the ascendancy, Brazil now attempted to throw down the gauntlet to Argentina, each attack drawing a collective gasp from the Mendoza crowd, who realised that the task facing their team was becoming more difficult. A break from Brazil's own half saw Cerezo fire a shot across Kukla, who managed to save with his legs. Both teams exchanged shots in the final five minutes before the referee blew the whistle signalling the end of Poland's World Cup. It was a campaign that began with much promise but ultimately ended in disappointment as they finished in third place in the group, outside the third-place play-off position.

Brazil at this point were blissfully unaware of what their 3-1 win meant. The few Brazilian fans in the crowd, greatly outnumbered by the supposed 'neutral' Argentina fans, waved their flags and cheered on their team, as if trying to counteract the nervous body language of the players departing the field in uncertainty. Had they done enough? Argentina and Peru would kick off in less than an hour, the hosts requiring a four-goal margin of victory to leapfrog their bitter South American rivals. The answer would arrive nearly 1,000 kilometres east in Rosario.

Argentina vs Peru: 21 June 1978 – Estadio Gigante de Arroyito, Rosario

THE FINAL match of Group B took place in Rosario and saw Argentina face South American rivals Peru. The match is unquestionably the most controversial in the history of the World Cup, launching numerous conspiracy theories, ranging from accusations of intimidation, match-fixing and even attempted murder.

Argentina's route to the World Cup Final was meant to be a linear procession through Buenos Aires, playing all their matches at Estadio Monumental. However, their loss to Italy in the first stage, officiated by Israel's incorruptible, unflappable Abraham Klein, meant the gods of football sent them on a different route. On their detour to Rosario, they discovered their mojo and the prodigal son of Estadio Gigante de Arroyito had found his shooting boots.

Following Brazil's 3-1 triumph over Poland, Argentina required a winning margin of four goals to leapfrog their neighbours and take their place in the final. The fact that Argentina took to the pitch with this knowledge is a bone of much contention between the two South American giants. Scheduling of the tournament meant that Argentina always played their matches in the evening to ensure the largest number of viewers. However, this handed them a huge advantage as they knew what was required of them at 7.15pm on 21 June. Brazil, by contrast, had taken to the field against Poland at 4.45pm with a blank canvas, with no idea of what their rivals may do later.

The Brazilian football federation, led by Admiral Nunes, sensing potential corruption, campaigned to the tournament organisers, EAM, to change the kick-off time, bringing them in line with one another and eliminating Argentina's advantage. The EAM refused this request so Brazil were left frustrated, agitated and paranoid. The organisers, hand in glove with FIFA due to the friendship of Lacoste and Havelange, remained steadfast that the match would kick off at the scheduled time, dismissing the possibility of simultaneous kick-off times.

Brazil were understandably enraged by this snub and, for the first time in the tournament, the Brazilian federation and the coach Cláudio Coutinho were on the same page. However, Coutinho managed to absorb the anxiety rather than transmit it to his players. Brazil were able to focus on their football and dispatch their opponents in style. Their win over Poland was made more impressive considering the same team had defeated them four years prior in the third-place play-off. If Brazil were to avoid playing in the play-off again in 1978 an Argentina team buzzing with nervous energy would have to fall short later that evening. Brazil had thrown down the gauntlet for their biggest rivals, so the pressure was now on Argentina. Menotti's previous declaration that a handsome win for Brazil could make Argentina nervous had come to pass, as the muggy atmosphere of the Rosario night was laced with anxiety.

Although the scheduling of the match was advantageous for Argentina, it's too much of a leap to suggest skulduggery on this evidence alone. Argentina taking to the pitch later than Brazil was undoubtedly fortuitous but, had things gone to plan, they wouldn't even have been on the same side of the draw as their neighbours. Instead, it's more likely that they happened upon a set of circumstances that suited them and had no desire to alter things in the interest of fairness. In fact, FIFA learned nothing from the scheduling debacle and found themselves in a similar situation four years later. Still under the stewardship of João Havelange, Spain hosted the 1982 World Cup. In a match dubbed 'The disgrace of Gijon', West Germany faced Austria, with both knowing a victory for the Germans by fewer than a three-goal margin would mean qualification for both teams. Inevitably, West Germany scored early through Horst Hrubesch and the two teams played out 80 minutes without any realistic attempt to trouble their opponents, securing qualification for both nations at the expense of Algeria. The on-field display was even more blatant than what took place four years prior in Rosario, as both teams were visibly unwilling to play any genuine football, aimlessly passing the ball around and running down the clock.

Following a strong display, topping a group that included Scotland and eventual finalists the Netherlands,

Peru were expected to perform well in the second round. However, with back-to-back losses against Brazil and Poland, they didn't live up to these expectations. The 6-0 capitulation against Argentina in Rosario was anomalous when compared to the rest of Peru's performances and meant the South Americans exited the tournament with a whimper. The nature of the result and what it meant for the hosts has caused many observers to cast aspersions on the integrity of the game. But even before the teams took to the pitch, something foul was afoot.

In preparation for their final match of the World Cup, the Peruvian team received a visitor in their dressing room. Just before kick-off, they were visited by none other than President of Argentina, General Jorge Videla. Videla brought with him a guest, former US Secretary of State and close friend of the dictatorship Henry Kissinger. Kissinger's relationship with military governments across Latin America is infamous, due to his role in spearheading Operation Condor. In declassified US state department files, Kissinger was criticised for his role as a high-profile American cheerleader for the Argentinian military junta. A 1978 memorandum stated: 'His praise for the Argentine government in its campaign against terrorism was the music the Argentine government was longing to hear.'[134] The presence of Kissinger in the dressing room suggests a show of power from the military. In infiltrating the sanctity of the dressing room, shoulder to shoulder with a man synonymous with the dictatorships around the continent,

---

134 Uki Goñi. 2016. 'Kissinger hindered US efforts to end mass killings in Argentina, according to files'. Guardian.com

the military undoubtedly sought to intimidate their visitors. The dictatorship would of course plead innocence, stressing that Kissinger was out of office at the time, a friend of the government and, crucially, a keen football fan.

However, the visit of Videla and Kissinger to the Peru dressing room was certainly abnormal. Since the revelation of their attendance, numerous commentators have understandably demanded to know the nature of their visit and what was said. Among those was Francisco Morales Bermúdez, who was president of Peru between 1975 and 1980. Speaking on the visit he said: 'Why did Videla visit the dressings rooms of Peru? I have tried to investigate this. I don't want to mention names, but there have been many subordinate things there. It was not strictly football. Videla intimidated them. Something happened and it seems that a little money exchanged hands. Everything suggests it was so. With these things there is no way to investigate, but there is almost the conviction of what I tell you. Although one does not get to prove it. It was anomalous. It was totally anomalous.'[135]

Exactly what was said in the changing room by General Videla to the Peruvians before the kick-off is unclear, but he is reported to have spoken about the importance of 'Latin brotherhood'. Whether the general was appealing for clemency from his rivals or intimidating them, Videla's narrative echoed former President of Argentina Julio Argentino Roca, who believed in the importance of collective Latin American interests. In 1904, attending a

---

135 'Morales Bermúdez – En el Mundial 1978 parece que corrio dinero'. Elcomercio.pe 2016.

match between Brazil and Argentina in the Copa Roca (a tournament named after himself), Roca reportedly urged his players to allow Brazil to win, declaring, 'Muchachos, we have to be diplomatic. Brazil is celebrating the anniversary of its independence. It's not fair they lose. We have to let them win. Do it for the peace of the Americas.'[136] In falling on their swords, Peru could allow Argentina to pass through unharmed to the World Cup Final in their hour of need.

Of course, Peru would need an incentive to step aside for their Latin brothers, and theorists believe these incentives took many forms, from the diplomatic to the financial. Investigative journalist David Yallop alleges that the call to bribe the Peruvians came from the very top, as General Jorge Videla gave tournament organiser Carlos Lacoste the green light to approach the Peruvian government with their proposal. Yallop claims that among the things offered were a grain shipment of 35,000 tons from Argentina to Peru, a $50m credit line and substantial individual bribes to members of the Peruvian military. The writer also alleges that individual players were paid $20,000 for their complicity in the fraud. However, Yallop declines to name any of his sources, claiming their willingness to be interviewed was under the strict condition of anonymity.[137]

It's disingenuous to dismiss Yallop's claims out of hand but the variety of allegations without a named source doesn't constitute a smoking gun of evidence. The book in

---

136 Andrew Flint. 'The clockwork of La Maquina, the team that reinvented Argentine football'. thesefootballtimes.com
137 David Yallop. 1999. *How They Stole Our Game*. Poetic Publishing.

which Yallop makes these accusations is littered with tropes about Argentinian football being a hotbed of skulduggery, including a needless attack on captain Daniel Passarella – who would later coach Argentina at the 1998 World Cup. Yallop claims the Argentine wouldn't last ten minutes on the pitch if he were playing 20 years later. Yallop's frequent references to Argentina's meanness of spirit hint at a bias and undermine his accusations, as the lack of sources undermine his investigative work.

The sheer volume of allegations of corruption mean that they must be taken seriously, but often the claims are contradictory. It beggars belief that the Peru team could have been simultaneously intimidated to the point they felt they had to throw the match, but also bribed to lose. Were they threatened? Were they paid off? Was it neither? Both?

In addition to rumours swirling around grain shipments and credit lines, there was also the accusation of the replacement of political prisoners. 'Videla accepted us as prisoners of war on the condition that Peru allow him to win the World Cup, something he needed to clean up Argentina's bad image in the world.'[138] This allegation was made by former Peruvian senator Genaro Ledesma Izquieta in an interview with Argentinian newspaper *Tiempo Argentina*. Ledesma alleges that the throwing of the football match was a key negotiation point in the transfer of political prisoners between the nations. As both countries were run by military dictatorships, sponsored by the CIA's Operation Condor, the transfer of political

---

138 'Plan Condor' in the 6-0 of 78, VOICES PERU21

prisoners was commonplace. Both governments sought to root out left-wing subversives and would have collaborated with one another. Again, this isn't a smoking gun but it's entirely possible that the result of a football match, so vital to the Argentinian junta, could be used as a bargaining chip. These accusations are corroborated by a member of the coaching staff. Luis Zacarías recalled in an interview with Argentinian newspaper *El País* that General Jorge Videla asked for assistance from the Peruvian team prior to kick-off, stating, 'You are our brothers since the time of San Martín, and we want you to help us so that this Argentine people is happy.'[139]

Although this match is now frequently cited as one of the most controversial in the history of the game, it took eight years for the allegations of bribery to first surface, as journalist Maria-Laura Avignolo first outlined the accusations in 1986.[140] Much of the controversy at the time centred around Peru's goalkeeper Ramón Quiroga. The naturalised Peruvian citizen was born in the city of Rosario and began his professional career playing in the very stadium where Peru would take on Argentina, representing Rosario Central for five seasons. For Brazil to be successful, the man from Rosario would have to thwart his homeland and restrict them to fewer than four goals. The Brazilian federation and fans were understandably anxious, considering Quiroga's eccentricity and catalogue of errors in the previous matches. As recently as 72 hours

---

139 Varios senadores peruanos pedirán una investigación por la goleada de
   Argentina a Perú en el Mundial 78. *El País* (elpais.com)
140 David Yallop. 1999. *How They Stole Our Game*. Poetic Publishing.

before the match against Argentina, Quiroga had drawn gasps from the crowd as he raced off his line in the final moments to join in his team's attacks against Poland. Peru inevitably conceded possession and Quiroga promptly rugby tackled Grzegorz Lato to prevent a certain goal. Brazil would be wishing for no more cavalier bursts upfield from the man christened 'El Loco' against his native country.

Quiroga's coach Marcos Calderón addressed the issue. In a show of faith in his stopper, he insisted, 'Quiroga is a naturalised Peruvian citizen, and he is also 100 per cent professional. He will play like one against Argentina.'[141] If the Brazilians were placated by claims of his professionalism and integrity, they were still alarmed about his eccentricity. However, Quiroga vowed his loyalty to his adopted nation, stating, 'It has always been my dream to come back and play international football against Argentina but I am sorry that it had to happen under these circumstances.'[142]

In the years following the match, Quiroga's perceived conflict of interests between the country of his birth and the country he represented took a back seat to the more explosive accusations regarding corruption. Zacarías's allegations of Videla's dressing-room request are far more damning than Quiroga's nationality, yet they weren't widely reported at the time. Challenged on why he didn't raise the issue, Zacarías stated, 'I did it at the time. I brought it to the attention of journalists. If they did not report it, then this matter is up to them.' As mentioned previously,

---

141 *Deseret News*, 20 June 1978.
142 David Miller. 1978. *World Cup: The Argentina Story*. Frederick Warne Publishers.

much of the media in Argentina at the time was under the strict control of the dictatorship. Except for the *Buenos Aires Herald*, it's unlikely in the extreme that a media outlet would have broken rank and published a damaging story that painted the military in such a light.

Carlos Ares worked for *El Gráfico* during the World Cup, the publication tasked with writing the official biography of La Albiceleste during the tournament. Ares spent a great deal of time with the team at their base in José C. Paz and was at the front line as whispers of corruption swirled. Ares claimed to have later raised these concerns with tournament organiser Carlos Lacoste, only to be told not to pull at that particular thread, for fear of his life. Ares claims, 'He threatened to have me killed. I had to go into exile in Spain.'[143]

Interestingly, some of the people present in the dressing room offer conflicting recollections of Videla and Kissinger's visit. Legendary striker Juan Carlos Oblitas categorically denied any intimidation or bribery occurred and insisted that Videla's visit to the dressing room actually took place after the match and his words were 'to raise our morale and nothing else'.[144] If Oblitas's version of events is to be believed, it pours cold water on the theory that the dictatorship influenced the outcome prior to kick-off. It's near impossible 40 years on from the event to unpick fact from fiction regarding this match, as each claim and counterclaim is added to the canon of conspiracy theories.

143 *How They Stole Our Game*. David Yallop. Poetic Publishing, 1999.
144 VaVarios senadores peruanos pedirán una investigación por la goleada de Argentina a Perú en el Mundial 78. *El País* (elpais.com)

With reputations at stake, nobody on the Peruvian side has taken responsibility for a bribe, with senator Ledesma alleging that the match was fixed by the highest figures in both governments. Contrastingly, President Francisco Morales Bermúdez himself demanded an independent investigation, suggesting he knew nothing of the incident. If there was culpability on the part of the Peruvian government, nobody is owning up to it.

As accusations, paranoia and fear swirled in the air, the teams took to the pitch. The atmosphere in the stadium had now reached its apex, as a cauldron of noise that had been bubbling steadily during the build-up threatened to spill over. Argentina's move from River Plate's El Monumental to Estadio Gigante de Arroyito meant the crowd was a lot closer to the pitch and gave the fans in the steep stands an opportunity to greet the Peruvians in a manner that bore no traces of General Videla's promised Latin brotherhood. If the military had yet to fully intimidate the Peruvians, then the Rosario crowd took up the mantle. In fine voice, they welcomed Cubillas and his fellow players to proceedings with a hostile cacophony of vitriol and peppered the pitch with ticker tape, the turf resembling a city centre nightspot at the end of a heavy night of merriment.

The electricity in the air and magnitude of the task ahead of Argentina brought enormous pressure, which Peru, much to their credit, adapted to far better than their hosts. In the opening minutes Argentina appeared shell-shocked. There was a fraught inaccuracy to their play as if the enormity of their situation had dawned on them. Peru, by contrast, seemed inspired by the atmosphere and created numerous chances early on.

Juan Carlos Oblitas, sensing the trepidation in the Argentina defence, carried the ball towards the penalty box. Centre-back Luis Galván hesitated, transfixed by the Peruvian's grace, unsure whether the striker would attempt to cut inside him or continue out to the wing, in search of a cross. By the time Galván was in position to challenge, Oblitas had found his way inside the box. The defender's challenge would have to be timed to perfection or he would concede a penalty kick. As the Rosario crowd froze with heavy-beating hearts in mouths, Galván proved equal to the moment and timed his lunge to perfection. Oblitas's final touch was his heaviest, perhaps purposely knocking the ball into Galván's range, inviting the tackle, as if to say, 'Come, take the ball off me,' knowing that, if the challenge was a fraction off, he would be placing the ball on the penalty spot. Galván obliged and flew into the tackle, which he executed expertly, sending the ball out towards the corner flag, and scything through his opponent for good measure.

The attack was a precursor for what was to come, as Peru dominated the early exchanges. They played with a refreshing abandon as they blocked out the whistles and jeers of the Rosario faithful. Their best chance came in the tenth minute as Muñante attacked from the right wing. He blazed past the left-hand side of Argentina's defence, containing captain Passarella and left-back Tarantini. The captain's trademark assurance at the back was absent as he stumbled over the through ball, allowing Muñante to ghost past and find himself facing the whites of goalkeeper Fillol's eyes. Muñante hurdled the keeper and raised his hands to the sky like an eagle, soaring above the Rosario bear pit, expecting his chip to sail into the net. The ball belied the striker's vision and instead bounced back off the upright, allowing the retreating Galván to collect it and clear.

Five minutes later, the Argentinian defence was called into action once more. A delicious lofted pass from the left foot of Cubillas dropped just inside the penalty box. Oblitas had anticipated it and sped off, a half-step quicker to the action than defender Jorge Olguín. Oblitas struck a left-foot shot across goal on the half-volley, but this time Fillol showed great composure. Staying on his feet for longer than he did for Muñante's effort, the goalkeeper parried the shot around the post to safety. Oblitas stood hand on hips, incredulous that Peru had spurned another opportunity. His expression displayed a foreboding sense that Peru would be made to pay for their impotence in front of goal.

Unfortunately for Peru, this impotence was made more apparent by the deadliest finisher in international football at the other end of the pitch. A pass from Passarella bounced up to Mario Kempes around 25 yards from goal, between the lines of Peruvian midfield and attack. The ball sat up at a perfect height for the striker, inviting the fabled long-range sharpshooter to volley the ball into the net. However, noticing the centre-backs had split, leaving acres of space to charge forward, Kempes dummied his shot, drawing centre-back Manzo into a challenge. Manzo threw himself at Kempes, all limbs spread out to maximise the block, earnestly buying the dummy. Kempes swept past the defender, leaving him in a heap on the ground, the way a magician draws in their mark with their sleight of hand. The Valencia striker charged forward into the penalty box as the remaining defenders trailed in his wake. Kempes slid the ball underneath the advancing Quiroga and into the empty net. As the ball spiralled across the grass, collecting ticker tape on the way into the goal like a gathering snowball, Kempes ran away with arms aloft. The touchpaper had been lit and Argentina were a quarter of the way there.

Kempes was now a man possessed. Unshackled by Menotti, Argentina's goal-getter in chief was now positively salivating at the prospect of adding more goals to his and Argentina's tally. Menotti threw caution to the wind, switching to three at the back and converting Passarella from the traditional sweeper role into a deep-lying midfielder to sit between the back three and the two in midfield. Passarella's role at the base of a triangle that contained Américo Gallego and Omar Larrosa allowed Kempes the freedom to wreak havoc on the Peruvian defence as part of a four-man attack.

The die had been cast and, once the first goal was scored, a rampant Argentina went in search of more as Peru tried in vain to prevent them. Five minutes after the opening goal, Leopoldo Luque sought to add another. Receiving the ball from Larrosa at the edge of the penalty area with his back to goal, he motioned to take the ball inside, drawing a challenge from Manzo. The defender, who had moments earlier been tormented by Kempes's trickery, was once again bewildered by a shaggy-haired Argentina forward. This time Kempes's compatriot swivelled his hips, feinted inside and then dragged the ball back with his right foot. Luque accelerated past the defender, who had again lunged in, limbs flailing, attempting to make himself as big a target as possible, only to collide with thin air. The River Plate hitman took another touch in the box before firing a powerful left-footed drive across Quiroga that cannoned off the post, to the relief of El Loco.

Within 90 seconds Luque had fashioned another opportunity for Argentina. Capitalising on hesitancy in the Peruvian defence, he stabbed a pass through to defender Olguín, who had found himself in the unfamiliar position of centre-forward. Olguín's first touch caused the ball to pop into the air and, opting for power over precision, he blasted his volley against the crossbar and into the Rosario sky. The time the ball spent in the air after hitting the bar was scant reprieve for an overwhelmed Peru. Their lungs were burning and legs filling with lactic acid as Argentina laid siege to their goal, seemingly creating a chance with every attack.

On 38 minutes Argentina felt they should have been awarded a penalty. Bertoni controlled the ball on the byline, expertly keeping it alive. He moved the ball back towards goal, only to be felled by a flying tackle. Much to the bemusement of the crowd, the referee waved away the appeals for a spot kick and the game continued. The home nation's brief appeal for a penalty bought Peru just 60 seconds before facing the next attack as they found themselves in trouble once more. Firmly camped in

Peru's half, Argentina were able to launch attacks from the halfway line at will. Luque, with his back to goal, controlled a clipped ball forward from Larrosa, receiving the ball at hip-height and controlling the awkward pass expertly. He juggled it over the head of Peruvian captain Chumpitaz, who was suffering a torturous first half. This time Luque couldn't find the composure he had shown with his earlier strike and dragged his effort wide.

Argentina again felt they were denied a penalty on 41 minutes as Passarella rose highest to meet a booming cross from out wide. As the skipper took flight he was clattered into from behind, which caused his header to drift harmlessly wide. The referee clearly believed the fact that Passarella made contact with the header meant that he wasn't sufficiently denied a goalscoring opportunity.

As half-time approached, Peru were desperately watching the clock, hoping that the referee's whistle and half-time intermission would allow them to regroup and stem the tide of Argentinian attacks. Unfortunately for the visitors the mounting attacks bore fruit just before half-time, Peru's desperate defence finally submitting to the sheer volume of chances. Kempes and his compatriots had been running riot, picking the ball up between the lines and carving Peru open, so Peru would have been bitterly disappointed to concede from a set piece. The cross in was headed back across goal by defender Alberto Tarantini. He was the unlikeliest member of the squad to find himself on the scoresheet but the defender showed the instinct of his esteemed striking colleagues, heading the ball across goal in the direction from which it came for his only goal in the shirt of Argentina. Tarantini reeled away after having scored, soaking in every second of the celebrations. He pumped his fist and cheered as his trademark curly mop of hair seemed to pulsate. He and his team-mates exuded a sense of relief that all their first-half pressure hadn't been in vain. Those in the Rosario crowd were now the loudest they had been during the first half, determined to drag their men over the line with their partisan support. They carried this support through to half-time and waved their flags with even more fervour as the referee blew to signal the end of the first half. At the halfway point Argentina were halfway there.

There was no Argentinian delegation in the Peruvian dressing room at half-time; instead they were left alone with their thoughts, wondering how they would survive the inevitable onslaught on their goal in the second half. In the back of their minds, they must also have been juggling the dilemma of even if they could survive the Argentinian attack in the second half, could they survive the Rosario crowd? Perhaps the intimidation perpetuated by the hosts had finally taken its toll as Peru capitulated after the break. In truth, for the second 45 minutes they looked like a team that no longer wanted to be there. With nothing left to play for, Peru looked like a side running on fumes. Exhausted, intimidated and looking for the exit door. But before they were granted safe passage out of Rosario, they would be subjected to further humiliation.

As mentioned previously, the historic hierarchy of football in South America places Argentina, Uruguay and Brazil ahead of all the others. In this instance, the rivalry proved to be self-fulfilling as, after a successful tournament, Peru seemed happy to fall into line. Unable to qualify for the final, their race was run. Another loss at the group stage, against a nation that had traditionally dominated them in football terms, wouldn't do much damage to their reputation. They were expected to roll over and have their tummies tickled by Argentina, and in the second half they obliged with their obedience. Peru achieved much both on and off the field at the 1978 World Cup, and the notion of nation-building by integrating the non-European players into their cultural identity was complete.[145] This would have political and social implications in Peru and, crucially, served as a distraction from the struggling economy. All that was remaining was to leave Rosario in one piece, with their pride intact. They succeeded in at least one of these objectives.

Daily Express writer David Miller observed an 'inborn sense of inferiority' in Peru when they faced the giants of their continent. This is interesting since they had done themselves proud, drawing with the great Netherlands team of 1978 in the first round, a team equal to Argentina. However, when they faced their Latin American cousins, they were humiliated. For all the accusations of corruption, it's entirely possible that Peru simply conformed to the football hierarchy, and the intimidation they felt when taking the pitch may have been psychosomatic. Their lack of confidence reinforced by a generational belief that they were simply inferior to the schoolyard bullies of the continent.

---

145 Interview with Dr Peter Watson 2021 – teaching fellow of Latin American studies at the University of Leeds.

The siege of the Peruvian goal prior to half-time certainly hadn't raised confidence in the Peru dressing room and they returned to the field for the second half apprehensive about what further punishment awaited them. Argentina wasted no time in turning the screw on their torture machine and within three minutes of the restart had scored their third. Argentina were awarded a free kick near the touchline for a foul on Daniel Bertoni by José Velásquez. Bertoni sensed the presence of the Peruvian nearby and dropped theatrically to the ground, using the cries of the partisan crowd to draw a decision from the referee, who produced a yellow card for Velásquez, which seemed harsh in the extreme.

From the subsequent booming cross into the box, Kempes controlled the ball on his chest before playing a smart one-two with Bertoni. As the defence rushed towards Bertoni, his stabbed return to Kempes found El Matador all alone in the six-yard box with the goal at his mercy. The prolific striker scored his second of the match, and fourth of the tournament, firing a left-footed shot low into the bottom corner. Kempes collected the ball, embraced his team-mates and ran back to the centre circle. Argentina had to maintain their energy now that Peru were reeling. They required one more goal and had 40 minutes to find it.

That 40 minutes may have seemed like an eternity to Brazilians watching from home as they questioned whether Peru could hold on. As things stood, Brazil would qualify for the final on goals scored. However, the Brazilian spectators who had crowded around television sets only had 60 seconds to wait for their answer, as the Peru defence was breached yet again from the next phase of play.

Continuing his impressive display in midfield, Larrosa drove forward on the left wing and whipped a cross towards the back post. Arriving at the opportune moment to soar over his Peruvian opponents was, of course, Mario Kempes. He nodded the ball back, looping his header over Quiroga and across the goalmouth. Storming towards the goal line was Leopoldo Luque. An insurance policy dressed in a 70s moustache and flowing locks of black hair, Luque made sure by powering his header over the line from a yard out. The goal was soundtracked by the deafening roar of the Rosario crowd. They had witnessed the goal that would fire their beloved national team into the World Cup Final.

However, elsewhere in Argentina, the roar of the television was drowned out by the detonation of a bomb in the residence of finance minister Juan Alemann. The brother of Roberto, the future minister of the economy, Juan was a civilian in the military government. Despite his loyalty to the regime, Juan Alemann was critical of the expenditure incurred by the World Cup. As Luque scored the fourth goal, a bomb exploded at Alemann's home, the two events occurring simultaneously. The events could be coincidental; however, conspiracy theorists cite this as circumstantial evidence that the junta knew Argentina would score the required four goals. Of course, there is no way of knowing whether the bomb would have been detonated regardless of the score but Alemann is in no doubt as to who was responsible for the explosion: 'The match against Peru cost me the bombing of my home. A present from Massera.'[146] A civilian among military men, the austere Alemann had made a high-profile and powerful enemy in Massera, who valued the hosting of the World Cup above all other domestic issues. The bombing of Alemann's home was a message to him that a lack of faith in the World Cup was a sin punishable by death.

Not satisfied with four goals, Argentina pressed forward for more. Peru survived a further 15 minutes before they were punished again. Kempes picked up the ball on the left, glided forward towards the penalty area and found himself one on one, yet again, with Manzo, whose presence in the Peru defence was beginning to look merely ornamental. The beleaguered Peruvian now had lead in his legs and was no match for the jet-heeled Kempes. The Valencia forward powered past the defender and fired a low cross into the box in search of substitute René Houseman. The fresh legs of the Huracán man were too strong for Peru's defence and he was first to meet the cross, sliding the ball into the net. As soon as the ball crossed the line, Houseman set off towards the halfway line, sprinting, with fists pumping in jubilation.

Now that the game was beyond doubt, a fatigued Peru struggled to lay a glove on the buoyant hosts. They braced for further impact as best they could and invited Argentina on to them. A mix-up in defence, as Peruvian defenders stumbled over their feet, allowed Larrosa to pick their pockets. He drove forward and played in Luque, whose low shot found the bottom corner and ended Peru's

---

146 *A Dirty Game*. Documentary dir. Jaap Verdenius and Kay Mastenbroek, 2002.

misery. 6-0. La Albiceleste were in their maiden World Cup Final, which would take place back in the capital city's El Monumental stadium.

The collective gasps from the stands in the first 15 minutes soundtracked a crowd on the verge of collective hyperventilation. Once Argentina were safe and sound, six goals under their belt, the gasps were replaced with the cheers of unbridled, patriotic joy. The ecstasy in the stands was mirrored by that of the players in Argentina's dressing room. The sounds of the celebrations reached such a crescendo that some cynical observers suggested that the players must have been under the influence of drugs. In fact, throughout the tournament, Argentina's squad was dogged by allegations of drug abuse, and some claimed they were 'doped up to the eyeballs' on amphetamines before facing Peru.

David Yallop alleges as much and criticised the organisers for not investigating or clamping down on drug use. He stated, 'The fact that there is strong evidence that many of the Argentinian World Cup team were on drugs, not merely during this match but throughout the World Cup, seems to be an almost irrelevant postscript.'[147] The fact remains that no Argentinian player returned a positive drug test during the tournament; however, many observers have poured scorn on the diligence of the drug testing. Yallop claims that every urine sample that the Argentinian team provided came from a single source, their water boy, Ocampo, meaning the players were free to consume any

147 David Miller. 1978. *World Cup: The Argentina Story*. Frederick Warne Publishers.

substance they wished without fear of detection. Another commonly reported story that highlights the corruption during testing is that, upon inspection of the urine samples, a FIFA official discovered that one of the Argentina players was pregnant.[148]

FIFA's laissez-faire approach to drug use at the tournament takes us back to the opening group stages and Willie Johnston's failed drugs test for Scotland. On this occasion, the rules stated that the team whose player failed a drugs test would forfeit the match 2-0. FIFA also possessed the power to expel the offending team from the tournament. However, as Scotland had already suffered a loss to Peru by a two-goal margin, there was no need to alter the result or disrupt the group by expelling them. The discovery and subsequent expulsion of the player was fortuitous for FIFA logistically, with some in Scotland even suggesting that the discovery was orchestrated by FIFA.

In his book *'78: How a Nation Lost the World Cup*, Scottish writer Graham McColl says that Johnston believes he was a marked man – carefully selected by the organising committee. Despite Archie Gemmill being initially chosen by the organisers to provide a sample, it was Johnston who ended up providing one. Johnston's positive result provided the world with the evidence that FIFA had dealt with the issue of drug taking and served as a warning to the rest of the competing nations that they were taking what was becoming an issue of 'growing concern for the

---

148 Will Hersey. 2018. *Remembering Argentina 1978 – The Dirtiest World Cup of All Time*. Esquire.com

governing body' seriously.[149] McColl raised the possibility that Johnston 'could have been a wanted man', and now that the issue had been publicly dealt with and a scapegoat found, Argentina were able to continue to dope without consequences.

This theory is bolstered further by a reported conversation between Leopoldo Luque and Willie Johnston a year before, during Scotland's tour of South America. When Scotland faced Argentina at Boca Juniors' La Bombonera, the gifted Johnston drew the ire of the Argentina defence in a foul-tempered encounter. Subjected to a focused assault from full-back Vicente Pernía, the Scottish winger was spat at, punched in the ribs and generally physically harassed before the referee inexplicably sent off both men. Johnston's display drew the attention of striker Leopoldo Luque. Johnstone recounts, 'Afterwards their guy [Leopoldo] Luque came looking for me. "John-ston," he said, "you're a good player. But do not come back to Argentina."'[150] Of course, Luque's warning could be merely an attempt to intimidate the young man in the cauldron of La Bombonera, but the foreboding message adds another stitch to the tapestry depicting Johnston as a marked man. His 1978 World Cup ended in disgrace and marked the end of his international career, so the Rangers man may have regretted not taking heed of Luque's advice.

149 Graham McColl. 2006. *'78 – How a Nation Lost the World Cup.* Headline.

150 Aiden Smith. 2014. Interview: Willie Johnston, ex-Scotland winger, *The Scotsman.*

The allegations of drug use add to a catalogue of theories that Argentina's 6-0 demolition of Peru and subsequent qualification for the final was down to collusion between organisers and the military. However, to date, there is no unequivocal piece of evidence that proves the game was rigged. The scoreline may be somewhat surprising, considering Peru's strong performances earlier in the tournament, but it's worth remembering that Peru had nothing to play for. Intimidated, disorganised and desperate for a ticket out of the bear pit of Rosario, it's well within the realms of possibility that Peru crumbled under the pressure of the home favourites, who had everything to play for.

Speaking 40 years later, Ricardo Villa recounts, 'I can say that Peru is not a tough team. It's not hard to score against Peru.'[151] After all, better teams than Peru have suffered heavier losses when they faced a team with much better motivation. What is undisputed is the sheer volume of factors the hosts stacked in their favour against their opponents. The staggered kick-off times and the foreboding visit of a murderous dictator to the Peru dressing room beforehand may not be evidence of corruption but they certainly can't be considered to be within the spirit of the game.

The hosts used every advantage possible to ensure that it would be them taking their place in the final at Estadio Monumental five days later, and people's opinion on whether this was by foul or fair means is down to their

---

151 *Pele, Argentina and the Dictators*. Goalhanger films. 2020.

moral compass. As for the accusations of bribery, drug use and collusion between the dictatorships – it's unlikely we will ever discover the truth. What is unquestionably true is that Argentina's final step on the path to their home final was the most controversial 90 minutes of football ever to take place in the history of the World Cup.

The Campaign Against
the Tournament

WITH THE tournament on the horizon, opponents of
the dictatorship were split on one key issue – should the
World Cup take place in Argentina? Within Argentina,
in the most part, enemies of the dictatorship broadly
supported the staging of the tournament. The swelling
sense of patriotism during the World Cup was a force that
opponents of the junta didn't want to battle directly, as it
had successfully tied the success of the tournament to the
growth of the nation. Marina Franco, of the University
of Paris, states: 'The World Cup was used, internally, as a
factor of "patriotic" mobilisation to renew military support
… and curb growing external opposition.'[152]

For domestic opponents of the dictatorship, the World
Cup was a key battle ground, as important to them as
it was to the junta. If they were able to use the foreign
press to amplify the atrocities of the regime to the rest
of the world, perhaps they could gather enough domestic
support to topple the dictatorship. For one such opponent

---

152 Marina Franco. 2007. 'International solidarity, exile and dictatorship
around the 1978 World Cup'. *Ediciones del Zorzal.*

of the junta, Osvaldo Bayer, a writer and political refugee exiled in Germany, alerting the foreign press about the atrocities in Argentina was a key objective. Bayer insisted, 'Our highest priority was to inform Europe about what was going on in Argentina.'[153]

Opposition groups sprung up across Europe: Sweden, Belgium, Spain, Israel and France. The groups were a blend of Argentine exiles and European citizens, whose primary objectives were to inform the world of the atrocities taking place in Argentina and potentially disrupt the staging of the World Cup.

Sweden

The first, mobilised opposition to the staging of the World Cup took place in Sweden. The Argentina Komité in Stockholm launched a campaign to boycott the tournament. Left-leaning Swedes were already experienced in the notion of boycotts, led as recently as 1976 by Prime Minister Olof Palme of the Social Democratic Party. Palme was highly critical of the American-sponsored military dictatorships of Latin America and also mobilised boycotts of apartheid-era South Africa. Initially the Komité enjoyed a harmonious relationship between Swedish and Argentinian members but, as 1978 rolled around, the Perónists in their ranks gradually turned against the idea of a boycott. Football was deemed a fundamental human right to Argentines and one of the few freedoms enjoyed by Argentina's citizens. Without the support of the exiles the boycott

---

153 *A Dirty Game.* Documentary dir. Jaap Verdenius and Kay Mastenbroek, 2002.

lost momentum. The campaign was derailed and never recovered.

Belgium

In Belgium the 'Comite Belge contra la repression en Argentine' (COBRA) favoured a policy of boycott throughout 1978. A spokesman declared that the 'boycott is achievable' provided 'public opinion (under pressure) becomes aware of the situation'. The committee dealt with dissenters by simply kicking them out, as the group gradually became exclusively Belgian following the expulsion of the Argentine exiles who opposed a boycott.

The Belgian campaign fell victim to a lack of public awareness due to the national team's failure to qualify for the tournament. Without the support of Belgium-based Argentines, the absence of the Belgian Red Devils at the tournament meant the campaign couldn't capture enough public attention to gather momentum.

Spain/Catalunya

The Spanish opposition centred in the north-eastern region of Catalunya. In contrast to many of the other nations, the 'Catala D'informacio i Solidaritat amb el Poble Committee Argentino' (CCISPA) didn't campaign for a boycott, instead focusing on solidarity with victims of the Argentinian dictatorship. They highlighted the importance of foreign press being given the opportunity to report on the realities of Argentina for the first time and warned that disruption of the tournament may serve only to lock them out. They stated that 'non-participation was not healthy because, if conscientious journalists did not attend, they would be replaced by others less prepared to understand the Argentine reality beyond the field of play'. According to CCISPA, the World Cup gave the foreign press an opportunity to investigate the stories ignored by Argentina's military-controlled media.

In Madrid a 'committee of boycotting the football World Cup' was established. Headed by Eduardo Luis Duhalde, the committee struggled to maintain the support from Argentine exiles as the World Cup drew nearer. One member of the committee remembers how difficult it was for the Argentine members to disassociate themselves from the national team as the tournament approached: 'I remember one of the games in which my Madrid kitchen was filled with the voices of Argentine exiles. All exiles that had bitched against the World Cup. When the tournament began, they did not miss a game and suspended work if it was necessary to watch the game.'[154]

Israel

The relationship between Israel and Argentina's military junta is an extremely complex one. The junta received military support from Israel, albeit with significant diplomatic caveats, including the release of political prisoners of Jewish background. Although the numbers are disputed, Raanan Rein of the University of Tel Aviv estimates that as many as 400 arrived in Israel. These

---

154 Marina Franco. 2007. 'International solidarity, exile and dictatorship around the 1978 World Cup'. *Ediciones del Zorzal*.

prisoners were not hard-line Zionists and many scattered throughout Europe or returned to Argentina once the dictatorship had been toppled.[155]

Despite Israel's role as 'one of the major providers of arms to Argentina',[156] Argentinian administration's historic antisemitism was problematic for many Israelis. The delegation of Argentine–Jewish associations allege that 1,300 Jews disappeared under the dictatorship, which could be as much as 10 per cent of the total figure of 'disappeared people' – highly disproportionate to the number of Jews in Argentina, which is less than 1 per cent of the total population. This targeting of Jewish people supports Robert Cox's belief that the dictatorship was inspired by and emulated Nazism.

In the years following the coup, in the lead-up to the World Cup the 'Israeli Committee of Solidarity with the Argentine People' (COSPA) was established, founded by Argentine exiles. The main problem encountered by COSPA was the surveillance of the Israeli security services, who had been ever-present since the very first meeting of the opponents of Argentina's dictatorship in Tel Aviv. COSPA organised a demonstration outside Tel Aviv's Argentinian embassy in March 1978. The protestors numbered in their hundreds; however, fearing reprisals for family members back in Argentina, all those with links

---

155 Raanan Rein and Davidi, Efraim. 2009. 'Sport, politics and exile: protests in Israel during the World Cup (Argentina,1978)'. *International Journal of the History of Sport*, 26(5): 673–92.

156 Mordechai Gur, ex-chief of staff of the Israeli armed forces, Kafra. 'The Devil's Dilemma'; and Bishara Bahbah. 1986. *Israel and Latin America*, 126.

back to their homeland wore masks for anonymity. The protest was successful, leading to a dozen articles being published on the subject that month.

COSPA remained active in solidarity with the opponents of the junta until the Falklands/Malvinas conflict and subsequent collapse of the dictatorship.

France

The epicentre of the gathering wave of protests was in Paris. The group known as 'Boycott du Mondial Committee of football in Argentine' (Committee to boycott the World Cup in Argentina) or simply COBA emerged in late 1977. COBA was a mixture of Argentine exiles and European citizens who organised protest marches and distributed literature condemning the atrocities in Argentina. Their goal was to raise awareness of the crimes of the dictatorship and encourage a mass boycott of the event.

Liliana Andreone was a member of COBA and partner of famous critic of the junta, Elvar El Kadri. El Kadri was a marked man in the eyes of the military due to his role as a founding member of the left-wing militant group 'Fuerzas armadas Perónistas' (Armed Perónist Forces). Andreone speaks of the anxiety felt as the dictatorship attempted to root out left-wing subversives following their ascent to power:

'My partner [El Kadri, whom she affectionately refers to as Cacho] had to leave. He was given information that he was a wanted man. I helped him leave with fake papers. First, he left for Uruguay, and from there to Lebanon as his father was Lebanese. They were in touch with a Palestinian group that were also involved in politics. Cacho thought it would be a good idea to go to Lebanon as he wanted to write a book on the history of Palestine. Cacho decided to leave Lebanon when the armed conflict intensified. He didn't want to be exiled from Argentina only to die in the Middle East.'[157]

At this point in the story, realising that as a known associate of Cacho, she was in grave danger, Liliana joined her partner in Europe. 'I was a lawyer. We chose to go to Spain because there was legislation that allowed me to continue my work as a lawyer. But we had problems there.' For Cacho and Liliana, Spain seemed like a good solution. Fluent in the language and with an existing network of Argentine associates, they thought they would settle easily. However, Cacho soon found himself detained by the Spanish authorities. A hangover from the rule of recently deceased fascist head of state, Francisco Franco, the Argentinian government had many friends in Spain and Cacho was tracked down by the Spanish Civil Guard.

The detention of an Argentine citizen on Spanish soil drew the attention of Amnesty International and, with the assistance of Andreone, a practising lawyer, they were able to free Cacho. However, she insists that the Spanish government found it hard to accept the situation and never admitted culpability for detaining Cacho. Instead, they dumped him at the French border and washed their hands of the situation. Amnesty International took care of the couple's transport to France. Liliana insisted that they

---

157 Interview with Liliana Andreone, 2021.

never chose to live in Paris but circumstances took them there. The primary drawback of the move was the fact that the reciprocal agreement between Argentina and Spain regarding employment didn't exist with France. Thus, Andreone couldn't work as a lawyer. With her professional life now at a crossroads and their friends left in Argentina and Spain, Liliana and Cacho required a new support network. They sought out the Argentine community of Paris and discovered a group of like-minded individuals, located at the inconspicuous number 14 Rue Nanteuil, Paris – the residence of COBA.

COBA sprung organically from a group of left-leaning Parisian students and at its peak boasted 200 smaller committees across the length and breadth of France. The group picked up the baton from a 1977 edition of *Le Monde* magazine, which called for the boycott of the World Cup. COBA's initial publications centred around the fact that the World Cup was taking place against the backdrop of state terrorism. The publications focused on the detention centres that imprisoned, tortured and murdered enemies of the junta. A stone's throw from the stadiums where the football would take place were the brutal detention centres, hidden in plain sight.

The message of COBA was clear: 'Will the World Cup, planned for June 1978 in Argentina, take place amongst concentration camps?'[158] The group created artwork and posters lampooning the military junta, tearing down the façade of peace and placing images of football

—
158 Luciana Bertoia. 'The boycott of the 1978 World Cup: the failure that was a success'. papelitos.ar

257

alongside images of torture. One of the most evocative pieces was the image of the World Cup logo flanked by barbed-wire fences synonymous with Nazi concentration camps. The poster came with the tag line: 'No football amongst concentration camps'. Other posters drew on this comparison with Nazi Germany, one depicting SS guards alongside a German shepherd dog guarding a football, the words 'Mundial Non. 1936 Berlin. 1978 Buenos Aires' written above, drawing a comparison between this World Cup and Hitler's Olympics of 1936.

At the dawn of the new year, with the World Cup a mere six months away, COBA publications were reaching the zenith of their popularity, selling almost a quarter of a million copies in the first half of the year.[159] The burgeoning growth of the movement and the swell of opposition towards the World Cup had spooked the dictatorship. Leading the propaganda war at home, due to their control of the media and iron curtain of silence, the dictatorship launched a counter-offensive in Europe. On the orders of the leader of the navy, Admiral Emilio Massera, the Argentinian embassy in France was given $100,000 to set up a counter-intelligence campaign designed to derail the growing momentum against the military. A branch of ESMA, named 'The Pilot Centre', was established in Paris. According to Liliana Andreone, the centre was a 'screen' for the military, a clandestine surveillance group under the guise of a cultural centre for Argentines abroad. Liliana comments: 'They organised cultural events in order

159 Marina Franco. 'Human rights, politics and football'.

to discover people's politics. To root out the socialists. The objective was to stop the bad PR campaign against the military. There was big focus here in Paris. That's why they set up the flight centre near the embassy.'[160]

The military considered the anti-military committees in Europe, fuelled by Argentine exiles, to be a significant part of a smear campaign against Argentina. Undersecretary of foreign relations, Gualtar Allara, spoke of the campaign during a 1978 seminar in Buenos Aires, saying, 'Argentina faces a strenuous campaign implemented from abroad that tries to plunge into discredit and isolation.'[161] Naturally, the junta's vice-like grip over domestic media didn't extend beyond their own shores – marking the exiles messaging in Europe as a great cause for concern. Juan Alemann, the former finance minister, believes that 'in Europe they still claim facts that aren't true. There were 7,000 prisoners, no more, no less. The Montoneros launched a good campaign across Europe. Together with other leftist movements, the guerrillas got much support from Europe. The generals were not used to dealing with their public relations. There was a war going on – 7,000 terrorists got killed.'[162]

The anxiety the junta felt at the burgeoning campaigns across Europe contrasted heavily with the war they were fighting on their own shores. Feeling increasingly confident that they had secured control, the junta had succeeded in forcing left-wing militarism to the fringes. Los Montoneros

---

160 Interview with Liliana Andreone, 2021.

161 Marina Franco. 'The "anti-Argentine campaign": the press, military discourse and consensus building'.

162 *A Dirty Game*. Documentary dir. Jaap Verdenius and Kay Mastenbroek, 2002.

were broadly in exile and the political assassinations on the streets of Buenos Aires were far less frequent (hence the shock when General Actis's murder was originally attributed as a left-wing guerrilla hit). Raanan Rein, professor of Latin American studies at the University of Tel Aviv, claims, 'The guerrilla movements had to reach a truce with the military dictatorship and make it clear to world public opinion that they would not try to sabotage the games and that teams arriving in Argentina for the games should have no reason to fear violent clashes during the tournament.'[163]

The truce was secured due to a 1977 meeting in Paris between Admiral Massera and Los Montoneros leader Firmenich. Montoneros elder Rodolfo Galimberti shed light on the meeting during an interview with French newspaper *L'Express* in April 1978. Galimberti stated that, along with the boycott being an unrealistic policy, the Montoneros agreed to take no violent action during the World Cup, stating, 'We will take no action that might endanger athletes or journalists.' Massera and Firmenich had a common interest in the world's media receiving safe passage around Argentina, although both hoped to influence the contrasting stories that would be told.

Of course, the vow not to sabotage the tournament didn't extend to the television or radio transmission as two of Argentina's matches were disrupted by Los Montoneros hijacking the audio. The organisation succeeded in

---

163 Interview with Raanan Rein, Professor of Latin American studies at the University of Tel Aviv, 2020.

transmitting their message over the sound waves as citizens watched the matches, soundtracked by Mario Firmenich's commentary – he sought to broadcast the 'painful reality' of the dictatorship's crimes. The propaganda war was in full swing, as both sides attempted to use the World Cup to showcase their opposing views.

What remains is to assess whether the campaigns against the dictatorship during the World Cup were successful. On the surface at least, they failed. The World Cup took place, conducted in peace – to the naked eye – and Argentina triumphed. General Jorge Videla handed the trophy to Daniel Passarella as the stands sang the name of the dictator. However, the scope and success of the protests was unprecedented. COBA received 150,000 signatures on a petition to suspend the World Cup. Meanwhile, increased pressure on the Argentinian government, fuelled by COBA's non-stop messaging and literature, led to the release of four French detainees.

More significant perhaps was the success of the campaigners to place the issue of Argentina's disappeared people into the global public conscience. The hosting of the world's most watched sporting event meant that the plight of foreign people in a foreign land was put into a human context for observers around the world. The protestors in Plaza de Mayo, once regarded as the 'mad women', were now well-known globally, enough for tournament organisers to ban players from associating with them. Soon, investigations into the disappeared people would begin, as in 1979 the International Court of Human Rights would send a delegation to Argentina.

Third-Place Play-Off: Brazil vs Italy, 24 June 1978 – Estadio Monumental, Buenos Aires

TWENTY-FOUR HOURS before the main event at the same venue, Italy and Brazil took to the pitch for a match that, in truth, nobody really wanted to play. The 22 men wondering what they could have done differently to be contesting the final were joined by referee Abraham Klein. Klein could surely relate to the players, having been overlooked for the final himself.

There was no denying who the home favourites were. Italy were cheered on to the pitch by the Buenos Aires faithful, a high percentage of whom could point to Italian lineage as a reason for their vocal support. Brazil arrived to a cacophony of abuse. The Brazilians had made no secret of their disapproval of the circumstances that led to Argentina's 6-0 win over Peru, which ruled Brazil out of the final. As accusations of corruption lay thick in the air, the Argentine fans may have felt stung by questions of their integrity. However, following the recent 'battle of Rosario' contested by the teams and the nature of the rivalry, the boos that greeted Brazil's arrival at Estadio Monumental would have been deafening regardless of what had been said beforehand.

It was Brazil's second consecutive third-place play-off, following their 1974 loss to Poland. Their eight-year absence from the main event required some awkward soul-searching in the national game. Some critics believe the willingness to cry foul meant they weren't confronting the real issues in their game. The hero of 1970, Pelé, was one such critic, lamenting, 'Must we, as Brazilians, sink so low to allow a smokescreen to hide the real reason for Brazil's failure to reach the final? The truth is that we were not good enough.'[164]

Pelé's pragmatism wasn't shared by his former team-mate Rivellino, who claimed, 'Everyone knew that it was fixed for Argentina to become world champions.'[165] Rivellino's frustrations at the tournament were mounting: in and out of the team, at odds with the manager and bitter at the perceived injustice faced by his team. Despite their clashes during the tournament, Coutinho extended the olive branch to Rivellino, allowing him to make a final World Cup bow in the Brazilian shirt, coming off the bench for half an hour, replacing Cerezo in midfield.

The match began with Brazil in the ascendancy. Either riding the wave of their fluid performance against Poland or fuelled by a sense of injustice, their attack was functioning effectively in the opening half hour. The team that would

————
164 David Miller. 1978. *World Cup: The Argentina Story*. Frederick Warne Publishers.
165 *Pele, Argentina and the Dictators*. Goalhanger films. 2020.

be inherited by Telê Santana a year later were beginning to show the potential for fluid, total football so desired by Coutinho, but so absent in Mar del Plata. Twice Roberto Dinamite was felled in the penalty area, and twice referee Klein waved away Brazilian protestations, uninterested in awarding a penalty.

Granted mercy by Klein's leniency, Italy struck first shortly before half-time. Brazil's fluidity in attack was undermined by their disinterest in defence. Their slow-footed reaction to Italy's attack suggested that they weren't fully focused on the task at hand, not affording the third-place play-off the attention they would have to the final. Forging his reputation as one of Europe's most exciting attacking players, Paolo Rossi received the ball on the right wing. He stood directly in front of defender Amoral and quickly shifted the ball to his right, dropped a shoulder and glided effortlessly past the flat-footed defender. Rossi's floated cross into the box was met by the onrushing Causio, who had eluded the Brazil defenders, who were unaware of his presence. From close range Causio nodded past Leão, who lay on the ground as his defenders fished the ball out of the net, avoiding eye contact with the goalkeeper they had left helpless.

Now that the Italians had established a foothold, they pressed for a second, hoping they could take a two-goal lead into the dressing room. Rossi continued his fine form, rounding the goalkeeper only to fire wide, while Causio shook the crossbar following up from a Leão save. Brazil, eager to hear the whistle for half-time, managed to keep the score to 1-0 as the teams trudged off at the interval. The atmosphere had now cooled in Estadio Monumental as both teams were warmly applauded off the field, following 45 minutes where both sides played in a positive manner.

Following the break, Italy reverted to type. Echoing their performance against the Netherlands in their previous match, they tensed up and attempted to protect their lead, now they had something tangible to hold dear. Italy's reluctance to attack invited Brazil into their half and they were rewarded for their progressive play just after the hour mark. Nelinho, fresh from his goal in the previous match, received the ball at an impossible angle on the right-hand side of the 18-yard box. The defender was in position to strike a cross into the box but instead elected to fire a shot with the outside of his right boot. The ball curved away from goal, before swerving violently to the right, out of the reach of Zoff and into the net. Nelinho's scarcely believable banana shot caught the whole defence by surprise, seemingly defying the laws of physics and leaving the 67,000 in attendance open-mouthed by what they had seen.

Wearing the famous No.10 shirt, Rivellino entered the play. Sensing time running out on his storied international career, the moustachioed midfielder set straight to work. The veteran immediately put himself on set-piece duty, as Italy's stretched defence began conceding free kicks. On 70 minutes, Rivellino stepped over the ball, shifting it from his right to his left foot. The exhausted Italian defence stood off, allowing him to loft a pass into the box to the unmarked Mendonça, who miscontrolled the ball on his chest, forcing him away from goal. The ball found Dirceu at the edge of the penalty area, poised to strike. The attacking midfielder netted his third goal of the tournament, sweeping a beautifully struck half-volley that faded away from Zoff, inside the post and into the net.

Unable to switch momentum back their way, Italy relied instead on heavy-handed tactics to deal with Brazil's attacks. Claudio Gentile received a yellow card from Klein for a dangerously high challenge on Rodrigues Neto. His stamping motion drew the anger of the Brazilians as Neto reached a bouncing ball before him. Gentile raised his arms apologetically, acknowledging the severity of the challenge, but still glanced a disappointed look at Klein for having the temerity to reach for his card. Worse would come from Scirea and Sala. The players from either side of the Torino derby seemed to be in competition for who could commit the most egregious foul, as the Juventus man's two-footed lunge trumped the Torino player's clothesline.

Brazil, having had enough of being bullied, were beginning to match Italy's physicality as the match threatened to spill out of hand. After 90 minutes Klein was relieved to blow the final whistle, signalling the end of the match. Italy, who began the tournament so strongly, defeating the hosts in the first group stage, would have to settle for fourth. Brazil claimed a bronze medal, going one better than their previous World Cup. For them of course, this was not deemed good enough and Coutinho would soon leave his role as coach, to be succeeded by Telê Santana, whose appointment heralded a revolution. The Brazil team in transition would be refined, sprinkled with the stardust of an inspirational new captain in Socrates and win hearts and minds at the next World Cup.

At least Coutinho's Brazil finished the World Cup on a high. Emerging from the quagmire of Mar del Plata, surviving a near insurrection that saw the coach degraded and disrespected, they left Argentina the only undefeated team, declaring themselves the moral victors of the World Cup.

The Final: Argentina vs Netherlands, 25 June 1978 – Estadio Monumental, Buenos Aires

AN INCH-PERFECT through ball from substitute Wim Suurbier is pumped deep into Argentina's penalty area. The ball evades the defence and finds Rob Rensenbrink unmarked at the edge of the six-yard box. Argentina goalkeeper Ubaldo Fillol is off his line instantly, realising that the last opportunity to win the match in regular time is falling at the feet of a Dutchman. The crowd in El Monumental, who have created a cacophony of patriotic clangour, fall eerily silent, willing their compatriot to reach the ball before Rensenbrink. With bated breath, everyone in the stadium realises simultaneously that the Anderlecht striker is reaching the ball first. He calmly side-foots the ball past the goalkeeper, sending it bouncing towards goal. With every revolution of the Adidas Tango ball, christened after the dance that originated in the streets of Buenos Aires, another question hangs in the air unanswered. What would become of the Argentina team that lost on their home soil? How could the junta unify a divided country, without a national team to hang its success upon? Would the Netherlands team make it out of Buenos Aires unscathed?

The questions remain forever unanswered, as Rensenbrink's shot, with the goal gaping, finds the width of Fillol's post, before ricocheting to safety. The match ends a goal apiece in regular time, so a further 30 minutes of extra time will be required to separate the teams. The width of a post is all that separated the Netherlands from winning a World Cup Final at the second attempt, from nearly men to heroes. It was also all that separated Argentina's military, on the brink of a national outpouring of patriotic jubilation, from devastation and humiliation under the global gaze. The width of the post isn't much but, in this instance, it is symbolic of the crossroads where both teams found themselves.

A month after General Jorge Videla declared the World Cup open, promising a 'sporting confrontation, characterised by chivalry', 16 teams had been whittled down to two, and only one battle remained to be contested. The images of the 1978 World Cup Final are some of the most evocative in the history of the tournament. The misty eyes of nostalgia easily recall the turf of River Plate's El Monumental littered with ticker tape and the colour contrast between the Oranje and La Albiceleste, both wearing much-loved Adidas versions of their iconic kits.

The 1978 tournament was in many ways a transitional tournament, from the old-fashioned model to what we recognise today, characterised by its marketing and commercial partnerships. One of the most memorable aspects of this particular World Cup was the ball that was used. The Adidas Tango was an instant favourite and a must-have for memorabilia collectors, cementing the commercial aspect of football. Sensing the developing commercial opportunities of sport, the world's governing body had pulled the trigger on the marketability of the tournament. For the first time in its history, the tournament was in the hands of its sponsors, as the 1978 version was the first to be delivered in 'proud partnership with Coca-Cola', due to a deal brokered by FIFA President João Havelange, Horst Dassler of Adidas and PR executive Patrick Nally.

The three men sold the marketability of the tournament to investors and, following the 1978 edition, they sought to grow the World Cup, expanding the number of teams, promising to develop the game's global reach. For Horst Dassler, this meant a tournament clad entirely in Adidas, from the boots worn to the iconic football used. The memorable Adidas Tango was said to be inspired by the dance culture of Buenos Aires, and its 12 panels were meant to dance across the ticker tape like a tango dancer on the streets of La Boca. The much-sought-after accessory also featured different brandings for the cities where matches took place, with the Adidas Tango Rosario a particularly popular version of the ball.

Havelange was under enormous pressure to deliver the world's first World Cup in colour, as he had promised during his campaign to become president. In 1978 in

Argentina it would have been almost impossible to have watched the tournament in colour, as the matches were only transmitted in colour internationally. Unless you were a friend of the military or invited to one of the exclusive lounges in television studios, you would have watched the game in black and white. However, as time has passed, much of the mythology of the World Cup revolves around the introduction of colour TV in the country.

Many Argentines equate getting their first colour TV set from electronics store Fravega with watching the World Cup. 'Si, vi la final en color (yes, I watched the final in colour)' is a common trope in Argentina. Many people will claim that they watched the final at home, in colour, despite this being broadly impossible. The collective misremembering of the event may be due in part to the iconic images of El Monumental, replayed ad nauseam in the decades that followed. The pitch bathed in white ticker tape, the deep orange of the Dutch kit and the crisp blue and white of Argentina's are hugely evocative of a significant moment in time.

The ticker tape on the turf is also memorable. The throwing of *papelitos*, as this is known, is a ritual of Argentinian football. If you attend a match nowadays at Boca Juniors' La Bombonera stadium, upon entry you may be handed a newspaper. Tradition dictates that at kick-off the fans tear up the newspapers and throw them skywards. Now a mainstay of Argentinian football, some of the more conservative figures in their game were angry with the practice. Commentator José Maria Muñoz was horrified with what he was seeing during the early stages of the tournament, declaring it as Argentina displaying its 'ugly face to the world'.[166]

Of course, with the torture and murder taking place less than a kilometre from El Monumental in the detention centre of ESMA, it was completely ludicrous that Muñoz defined the ugly face of Argentina as fans throwing confetti around the stands. The newspaper *Clarin* lampooned Muñoz's pomposity in its 'Clemente' cartoon strip. The famous cartoon character mocked the commentator with his phrase 'Tiren papelitos, muchachos (throw the *papelitos*, guys)'. The throwing of the *papelitos* became more and more popular with fans, until organisers eventually decided to adopt the phrase themselves, displaying the 'tiren papelitos' message on the big screens during the final.

Despite the severity of military rule, the image of confetti being thrown in the stands portrays a party atmosphere and supports claims made by Clive Thomas, referee of the first phase match between Brazil and Sweden, that the atmosphere in Argentina became more fun and relaxed as the tournament continued. Perhaps the military were becoming more confident that they were in control and as a result were able to afford spectators more freedom.

The freedom given to the people of Argentina, however, had yet to be extended to the Dutch team. Hidden away by the KNVB for fear of being embroiled in a politically charged atmosphere, their first experiences of Buenos Aires were difficult. They had defeated Italy on their first visit to the city but facing the hosts four days later was a completely

---

166 Interview with Fernando Spannaus, 2020.

different prospect. Their coach was diverted through side streets en route to the final and their bus was pelted with objects and jeered, the intimidation tactics of the hosts again in full swing. The Dutch squad were becoming increasingly frustrated with their hosts, following the publication of Rudi Krol's forged letter. It was a case of out of the frying pan and into the fire for the Oranje, who went from the eerie isolation of Mendoza and Córdoba to the cauldron of Buenos Aires, at the mercy of the partisan crowd who lined the streets to 'welcome' them.

When the day of the final arrived, Buenos Aires was braced for what coach César Menotti had promised would be a festival of attacking football. To those who believe in such things, there was an air of destiny about the final. Menotti, tasked with guiding Argentina to glory in their homeland, faced the nation, whose philosophy he so admired and whose brand of football he emulated. How appropriate that, to claim their much-coveted maiden World Cup win, Argentina would have to defeat the team that humiliated them four years previously in West Germany, a loss that would cause the AFA to rip up the rule book, start from scratch and appoint a coach so at odds with the military dictatorship that arrived in 1976. A World Cup Final is always the biggest challenge of anyone's career, however, and Menotti's Argentina had to vanquish not only the world's best football team but overcome their own history and exorcise the ghosts of Gelsenkirchen.

For the Dutch, it was their own shot at redemption. They were so heavily favoured to beat West Germany in the final four years previously that they 'forgot to score a second goal', ultimately losing 2-1 to the hosts. Four years later in Buenos Aires they once again faced the host nation, this time in front of an even more hostile crowd. But, enough about destiny and the swirling winds of fate. What about matters that were in human hands, such as selection?

Menotti made a change from the 6-0 demolition of Peru, replacing midfielder Omar Larrosa, whom he had worked with at Huracán, with Osvaldo Ardiles. Larrosa may have felt particularly hard done by as he had performed magnificently against Peru in their de facto semi-final. Larrosa had clipped numerous balls beyond the Peruvian defence, finding Kempes and Luque to devastating effect. However, he didn't possess the ability of Ardiles to carry the ball forward at pace. Menotti had clearly identified that the Netherlands' midfield would be more vulnerable to being run through than passed around. To compete with the Netherlands' undeniable quality in possession of the ball, Argentina sought to increase the pace of the game and dictate from the front foot.

The Netherlands' only change from their victory against Italy was in goal, with Jongbloed replacing Piet Schrijvers in the starting XI after coming off the bench for him 20 minutes into the previous match. Familiarity was key for the Dutch, whose team contained eight players from the World Cup Final in Berlin four years earlier.

The final matter for selection was to be who would officiate the final. The Israeli referee Abraham Klein was the obvious choice, a senior professional who had displayed great nerve and grace under fire when refereeing Italy versus Argentina in the first round. As mentioned earlier, he had proven that he was a fair referee, unable to be swayed by pressure from the home team. Klein had also refereed Austria's shock win over West Germany in Córdoba and had been praised for this performance. He was trusted, honourable and in good form. A veteran of 1974, Clive Thomas was also heavily tipped to be the man in the middle prior to the tournament taking place; however, his decision to disallow Brazil's goal in their opening game had marked his card. The manner in which the officials took against Thomas meant he was no longer in consideration. Instead, the match was awarded to Sergio Gonella of Italy. Gonella and Klein were identified as the two referees who would officiate the two final matches at the tournament, namely the third-place play-off and the final. The AFA were reportedly unhappy with the idea of Klein refereeing the final, the reasons given being the perceived links between the Netherlands and Israel, and Klein's personal links with the Netherlands.

Abraham Klein was born in Timişoara, Romania and spent the Second World War there. As many of his relatives were murdered in the Holocaust, Klein was eventually able to leave Romania for Israel. Before arriving in Israel, he spent a year in Apeldoorn in the Netherlands. He adored this year of his life and speaks with great gratitude and affection about his time there: 'There are things in life that you cannot forget. When, after the Second World War, a country like Holland gives you the feeling that you are at home; when they give you everything: food, education, sport, these are things that you cannot forget.'¹⁶⁷ Klein clearly shared a great affinity with the country; however, to suggest that this was a relevant reason not to award him the final is to reinvent history. Klein recalls, 'Nobody at the Argentinian government or FIFA knows about it, so this cannot be true.'¹⁶⁸ Since Klein has gone on record and spoken about his love of the Netherlands, attempts have been made to cite this as a reason he wasn't awarded the World Cup Final but, at the time, no one in the organising committee would have known about Klein's relationship with the nation.

If links between nations are to be used as a reason to question a referee's integrity, then Sergio Gonella's appointment would have raised more concern than Klein's. The social and historical links between Italy and Argentina are common knowledge, as Italians have historically formed a huge percentage of Argentina's migrant population, particularly in Buenos Aires. A cursory glance at Argentina's squad names would reveal names of Italian descent, such as Bertoni, Tarantini and Passarella. However, Gonella's heritage wasn't deemed as detrimental to his integrity.

In truth, far more important than the referee's honesty or nationality was his personality. To survive the hostile atmosphere of Estadio Monumental on this day, the referee would need to be incredibly confident, resilient and rhino-skinned. Otherwise they were easy prey for the partisan home crowd and easily manipulated by the streetwise

167 Rob Smyth. 2012. 'The forgotten story of Abraham Klein, the "master of the whistle"', *The Guardian*.
168 *Ibid.*

home team. Klein had already displayed these qualities, officiating Argentina's defeat to Italy, thus making him undesirable from the dictatorship's point of view. They needed a man who would be influenced by the occasion and liable to award decisions to the home team when pressured to do so by the home crowd. Under sufficient pressure from the military and the EAM, FIFA appointed their man in Gonella.

Gonella faced unprecedented pressure before the match had even started, as an Argentinian power play made clear who was in control. Taking over the mantle from the legendary Johan Cruyff, Ruud Krol led out his countrymen to face the hosts in the World Cup Final. Except this time, the hosts had yet to take the field. Ten minutes of confusion followed, as 11 Dutch players stood isolated in the middle of El Monumental, their only company the ticker tape blowing around on the pitch and 71,000 Argentines in the stands baying for their blood. Argentina would eventually take to the field but not to play football, not unless it was on their terms.

Argentina's captain Daniel Passarella appeared with his compatriots after the delay, unprepared to begin the match, as long as René van de Kerkhof was wearing a protective cast over his injured wrist. The fact that he had worn this cast in every match since a collision in the Netherlands' opening fixture versus Iran clearly meant that this was a display of gamesmanship by Argentina. The home team drew a line in the sand and remained steadfast in their assurance that the final wouldn't begin until their demand was met. This had two intended outcomes: to frustrate the Dutch and intimidate the referee. It was ultimately successful on both counts. Poor Sergio Gonella found himself between a rock and a hard place, pleading for the teams to come to a compromise, as the stands simmered with nervous energy and frustration. Gonella's authority was severely undermined and he was left with no doubt that he wasn't the man in charge of what was taking place.

Johan Neeskens, plying his trade in La Liga for Barcelona, fluent in Spanish, challenged Argentina captain Daniel Passarella on his team's refusal to begin the match. Speaking with Hugh McIlvanney of *The Observer*, he recalled, 'I asked Passarella what kind of regulations could allow René to play five matches with the covering on his hand and then ban him from the field a minute before the World Cup Final.'

The Dutch, already made to wait for the beginning of the final, alone and confused on the pitch, were incandescent. Skipper Krol threatened to walk his team off the pitch, such was their exasperation with the situation. 'They were trying to unnerve us,' said Krol of the incident, fully aware that it was a psychological ploy from their opponents.[169] Their bluff called, Argentina finally relented and the match began once Van de Kerkhof had applied a light dressing to the cast.

Unsurprisingly, the delay had done nothing to simmer temperatures among the players and the final took off in fractious fashion, with challenges flying in early on.

---

169 David Winner. 2000. *Brilliant Orange*. Bloomsbury.

The Dutch sought to impose themselves physically, to emphasise that, although they were a technically gifted team, they intended to be physically dominant over their South American hosts. Arie Haan's foul on Ardiles early on drew the ire of the Argentines as they felt their diminutive midfielder had been unfairly targeted. Happel's men had fired a shot across the bows, demonstrating to their hosts that the Argentinian midfield wouldn't be able to run through them if they had no legs. Ardiles, small in stature, but a frame filled out with positive attacking intent and the ability to power forward, was the key man in Argentina's midfield. Despite nursing a slight ankle injury, the man from Córdoba was identified as a key player by both teams and his ability to negotiate the midfield war zone would be a microcosm of the story of the final.

Much of the focus of the build-up centred around whether Argentina would be able to cope with the physicality of their opponents, something that was referenced frequently in interviews with both camps. Alberto Tarantini addressed the physicality of his opponents when he stated, 'Holland are hard. They tackle powerfully. I'm not saying they have evil intent, but we are worried about what we saw in the Italy–Holland match.'[170] Whether Tarantini's words expressed genuine concern or whether they were said to place an idea in the heads of officials prior to the match is unclear. But Haan's heavy treatment of Ardiles in the opening minutes meant that Tarantini's words weren't without merit. 'Certainly, the

---

170 David Miller. 1978. *World Cup: The Argentina Story*. Frederick Warne Publishers.

spirit in which this match has started has changed the whole World Cup scene,' said BBC commentator David Coleman at the time, highlighting that Menotti's promised 'festival of attacking football' hadn't been delivered in the opening minutes.

Rensenbrink was presented with the game's first goalscoring opportunity. Arie Haan, a master from long range, following two thundering top-corner strikes already in the tournament, turned provider. He clipped a free kick into the area between six-yard box and penalty spot. The only man to rise to meet the cross was Rob Rensenbrink, soaring above three stationary Argentines. The defenders seemed frozen by fear as they remained rooted to the spot, the footsteps of Rensenbrink drawing near until it was too late and the Dutchman was in position to meet the cross. The goal at his mercy, Rensenbrink headed downwards, as all forwards are taught to do, but his powerful header bounced the wrong side of the foot of the post.

As the ball thundered down into the turf, narrowly bouncing out for an Argentina goal kick, it drew attention to the base of the goalposts. An unremarkable piece of hardware, the goalposts are usually only noticed when the ball is struck against them. However, there was something different about these goalposts: a small black band painted around the base of the post. The black paint on the goalposts was the work of groundsman Ezequiel Valentini, who in 2017 revealed the hidden message behind the paint. FIFA had paid particular attention to the goalposts for the World Cup and had two clear demands of the ground staff: there would be no hardware behind the goal, and the stanchions (which connected crossbar to posts) be uniform across the tournament venues. The second request was naturally ignored as Valentini pointed out the rebellious nature of the Argentine people meant they were 'just not a uniform people'.[171]

FIFA's attention to detail on such matters alerted the ground staff to one simple fact – the goalposts would be seen on television screens around the world. With this came an opportunity. Valentini painted the black bands around the posts to symbolise black armbands. Sometimes mistakenly seen as a protest against the military, rather, they were a tribute to the disappeared people of Argentina during the dictatorship. Valentini recounted, 'Everyone knew someone who knew someone that had disappeared. The staff all wanted to protest. By now the mothers were marching in Plaza de Mayo and we knew the world was watching. We discussed cutting a message into the grass, or painting a message on the advertising hoardings, something the TV cameras would see.'[172]

The black paint around the goalposts was a more implicit offering than a message cut into the grass but its message was nonetheless profound. In fact, it's highly unlikely whether an explicit message would ever had been allowed, as no doubt a member of the military would have realised and prevented such an act of defiance. The black band didn't go unnoticed by officials but ground staff were fortunate that the military's ignorance on football matters

171 David Forrest. 2017. 'The political message hidden on the goalposts at the 1978 World Cup'. In Bed with Maradona.
172 *Ibid.*

meant they were easily fooled. Valentini insisted the black
bands were a tradition of El Monumental, and the men in
uniform were sufficiently placated.

The groundsman expressed disappointment that the
players themselves didn't stage their own tribute, insisting,
'Every single player on each team should have publicly worn
a black armband to remember the dead.' However, it's
worth remembering that every effort was made to keep the
competitors in a protective bubble, away from the realities
of the outside world. Players were banned from attending
sites of potential protest and meeting with political figures.
As a result, the task of weighing up ethical dilemmas often
fell on the shoulders of coaches such as Menotti, who
struggled to balance the pressures of the military and the
expectations of their countrymen. Ardiles later observed
that Menotti 'completely isolated us. He didn't allow
anything political.'[173] Much like their Dutch counterparts,
every precaution was taken to keep the Argentina team in
a protective bubble.

Valentini's frustration with the players competing
was nothing compared to his revulsion of the military.
The groundsman spoke of the shameless way in which
the military conducted their atrocities under the noses
of terrified civilians. 'The junta sited their so-called
clandestine torture centres in full view of the public. We
remembered our dead in full view of the world. Like those
centres, our act of remembrance was hidden in plain sight.'[174]

173 *Pele, Argentina and the Dictators.* Goalhanger films. 2020.
174 'The political message hidden on the goalposts at the 1978 World
    Cup.' David Forrest, In Bed With Maradona, 2017.

A part of the legend of the 1978 World Cup, the black bands at the base of the posts serve as a poignant reminder of the men and women who were tortured and killed a kilometre away from the jubilation in El Monumental. The bold black bands contrast with the ticker tape that littered the pitch, swirling around the ankles of the players and shimmering under the moonlight of the Buenos Aires night sky.

Following Rensenbrink's missed opportunity, Argentina struggled to establish themselves in the match. On 15 minutes, striker Daniel Bertoni attempted to push Argentina further up the field. He received the ball in the middle of the park and powered forward, eluding a flying challenge. Bertoni reached 30 yards from goal before being crudely hacked down by Dutch captain Rudi Krol. The challenge drew a yellow card from Gonella and a 'hijo de puta' from Bertoni, as the unimpressed player let Krol know exactly what he thought of his tackling technique.

Once Bertoni's red mist had lifted, he and the Argentina team had learned something from the Dutch's lunging challenges. Yes, they were imposing their physicality on their opponents, but the desperate lunges revealed something that Archie Gemmill had discovered at the edge of the Dutch box in Mendoza: they were vulnerable to direct runs by tricky players. This explained Menotti's selection of Ardiles, Argentina's best direct runner, in the middle of the park. In a passing game, Argentina ran the risk of getting lost on the Dutch carousel. But they were able to hurt the Oranje with direct football. Not aimless long balls to a target man but high-octane, cut-throat football played at pace – typified by the metronomic Ardiles and his telepathic relationship with the eruptive Kempes.

As Gonella turned to give Krol a deserved yellow card, Bertoni was still bubbling with frustration following the challenge. Behind the back of the referee, a seething Bertoni dug a fist into the ribs of Johan Neeskens. Like a well-rehearsed Marx Brothers. routine, the referee turned back to see Neeskens on the ground, the perpetrator absent, while Mario Kempes stood nearby with the ball, scratching his head, feigning bemusement at the incident. Then, from the subsequent Argentina free kick, Jongbloed made his first save, dropping on a skidding free kick from the Argentina skipper Passarella. Bertoni's reaction to Krol's tackle inspired the crowd, who now had an incident to raise the temperature inside the stadium, which in turn encouraged Argentina's players.

Two minutes later a cross into the box was nodded down by Mario Kempes. The header evaded the intended receiver Leopoldo Luque and Dutch defenders alike. Daniel Bertoni was the man most alert and raced to the byline to collect the ball. As Jongbloed rushed out to narrow the forward's angle, Bertoni cut the ball back to Luque, who had found a position at the edge of the six-yard box. Luque's first-time strike was blocked, fortunately for the Dutch, at point blank range as the goalkeeper scrambled back towards his goal.

San Lorenzo full-back, Jorge Olguín was beginning to have an influence in attack as well as defence. On the right touchline near halfway he drew challenges from Neeskens and Haan, quickly shifting the ball between his feet and slaloming past the Dutch midfielders. Olguín wasn't satisfied with mere showmanship as he set up Passarella for Argentina's best chance of the opening 20 minutes, lobbing a pass across the Dutch penalty area. The ball was weighted perfectly, as a galloping Passarella didn't need to break stride, opening his body up, side-footing his volley towards goal. The defender's strike wasn't equal to the pass as he blazed his effort over the bar, much to the relief of the helplessly exposed Jongbloed in goal.

The fractious opening had given way to an exhilarating game of football, with chances at either end. The festival of football assured by Menotti had come to pass. Two minutes after Passarella's volley, the Argentina skipper was called upon to defend his own goal. A Wim Jansen cross from the right wing was floated into the penalty area with the sole intention of causing chaos among the defenders. The ball did exactly that as centre-back Luis Galván's clearing header ricocheted off the back of another Argentina player. The ball dropped kindly to Johnny Rep in the area, who, perhaps surprised to receive such good fortune in a crowded box, cushioned the ball on his thigh. Rep's body language portrayed a man in his back garden practising skills with his children, rather than one on the brink of firing his nation ahead in a World Cup Final, as he calmly controlled the dropping ball and arrowed a volley towards the top right-hand corner. Fillol flung himself to his left and, showing incredible reflexes coupled with wrists of steel, pushed Rep's volley high over the bar. The home crowd erupted; the save was as good as a goal as it seemed impossible that any keeper could stop a volley of such ferocity from such close range. Following Fillol's heroics, Argentina's attack rewarded the stopper with a few minutes' respite as they created a couple more chances up the other end of the pitch, Bertoni looking the man most likely to trouble Jongbloed.

On 38 minutes, at their most incisive, Argentina penetrated the Dutch defence to devastating effect. Receiving the ball on the left-hand side, Ardiles set off on a trademark run. Breaking through two Dutch tackles, Ardiles, at full stretch, maintained possession, stabbing the ball forward to Luque. The frontman, famed for his physicality, held off his defender and played the ball infield to Kempes. Anticipating the ball slightly earlier, Kempes had to check his run, the ball an inch behind him. However, Kempes's first touch was perfect as he swept the ball into his control and began his assault into the Dutch penalty area. The softest of nudges had split the two centre-backs and now Rudi Krol had no chance of tackling Kempes before he could get his shot off. Kempes slid the ball underneath the advancing Jongbloed and the ball rolled into the net, the white Adidas Tango briefly obscured among the ticker tape, which gave the goalmouth the resemblance of winter's first dusting of snow.

Kempes rose to his feet and sprinted towards the crowd, both arms once again aloft in his celebration that bore the resemblance of his countryman Juan Domingo Perón. In this moment Kempes was more famous, more iconic than any Argentine that had gone before him, as the cheers of El Monumental reverberated around the country.

The cheers could reportedly be heard within the walls of ESMA, where the torturers had downed tools to watch the World Cup Final arm in arm with their victims. Prisoner Adolfo Pérez Ezquivel paints a scene of chaotic celebration inside the walls of the detention centre, stating, 'When Argentina scored, everyone – the oppressors, the oppressed, prisoners and torturers – greeted and looked at each other with happiness.' The World Cup bubble that existed in Argentina, the superficial peace on the streets, had extended even to the detention centres. Such was the significance of Kempes's strike.

On the field, Argentina had expertly manged the emotion of the occasion, crafting a chance to double their lead from a set piece. Captain Daniel Passarella had evaded the attention of his marker as he sneaked towards the back post, only to head Kempes's floated cross into the grateful arms of Jongbloed.

The Netherlands carved an opportunity to equalise shortly before the interval as Willy van de Kerkhof and Johan Neeskens combined. A route-one ball, atypical for Ernst Happel's men, was headed down into the path of Rob Rensenbrink. At full stretch, he managed to get a good connection on the ball, firing the half-volley towards the corner of the goal, but Ubaldo Fillol was once again imperious between the sticks, smothering the shot at the near post and snuffing out the final attack of the half. As in their previous match against Italy, the Dutch went in to the changing rooms at half-time trailing by a single goal.

After 30 seconds of injury time, Gonella blew his whistle and brought an end to a pulsating first half. The beginning of the match had been characterised by heavy tackles and tentative attempts at goal but, as the half developed, thud and blunder gave way to the blood and thunder promised by the coaches. Speaking at half-time, ITV commentator and former World Cup winner Jack Charlton said, 'I think the Dutch defence are playing remarkably well. They're playing against very good players and have done a very good job on them. They've had one or two lapse moments but that's the way the Dutch play.' Despite Charlton's praise of the Dutch defence, their attack would have to create something if they were to spare themselves the fate of finishing second to the host nation in consecutive World Cups.

To be a fly on the wall in the Dutch dressing room at half-time. The interval in the bowels of River Plate's El Monumental stadium would be the final battle in the month-long power struggle between coach Happel and his assistant Zwartkruis. It was Zwartkruis who was tasked with motivating the players for the most significant 45 minutes in the shirts of their national team. Happel, the man whose brevity in team talks was legendary, left the motivational speeches for his assistant. Happel's job was to select the team, refine a game plan and work individually with the players on their responsibilities on the pitch. Much of the day-to-day running of the team still fell on the shoulders of Zwartkruis.

René van de Kerkhof revealed that at half-time during the previous match against Italy it was Zwartkruis who had read the riot act to the Dutch at half-time. Enraged by the tentative display, Zwartkruis demanded more decisiveness in attack. Pushing Neeskens further up the pitch, he reportedly bellowed, 'This is not Holland I have seen. You are not playing like Dutchmen.'[175] The Dutch players must have felt a sense of déjà vu, as four days later, in the same dressing room, they were receiving the same message from their former coach. To win their maiden World Cup they would once more need to fight back from a losing position.

It was Argentina who created the first chance of note in the second half. With 56 minutes on the clock, Daniel Bertoni was played through on the right wing. His run drew skipper Rudi Krol out of position to the right flank. Sensing the attention of Krol, Bertoni used his right foot to back-heel the ball, cutting inside Krol. The moment of trickery fooled the usually unflappable Dutchman, whose feet gave way beneath him. Leaving Krol on the floor, Bertoni powered towards the penalty area. Bertoni played a low cross through the gaping hole now at the centre of the Netherlands' box. The ball was equidistant between striker Luque and goalkeeper Jongbloed, as they both lunged for the Adidas Tango. As with his foot race against Kempes, Jongbloed, a few months short of his 38th birthday, was fractionally second best, allowing Luque to get a toe to the ball. Luque, perhaps in two minds, seemed to go for the ball with the outside of his boot, possibly attempting to round the goalkeeper. The ball rolled over Luque's toes, looped over the diving Jongbloed and rolled out of play to safety.

---

175 David Miller. 1978. *World Cup: The Argentina Story.* Frederick Warne Publishers.

Happel, or perhaps Zwartkruis, had seen enough, and Dick Nanninga was sent on, replacing Johnny Rep up front and offering a more direct threat in attack. Nanninga's presence began to create problems for Argentina's defence as La Albiceleste began committing cynical fouls to stem the tide of Dutch pressure, a number of which were inexplicably ignored by referee Gonella.

Dutch frustrations reached their boiling point 20 minutes from time. Winning a header in the middle of the park, Neeskens set off on a trademark rampaging run through the Argentinian defence. The Barcelona man was now the dominant force in the middle of the park, as Ardiles had been withdrawn for Larrosa, his injured ankle only lasting an hour. Neeskens took the bouncing ball towards the 18-yard box, splitting the centre-backs, before Luis Galván scythed him down from behind. The Talleres centre-back had denied Neeskens a clear goalscoring opportunity, yet the referee awarded nothing more than a free kick, which was squandered by the Dutch and Argentina breathed another sigh of relief. How many such breaths stood between them and winning the World Cup? The answer would be more than expected, as the Dutch pressure finally took its toll on the creaking home defence.

A pass from Arie Haan played René van de Kerkhof into space on the right-hand side of the penalty box. The right-sided forward hit his cross behind the Argentina defence, which was desperately racing back towards goal. Fillol was out of position, drawn to his near post to cover the angle as Van de Kerkhof had stormed past Tarantini, whom he had been tormenting in the second half. Running towards the cross was Dick Nanninga, whose eyes lit up as he timed his run perfectly, leaping into the air and powering his header into the centre of the goal. The Dutch were level and heading for extra time, unless they could find a winner in the remaining ten minutes. This golden opportunity fell to Rensenbrink, who saw all hopes of becoming the hero of the Oranje ricochet off the post with mere seconds remaining.

To crown the world champions, 30 minutes of extra time would be required. An emotionally exhausted Netherlands had no remaining energy reserves. Their dreams of lifting the Jules Rimet Trophy had ricocheted off the post in the final minute of normal time and they had neither the energy nor belief to forge another assault on goal.

Like a condemned prisoner spared from death row, Argentina began the additional 30 minutes with a new zest for life and looked the more likely side to win the match in extra time. Fresh from his pass that so nearly provided Rensenbrink with the winner, Wim Suurbier's next significant contribution would be an atrocious foul on Daniel Bertoni. Attacking from the left wing, Bertoni knocked the ball past the defender, only to be levelled by a knee-high, studs-first reducer on his standing leg. The tackle drew a yellow card but, in truth, should have been the substitute's last act in the final as Bertoni was fortunate not to suffer a serious injury. Poortvliet joined his countryman in the book minutes later as he cynically tripped Kempes, who had picked up a head of steam, carrying the ball dangerously into the Dutch half.

Poortvliet's instincts to identify Kempes as the danger man were correct. As the referee prepared to blow the whistle for the end of the first half of extra time, El Matador sprang into action. A through ball from Bertoni took two Dutch defenders out of the game. Receiving the ball at speed, Kempes was off. The prolific hitman powered into the Dutch penalty area, hips swerving and shaggy mane flowing, leaving one then another defender on the floor. The forward stabbed the ball underneath the goalkeeper and hurdled over him in one motion. A collective gasp was taken across Argentina, as inside the stands of El Monumental and within the walls of the detention centres time stood still. Initially running off in celebration, Kempes seemed to travel back in time, like a video cassette on rewind, as he returned to collect the ball, bobbling around having clipped the underside of the goalkeeper's body. The rest of the players, half a second behind Kempes, could only watch as the time-traveller returned to the present to fire the ball into the empty net.

El Matador's second consecutive brace, his sixth goal of the tournament, had given Argentina the lead in the World Cup Final for the second time. On this occasion there would be no response from the Netherlands. No words of encouragement from Happel or Zwartkruis could stem the gathering wave of Argentinian momentum, as they launched attack after attack into the Dutch half, with Bertoni and Luque unfortunate not to add to Argentina's tally.

Kempes and Bertoni then combined once again to hammer the final nail into the Dutch coffin. Bertoni fed

Kempes, who launched another trademark run into the Dutch 18-yard box. The defence had no answer to his power and precision and allowed the attackers the space to play a swift one-two, which fortunately fell to Bertoni, following a ricochet in the box. The ricochet completely wrong-footed Jongbloed, whose eyes understandably followed the man who had beaten him twice already, allowing Bertoni to roll the ball into the empty net.

The identity of the goalscorer was significant to one Buenos Aires man in particular. An academic paper written by Raanan Rein includes the testimony of an 'R.G.', a resident of Buenos Aires and a militant of the Marxist-Leninist Communist Party. R.G.'s reaction to the third goal typifies the harrowing dichotomy at play for Argentine citizens deemed subversives by the military. Speaking in 2007, he said: 'The dictatorship managed to make the people happy in the middle of a massacre! The player who scored the goal that won the game was named Daniel Bertoni. When I heard on the radio that Daniel Bertoni was the player who had won the game I felt a chill. Because I knew another Daniel Bertoni, who was kidnapped from the University of La Plata on 2 September 1977. Months after he disappeared, we found out he had been tortured to death in the concentration camp operating in the ESMA.'

R.G.'s account hammers home the fact that for so many in Argentina each moment of World Cup glory was tinged with sadness as the shadow of the disappeared loomed heavily over the triumph. Daniel Bertoni's moment of glory, which launched his international career into the stratosphere, took place a kilometre away from where his namesake took his last breath.

On the pitch, the Dutch had no answers and the match drifted away from them as the final moments were played out in a carnival atmosphere in front of the euphoric home revellers. The final whistle blew and the players sprinted around the field in all directions, fuelled by emotion, embracing anything in a blue-and-white shirt that moved. The bars and restaurants of Buenos Aires emptied as people took to the streets, desperate to be in each other's company, seeking a meaningful collective experience, fuelled by the intoxicating effects of patriotism. The roads of Buenos Aires were jammed with cars as fans drove around the streets blaring horns and chanting the infectious refrain of 'AR-GEN-TINA'.

For one of the more sadistic members of the military, the victory provided an opportunity to administer a cruel and unusual form of punishment on one of his prisoners. Captain Jorge Eduardo Acosta, nicknamed 'El Tigre', was infamous for his cruelty towards his victims. He is said to have taken a female prisoner on a tour of Buenos Aires during the celebrations that followed Argentina's victory. Acosta drove her around to show her that the people on the streets paid no attention to the disappeared, Acosta told her that people had forgotten her, the country had moved on and that everyone was happy and united together in celebration. The captain sought to juxtapose her misery with the jubilation of her countrymen. The prisoner is said to have requested Acosta to allow her to stand up and put her head through the car's sunroof for air. She wanted to scream 'I'm one of the disappeared' but feared her voice would get lost among all the celebrations. Or worse, her voice would be heard but ignored. This story supports *Buenos Aires Herald* editor Robert Cox's claims that the World Cup was so loud that it drowned out the suffering. Argentina fans in the stands punctuated chants of 'AR-GEN-TINA' with cries of 'Viva Videla' as they were momentarily swept along in the wave of patriotic ecstasy.

Menotti, to his credit, attempted to distance the victorious team from their associations with the military. Addressing his world champions, he reminded them of the pride they had given their countrymen, the everyday working men and women of Argentina. Reflecting on the victory, Menotti said:

'It was not the military junta, it was not the spectators at River. It was the people of José Carlos Paz, the people from villages, the people who came down on the trucks and taxis, and who blocked the streets. When I spoke out, I always ended by saying the same thing: "When you greet people, raise your head and you will know who you are playing for. The people are there, it's those people over there. They are your father, your brother, your friends, your neighbourhood, your people."'[176]

As the euphoric home fans bounced in the stands, they encouraged the whole of the nation to join them, poking fun at their defeated opponents by singing 'El que no salta es un Holandese' (He who doesn't jump is a Dutchman).

---

176 César Luís Menotti, *Mundial 78*. La Historia Paralela [DVD], Argentina, 2008.

The Dutch team were inconsolable. Shaking hands with their opponents on the field, they declined the offer to attend the post-match banquet, citing fears that the streets of Buenos Aires weren't safe in the aftermath of the final. The decision may have been perceived as a snub or a case of sour grapes in defeat, but Dutch fears were understandable considering their detour through the more unsavoury barrios of Buenos Aires on their way to the stadium. The organisers may have felt aggrieved by their no-show but they would have to make their peace with it. The KNVB was also stinging from the forged Rudi Krol letter and had little interest in rubbing shoulders with the press that had used them as the military's marionette.

Reflecting on their loss, Bram Vermeulen, who campaigned so passionately for the Dutch national team to boycott the tournament, said, 'Losing made things easier for them. They had everyone's sympathy. The Dutch were moral winners.' To many observers, the Netherlands team were the greatest one at the tournament. There is, of course, glory to be found in defeat, particularly if the victors are regarded as having won unfairly. In many ways, the Argentina team are also victims of the dictatorship. Their association with the military leaves a sour taste to the victory, which belies the fact that they were an incredible team. Mario Kempes, speaking 40 years after the event, remarked, 'I have come to terms with the fact we were champions during a dark time in Argentina,' conceding that memories of the time are tinged with sadness. To some of the people who suffered the abuse of power by the military at first hand, the silence of the national team in 1978 was viewed as ambivalence to their suffering. Adolfo Pérez Ezquivel laments that 'at no moment did he [Menotti] mention the suffering. The people who had disappeared. That's why I have always been critical of Menotti.'[177]

On stage with members of the military, the Dutch would have been awkward winners of the tournament. They feared that receiving the trophy from General Videla may have been construed as the Dutch team giving the dictatorship their endorsement. In losing the final, Rudi Krol, the Dutch captain, avoided the dilemma of whether to shake the hand of the military, which may have been some small solace following their defeat.

Videla's presence at the trophy presentation was a surprise to everyone. Beforehand it was widely expected that the trophy would be handed to the winning captain by FIFA president João Havelange but, perhaps sensing an opportunity to place the military at front and centre stage, there was General Jorge Videla, Jules Rimet Trophy in hand. The man who prior to the tournament had never set foot on a football pitch was now handing over the game's biggest prize. In almost every picture of Daniel Passarella lifting the cup, you see Videla in the background. The 'weasel with a pencil moustache', as described by Robert Cox, cuts the figure of an interloper on the patch of the athletes.

General Videla, flanked by his officials, had already broken the sanctity of the dressing room during Argentina's match against Peru, and here he was once more, a focal

---

177 *Pele, Argentina and the Dictators*. Goalhanger films. 2020.

point of Argentina's celebrations during the greatest moment in their sporting history. Videla's presence in almost every picture of the trophy-lift makes it seem as if he is a competitor, undermining the efforts of Passarella, Kempes and co. If 1970 was Pelé's World Cup and 1986 Maradona's, then by rights 1978 should belong to Mario Kempes. However, for far too many, it will always be regarded as the dictatorship's World Cup.

The final word on the tournament must go to Nora de Cortiñas, a member of Las Madres de Plaza de Mayo, whose son Gustavo was arrested in 1977 before his disappearance. She said, 'I watched the final at home. I cried the whole day. How is it possible everybody is so happy with the cup? The whole of Argentina is celebrating whilst my son is missing.'[178]

---

178 *A Dirty Game.* Documentary dir. Jaap Verdenius and Kay Mastenbroek, 2002.

Epilogue: The Legacy of 1978

Argentina vs West Germany: 29 June 1986 – Estadio Azteca, Mexico City

As the sun rose on the Azteca stadium, a vicious, blistering heat signified a new dawn for Argentina. Boasting the greatest player in the world, perhaps the greatest in history, the mercurial Diego Armando Maradona led them out to face West Germany.

There was nowhere for anyone to hide in the midday sun of Mexico City, as captain Maradona declared to his team-mates, 'In two hours we are world champions.' His countrymen didn't wilt in the heat of Mexico, as his words of motivation proved prophetic. A 3-2 victory meant they were World Cup winners for the second time. This time without the influence of the military. The dictatorship had ceded control of the country three years earlier and Argentina was now a democracy. They had also ceded control of the national team, which now belonged to Maradona. If 1978 was the dictatorship's World Cup, this was Maradona's. This was Maradona's Argentina.

The *pibe de barrio*, a boy from the slums of Villa Florito now stood with the world at his feet and the World Cup trophy in is hands. A familiar fairy tale, the boy from nowhere had cemented his status. National heroes exist all across the world but Diego Maradona's legend exceeded this heroic status as he became a cultural icon – the most famous Argentine since Juan Domingo Perón.

The fairy tale of Mexico City had catastrophic results for the memory of the 1978 World Cup. Aside from the 'hand of god' controversy of the quarter-final, Argentina's path to glory was paved with good intentions. They had won the sport's greatest prize fairly, allowing them to erase the memory of the trophy that many claimed had been won by foul means. A tournament as politically charged and culturally significant as the 1978 World Cup leaves quite a legacy. Some memories have faded, while others have been altered. Some scars healed, while some wounds remain open four decades later.

The erasure of the 1978 World Cup from the collective consciousness of Argentina in the years following the return of democracy was particularly tough on César Luis Menotti and his players. The memories of 60 per cent of Buenos Aires celebrating on the streets, fans drunk on the heady cocktail of patriotic ecstasy, chanting 'Viva Videla' quickly faded from memory. However, for the champions of 1978, the military were an albatross around their necks until the bittersweet relief of La Albiceleste's second World Cup win in 1986.

For two decades after the collapse of the dictatorship, Argentina struggled to accommodate their heroes of 1978. Perceptions of the team fluctuated as the country tried to come to terms with the trauma of the last military junta.

In 1983, when the dictatorship collapsed and democracy was returned to Argentina, writer Lívia Magalhães said that the perception of many Argentines was that 'victory in the field was also victory for the government. According to this point of view, players, technical commissions, and others involved on the field were seen as collaborators or supporters of the dictatorship.'[179] The notion of the 'Dictatorship's World Cup' gathered much traction and, fuelled by media perception at home and abroad, became the dominant perception of the event. This was a great shame for the competitors, who in truth had no relationship with the military, other than being paraded around Casa Rosada at times of triumph.

As Argentina emerged from its biggest-ever economic disaster at the dawn of the 21st century, perceptions shifted and stances softened towards the 1978 squad. In 2008, on the 30th anniversary of their World Cup win, the squad reassembled for an event organised by Buenos Aires's 'Space for Memory Institute'. The focal point of the event was an exhibition match between the 1978 squad and a team made up of current players, in El Monumental. Billed as 'the other final, the match for human rights and life', the match was part of a larger event organised as an act of reparation for victims of the dictatorship.

The presence of the 1978 squad at the same stadium where they became world champions, cheered on by their countrymen, echoed the electric evening of 25 June 1978. This time the cheers weren't conducted by the dictatorship

---

179 Livia Magalhães. '40 years after victory: disputing memories over the 1978 World Cup in Argentina, Soccer and Society'.

seeking to drown out the terror that was taking place in the adjacent detention centres. The cheers were both validation for the forgotten champions of '78 and a tribute to the disappeared.

The fortunes of La Albiceleste dovetailed with the fortunes of the dictatorship in the years following the 1978 World Cup. Four years later the national team travelled to Spain to defend their title. The tournament took place as the nation was at war, this time with Great Britain in dispute over the Falkland Islands/Islas Malvinas. A disastrous World Cup campaign for Argentina began with a chastening 1-0 loss to Belgium. The next day, Argentina surrendered control of the islands to Great Britain. Both events were crucial to Argentinian cultural confidence, and the humiliating losses suffered by the dictatorship hastened their downfall. It was a death knell for the junta and democracy would soon return to Argentina.

Many Argentines equate the losses to the crumbling façade of the dictatorship. Diego Maradona spoke of the betrayal felt by the public, who were told that their soldiers were winning the war, when in truth they were ill-equipped, freezing and let down by the military. Maradona, Passarella and other members of the squad took part in a public telethon to raise funds for the war effort prior to the World Cup. It later came to light that the funds were misappropriated by the dictatorship.

Maradona's World Cup bow in Spain was unsuccessful. Facing Brazil in Barcelona, he was kicked from pillar to post for 85 minutes before his frustrations boiled over and he was sent off in disgrace. Broadcaster Fernando Spannaus, who at the time had been volunteering in making care packages for Argentinian soldiers (which never made their destination), says that the loss was a relief: 'We should never have been there when our soldiers were dying. Thank God we lost. What if we had played England while at war with them?'[180]

The decades since the collapse of the dictatorship have been painful for Argentina. In the trial of the juntas, General Jorge Videla and Admiral Emilio Massera were sentenced to life imprisonment, only to be pardoned later. Their pardons were later revoked and Videla died in prison in 2013, having been convicted of crimes against humanity. It's no surprise that the inability to fully accept the crimes of the dictatorship meant that Argentina struggled to come to terms with how to remember the 1978 World Cup.

Members of the 1978 squad, although vehemently opposed to any connection with the military, accept that they aren't as loved as the 1986 squad and that their moment under the bright spotlight of El Monumental came during the nation's darkest period. César Luis Menotti and Mario Kempes, by a cruel quirk of history, will never have their names attached to the World Cup in the way that Pelé, Maradona and Ronaldo do. Rightly or wrongly, 1978 will to many always be viewed as the Dictatorship's World Cup.

---

180 Interview with Fernando Spannaus, 2021.